The Salamander

HORSE AND PONY MANUAL

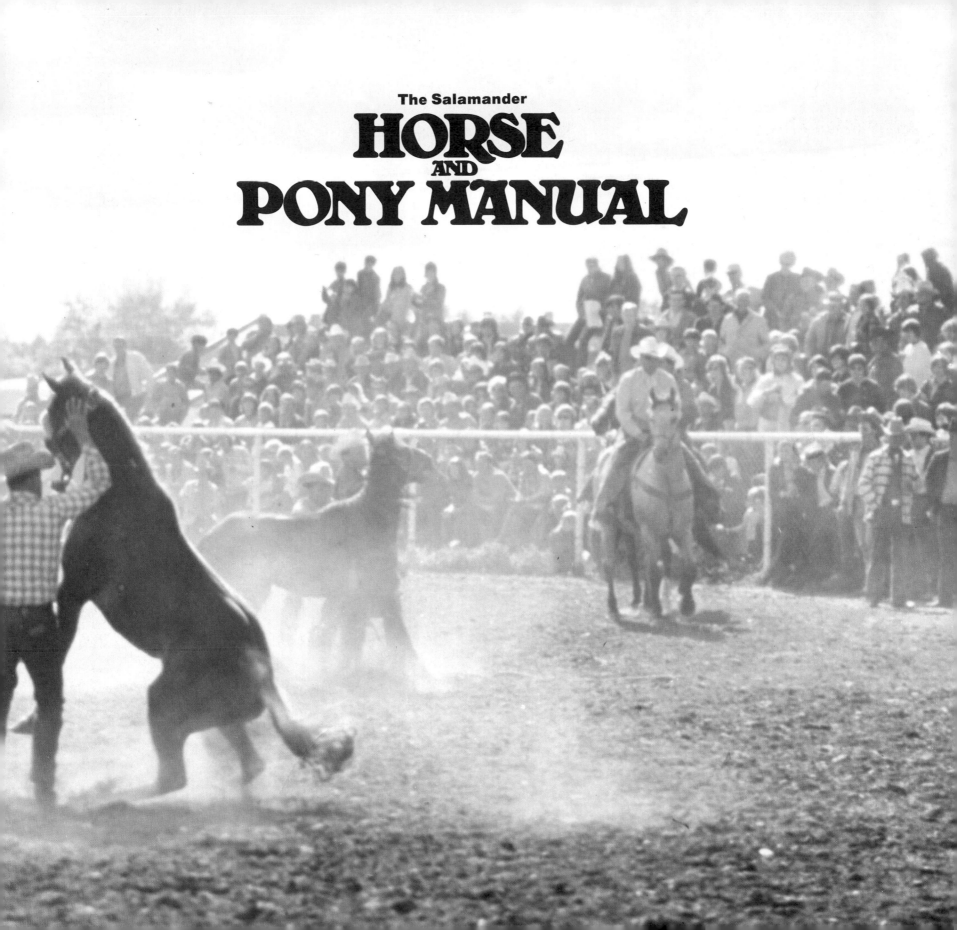

The Salamander

HORSE AND PONY MANUAL

A comprehensive guide to caring for, training and riding your horse.

Compiled by Jane Kidd
Foreword by Alison Oliver

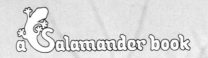

a Salamander book

Published by Salamander Books Limited
LONDON

CREDITS

A SALAMANDER BOOK

Published by Salamander Books Ltd.
27 Old Gloucester Street
London WC1N 3AF

ISBN 86101 002 7

Filmset by Modern Text Typesetting, Essex, England
Reproduced by Metric Reproductions Ltd., Essex,
England.
Printed by Henri Proost et Cie
Turnhout, Belgium.

All correspondence concerning the content of this
volume should be addressed to Salamander Books
Limited.

Editorial Consultant: Jane Kidd
Editor: Veronica Pratt
Designer: Steve Henderson
Artwork by Glen Stewart © Salamander Books Ltd.
Commissioned photographs by Bruce Scott.
For full details of all illustrations, please turn to back of
the book.

Consultant and Co-Author
Jane Kidd A former international show-jumping
competitor, frequent contributor to equestrian
publications and author of four books.

The Authors
David Hunt A leading trainer in Great Britain, and
international competitor in dressage.
Sheila Inderwick The chairman of The Riding Club
Committee, an international dressage judge,
contributor to various books and magazines and the
Chairman of the Long Distance Riding Committee.
Pamela Macgregor-Morris The equestrian
correspondent to *The Times,* contributor to *Horse and
Hound, The Chronicle of the Horse* and author of
more than twenty books.
Steven Price A partner in an equestrian publishing
company, author, and contributor to equestrian
publications.
Toni Webber The author of *The Pony Lovers'
Handbook, Pony Club Past and Present* and *Your
Stable,* and a contributor to *Riding, Light Horse, The
Horse* and other publications.

Note on the use of American terms
Wherever possible the terminology used has been
selected so that it is acceptable to both British and
American readers. It has, however, been necessary
sometimes to put the British equivalent in brackets after
the American word.

CONTENTS

FOREWORD

In recent years riding has become one of the fastest-growing leisure pursuits in the world and it is no longer the exclusive preserve of the rich. Thanks to the rise, internationally, in standards of living, and to the government subsidies given to equestrian sport in many countries, riding is now becoming increasingly available to people in all walks of life. All riders — and in particular the new, young riders of the future — should be able to take advantage of the facilities now available for education both in the art of riding and in the care of their horses.

It is very satisfying for me as a trainer to find that there is an ever-increasing demand for assistance and advice. This does mean, however, that there is seldom enough time to tell an individual pupil all that he or she needs to know about riding technique and care of the horse. I know too that there are many riders who have to keep their horses on a very limited budget and cannot afford much tuition.

There is therefore a great need for books that set out the fundamental principles of riding and horse care, clearly and concisely, without confusing the reader with too many complex ideas. *The Salamander Horse and Pony Manual,* simply and clearly presented and extensively illustrated with excellent pictures, fulfils all these requirements and should do much to help the riders of today.

Alison Oliver.

DEVELOPMENT OF RIDING

The earliest use of the horse was in harness, perhaps because his domestication followed that of oxen and wild asses, which were solely used for draught purposes. Riding proper began some time during the second millennium BC, at first by the nomadic tribes of Eastern Europe, later by all the peoples of the ancient world.

With systematic breeding and careful feeding, horses gradually became larger and more capable of carrying men for long periods. Their use was mainly confined to hunting and warfare. In places where war chariots could not operate, such as rocky hill country and heavily forested land, the mounted cavalry became an effective fighting force.

Although the role of the war horse varied from place to place and from age to age, the cavalry played an important part in all wars until this century. The development of the machine gun at the end of the nineteenth century marked the beginning of the end of the cavalry unit. Tanks and trench warfare finished it off. The last true cavalry charge occurred in 1939, when the Polish cavalry was cut to pieces by German tanks, and the only successful use of mounted troopers in World War II was the hit-and-run tactics of the Russian Cossacks against German reserve units immobilized on the Russian Front during the severe winter of 1943.

Riding techniques developed according to the purpose for which horses were required. The earliest manual on the care and training of horses, which is still in existence, was written by a Greek cavalry general, Xenophon (430-354BC). His book, *On the Art of Horsemanship*, contains a great deal on what to look for when buying a horse, and much good advice on how to handle horses, but comparatively little on the methods of bringing a horse to the degree of suppleness and obedience expected today. The Greeks rode bareback and used bits that a modern horseman would consider extremely severe. The only recognizable High School movements mentioned by Xenophon are the volte and pesade, and the training advocated by him was designed to produce a horse useful in battle, for the Greeks rarely rode for pleasure.

Little is known of how horses were trained either before or after Xenophon until the sixteenth century AD. Although Xenophon refers to earlier writers, only fragments of their manuscripts survive. Circus horses were popular for many centuries, however, performing a number of advanced High School movements. Some of the classical airs were supposed to have a military basis: the capriole, for example—a spectacular horizontal leap with the hind legs kicking out vigorously—could have been an effective means of dealing with an enemy approaching from behind, but it is doubtful whether any horse capable of executing so skilled a movement would have been allowed to take part in anything as dangerous as a battle.

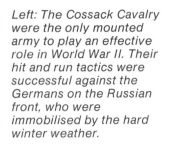

Left: The Cossack Cavalry were the only mounted army to play an effective role in World War II. Their hit and run tactics were successful against the Germans on the Russian front, who were immobilised by the hard winter weather.

Left: Charge of the 16th Queen's Own Lancers at Aliwal on the 28th January 1846 during the first Sikh War, from an aquatint by J. Harris.

Above: The Polish cavalry which was destroyed by German tanks in World War II. This ended the use of the horse as a major instrument of war.

This is one of the few complete sets of armour in existence and was made during the fifteenth century in Germany. Movement of mount and man was restricted by the weight of the armour.

Learning to ride
DEVELOPMENT OF RIDING

In 1550, a Neapolitan riding master named Federico Grisone published a systematic treatise on horsemanship, the first of a number of Italian books on academic riding. Riding became an art in itself and Naples the centre of a cult of formal riding that attracted young aristocrats from all over Europe. Horses were taught more and more dramatic movements, and the displays and carrousels performed by them and their noble riders were an important part of life in the courts of Europe.

By the seventeenth and eighteenth centuries, the French had taken over from the Italians in leading the world in classical riding. One of the greatest riding masters of this period was François Robichon de la Guérinière (1688-1751), whose principles of training a horse to be calm, light and obedient still form the basis of dressage today.

But while the techniques of riding in enclosed spaces continued to fascinate the European horseman and indeed were introduced into military training at cavalry schools, Englishmen favoured a much more dashing style of riding. This was partly fostered by the English passion for hunting, which with the development of fox-hunting during the eighteenth century meant riding hard across country, and—with the spread of enclosures—clearing obstacles in the way. Rivalry in the hunting field soon led to cross-country matches being arranged, and the first recorded steeplechase took place in Ireland in 1752. Made-up fences were soon introduced, and in 1837 the first Grand National was held.

Racing over fences was followed by arena jumping, and again it was the Irish who led the way.

In 1865 'leaping' contests were staged at the Royal Dublin Society's show, rapidly followed by similar events in other parts of the British Isles. In 1912, show-jumping became an Olympic sport.

In the USA, there were two influences at work on riding styles. The Western seat was a development of Spanish techniques following the introduction of horses to the American continent by the Conquistadors. Along the Eastern seaboard, however, the English hunting seat was generally preferred.

The strongest influence on modern riding has been Federico Caprilli (1868-1907), an Italian cavalry instructor. He advocated the forward seat, and the shortening of the rider's stirrups so that his centre of gravity was brought forward to coincide with that of the horse even when in the air over an obstacle. Caprilli's ideas were found to be effective and, following the success of the Italian show-jumping team before the first World War, the forward seat, with some modifications, was adopted all over the world. Today, riding is no longer confined to the rich and the army, and increasing numbers of riders are enjoying the thrill of learning about horsemanship. They all owe a great deal to the riders of the past who developed the ideas and methods generally practised today.

Right: Followers to hounds (right) in the nineteenth century adapted the classical seat, riding with long stirrups and leaning back over the fences.

Below: The Grand National was one of the first major steeplechases to be held in the UK and this depicts the fifth staging of the race in 1844.

Learning to ride
HOW TO LEARN

Since the war 'horse-fever' has become almost an epidemic in the Western world. No one is exempt and few ever recover once the contact is made. Why this should be so is hard to say—perhaps because the horse can be all things to all men; because riding is a shared adventure; because the horse's speed and agility, which so exceeds that of man, can for a short while be his; and because horses have such courage and gentleness.

Sadly the love and use of horses is not always to their benefit. Ignorance of the right way to care for horses can lead to unconscious cruelty.

The first stages

Much thoughtlessness can be avoided if newcomers are carefully instructed. The novice should start his riding career at a good riding school where he knows he will be safely mounted on horses suited to his ability. A few weeks' tuition at such an establishment, learning the basic seat and the use of the aids, will pay dividends in the future.

Riding is rated a high-risk sport, and the figures for riders and animals killed—especially on the roads—grow yearly. For this reason alone, it is not enough to get a few lessons from 'that nice young girl down the road', who may know very little more than her pupil.

A good school will always be willing to advise beginners on what to wear and will insist that their pupils always ride in a hard hat. Strong shoes or boots with a full-length sole and a low heel are also essential, and for comfort and looks either jodhpurs or breeches and a hacking jacket or polo-neck sweater should be worn. Jeans or loose trousers tend to make the rider's seat unstable and provide less protection from saddle-sores than breeches.

Another good reason for starting a riding career at a school is that faults in the rider's position will be corrected before they become established. It may also save the older rider from the painful back conditions that can spring from faulty posture. With a secure position in the saddle, a rider will gain confidence and will be able to use his reins to guide and control his horse rather than as a means of maintaining his own balance. He will learn to ride correctly over jumps instead of relying on the courage and speed of his horse to get him to the other side.

Owning a horse

Not until a rider is reasonably proficient should he think of acquiring his own horse. By then he should have ridden many different ones and will be able to assess what breed and size he prefers. He should have a much better idea of what is entailed in caring for horses, including the sort of saddle and bridle to buy. It is sometimes a good idea to keep the first horse at board (livery) for a while. Most riding schools welcome keen owners and encourage them to assist with the stable work, cleaning tack, etc. In this way, the rider will become more capable of caring for his horse at home, knowing when to get it re-shod or to call in a vet, and understanding the feeding of horses in relation to their work.

LUNGEING

Learning to ride on the lunge enables riders to forget about controlling the horse and concentrate on their position. Until confident and balanced it is wise to keep hold of the pommel.

A BADLY DRESSED RIDER

The hat is too big and will come off in a fall

Wrinkled jeans will rub

Bare legs get pinched

Shoes too large and the rubber soles easily catch in the stirrup.

In this exercise the rider swings the upper body and arms to face first one side then the other. This helps to make the hips and small of the back more supple.

When the rider finds it natural to sit in the correct position and is relaxed enough to follow the pony's movement without bouncing around then she can take her hands off the pommel.

Exercises help riders to relax and become more supple. Keeping the arms horizontal to the ground and swinging them backwards and forwards is good for the shoulders.

Touching the toes with both hands is impossible as this rider is finding out. The horse's neck gets in the way so it is best to touch one toe with the hand from the opposite side.

A lesson in progress. The boy on the pony is getting too close to the horse in front; he should have at least one length between himself and the next horse, otherwise he might get kicked.

Learning to ride
MOUNTING AND DISMOUNTING

The horse can be mounted in a number of ways. The athletic rider can vault on—springing up to lie across the horse and then swinging one leg over. Those too short to reach the stirrup (eg jockeys) can be legged up (see below), but the most practical and safest way is to mount using the stirrup on the nearside (left). It is a tradition in the horse world to use the nearside as opposed to the offside (right) of the horse, as much as possible. Buckles and girths are done up that side, saddlery is put on from the nearside and the rider mounts from there.

Accidents do happen when mounting, especially if the rider becomes careless. The three important precautions to take are: choose a suitable site that is relatively peaceful and on firm ground; check the girths, as a saddle that slips around can frighten the horse and off-balance the rider; if either the horse or rider is inexperienced it is best to get an assistant to hold the head, as the horse must stand still, both to avoid accidents and to establish discipline from the moment the rider gets on his back.

THE LEG-UP

The rider takes the reins in his left hand, holds the front of the saddle with his left hand and the back with his right, and bends his right leg ready to spring.

Upon a signal the assistant, who is holding the rider's left leg below the knee, lifts it upwards and the rider simultaneously springs into the air with his right leg.

MOUNTING

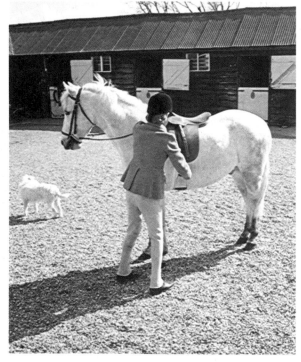

The rider faces the hindquarters, takes the reins in his left hand to place it by the withers and the stirrup in his right. The horse should remain still while the rider is mounting.

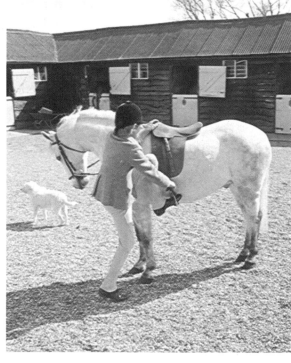

He places the left foot in the stirrup. It is important to keep the toe as low as possible lest it digs into the pony and encourages him to move off.

He puts his right hand on the offside of the saddle at the back and pulls on this arm at the same time as putting weight onto his left foot, ready to spring with his right leg.

The rider swings his right leg over the saddle to come gently down into the saddle, using his left hand to control the descent. Then he puts his feet into the stirrups.

The rider collects the reins in one hand and removes his right foot from the stirrup to swing this leg behind and over the saddle, taking his weight on his left leg.

This rider had taken his left leg out of the stirrup to land with both feet on the ground. Some experts however keep the left leg in the stirrup until the right is one the ground.

He swings his right leg well clear over the back of the saddle and hindquarters.

He lowers himself gently into the saddle and puts his feet into the stirrups.

THE CLASSICAL POSITION

The Classical position of the rider on a horse is wholly practical and yet elegant. It places the rider over the horse's centre of gravity, which lies just behind the withers and roughly in line with the point of his shoulder.

To achieve the classical position

The rider must first take hold of the front of the saddle and pull himself forward until he is sitting in the deepest part, which should be just behind the arch of the saddle. Old-fashioned saddles with shallow seats will handicap the rider, and so will those that are very wide in the waist. Modern saddles, which should fit both the rider and the horse, are designed to help the rider to slide easily into the correct position.

Once the rider is sitting in the lowest part of the saddle he should make himself as tall and upright as possible. This is achieved by raising the upper body and by reaching down with the legs. Then, providing the waist and hips are not allowed to collapse

backwards, his weight will come off the buttocks and on to the seat bones, the head will rise, the shoulders drop and the spine take up its natural line.

At the same time, the knee should be as low on the saddle as the rider's conformation permits, and the whole leg should lie close to the horse's side, with the toe higher than the heel. Once the rider has achieved this position it should be possible to draw an imaginary line from the lobe of his ear, through the point of his shoulder and his hip to the heel of the boot. He will then be in the basic position for all forms of riding on the flat, except racing.

If the imaginary line fails to touch the tip of the heel, the rider will be behind the balance and will probably have rounded his back and allowed his lower leg to swing forward. If the leg is behind the line, the rider is probably sitting on his fork. In other words, in the first instance he has transferred his weight back on to his buttocks, and in the second he has gone forward off his seat bones and is balancing

on his thighs. In neither position will his seat be stable and his weight related to that of the horse.

Even in the correct position the rider will not be able to maintain his seat once the horse is moving unless he is completely supple and relaxed. Any form of tension not only destroys his position but sets up a reciprocal stiffness in his horse, and this makes matters worse.

This particularly applies if he tries to grip with the knees or thighs. Contrary to what is sometimes believed this tends to weaken the rider's control by raising his seat out of the saddle. It defeats the whole object of the classical position, which depends on the united balance and harmony of horse and rider.

Thus, if the rider takes up the correct position and there is no tension in his body, he will be able to sink softly down into the horse's back on each stride (ie, as the hooves touch the ground). In this way the rider is carried up and gently forward by the horse's movement.

If, however, the rider is not seated over the horse's

COMMON FAULTS

By gripping with her knees this young rider has come too high out of the saddle and has to rest her hands on the neck and grip harder with the knees to keep her balance.

With the stirrups as long as this the rider finds it difficult to put any weight in them as he is only just reaching them with his toes. It is impossible for him to achieve a good position.

Although in a good position he is trying too hard and has stiffened up which will make it difficult absorb the horse's movement and maintain the position at faster paces.

With the stirrups as short as this the rider cannot use his back to control the horse, and if the head is down, this rounds the back and makes it more difficult to use the seat bones effectively.

Above: With the legs this far forward it will be difficult to use them to control the horse. With such long reins the hands are so close to the body that their movement is restricted.

Right: The rider is in a good position as a vertical line could be drawn from the lobe of his ear through the point of his shoulder and his hip to the heel of his boot.

A GOOD CLASSICAL POSITION

THE CLASSICAL POSITION

centre of gravity, the synchronization will be spoilt and the rider will have to maintain contact with the saddle by gripping and also to move his upper body to keep up with the horse's movement. Any displacement of the rider's weight that is out of harmony with the horse's natural balance is liable to set up mental and physical resistances, especially in the freedom of the horse's paces. Young animals in particular will be afraid of increasing their speed or lengthening their stride if they cannot rely on their burden 'to go with them'.

Providing his legs, and in particular the inner muscles of his thighs, are relaxed, the rider's knees will be deep on the saddle flap, and it is this depth that should help him to maintain his balance whatever the horse may do. At first, in his effort to lower the knee, the rider may find that his lower leg sticks out from the horse's side, but this tendency will correct itself once knee and leg are truly supple.

Then the rider will find that the inner side of his upper calf muscles automatically makes contact with the widest part of the horse's rib-cage, enabling him to give light unobtrusive aids. At the same time, because his upper body is upright and his shoulders are relaxed, the upper arms will hang down quite naturally until the point of his elbow lightly touches the hip bone. The rider has only to bring his fore arm up until, when seen from the side, there is a straight line from his elbow down the rein to his horse's mouth for his arms to be in the right position as well. The hands should be held as though he were reading a book, with the fingers closed on the reins, the thumbs on top and the back of the wrists facing outward. If the rider maintains his balance without tension he is then able to use his hands and reins quite independently of the rest of his body.

To remain in the classical position, no matter what saddle or horse the rider may sit on, takes years of practice and is best learned by riding without stirrups while on the lunge. But it is essential that the instructor should be very experienced.

A rider in the established position will find that by closing the angles of his hips, knees and ankles, he will be in the right place for jumping and galloping.

For these activities, the imaginary line becomes shorter and runs directly from the rider's shoulder to his heel with the knee in front and the hips slightly behind. The rider is still in harmony with the horse's centre of gravity, with the body adjusted to comply with the horse's extra speed.

The principal object of the classical position is to allow the rider to be motionless in relation to the movement of the horse and therefore for the two to work as one.

Below left: This rider is working hard with her seat to get some extension. It has led to her back coming behind the vertical and slipping back in the saddle.

Below: Inge Theoderescu from Germany is sitting well and in preparing her horse to turn down the centre line has slightly turned her shoulders.

Right: Patrick Le Rolland, from France's Cadre Noir who is considered to have one of the best seats in the world.

Learning to ride
THE WESTERN SEAT

The purpose of the Western (also known as the stock) seat is to permit a rider to assume a comfortable and relaxed position, so that he can spend many hours in the saddle, while still being able to control and guide his horse according to the demands of ranch and trail riding.

The high pommel and cantle of the Western saddle helps to achieve this by giving the rider greater security. The seat slopes backwards to the cantle so that the rider sits further back than is customary in the English style.

Western riders sit almost straight-legged, using longer stirrup leathers than in any other style of horsemanship. The leather must not be so long, however, that it is difficult to keep the heel below the toe. A deep seat enables the rider to brace himself in the saddle while roping and to effect the quick starts and stops needed in ranch work. The lower leg is vital to control and must be able to swing freely. Knees and thighs rest, but do not press, against the heavy stock saddle. The Western rider keeps his back upright, neither rigid nor slouching.

Both reins are held in one hand, because cowboys need a free hand for holding a rope or to flap a Stetson at a stray calf. The reins normally pass through the fist from over the index or under the little finger with the thumb up. However, when the ends of split reins fall on the nearside, then one finger can be placed between the reins. The free hand and arm should hang down in a relaxed manner, or the rider can hold the end of the split reins to keep them from swinging and to adjust the length of the reins.

Western horses are taught neck-reining, a term that describes changing direction through rein pressure on the animal's neck. To turn left, for example, the rider lays the reins across the neck to the left, and the horse will respond to the combination of direct and indirect reining. The reins can be held in either hand.

A good stock seat position is best learned on a responsive but gentle horse. Picking up the rhythm at all gaits is essential, because any stiffness or awkwardness on the rider's part will 'show daylight'

between him and the saddle. Unlike English-style equitation, Westerners do not post while trotting, so that a supple lower back and shock-absorbent legs are needed to sit down to a jog (the Western word for trot) as well as lope (the word for canter).

The aids should be imperceptible, and the weight of the rider must stay in the centre of the saddle.

The balance and responsiveness to a horse's rhythm learned in the early stages becomes more important in advanced work. This includes bending the horse in serpentines, turns on the forehand and haunches, and lightning starts and stops, all of which are needed in rodeo events, Western show classes, and actual ranch work.

Below left: Riding western style with light rein contact and the horse is being allowed to stretch and lower his head in the extended walk.

Below: This rider has a good position with a straight back and although the stirrups are long the heel is still well below the toe.

THE SADDLE SEAT

The fundamental aim of the saddle seat position is to display a three- or five-gaited saddlebred or a Tennessee walking horse to the best advantage. A gaited horse or walker is characterized by a high degree of leg, particularly foreleg, action that the rider wants to show off.

In the saddle seat position, the rider's legs are straighter than in the classic seat. Because gaited horses are trained to move forward with great energy, impulsion derived from leg pressure is less necessary in saddle seat equitation than in other disciplines. The rider is thus able to keep his legs ahead of the girth and slightly flared out at the knee, away from the horse's body, as if to frame the horse's forequarters.

To obtain the right position, the rider places himself comfortably in the saddle and finds his centre of gravity by sitting without irons and with slightly bent knees. The leathers can then be adjusted to the length needed to maintain the position. The iron is placed under the ball of the foot so that pressure on the centre of the iron is equal across the entire width of the foot. The feet point straight ahead.

The rider holds his body erect. Arms are held higher and elbows stick out further than in the classic position. The purpose of this is to influence the horse's head carriage directly through rein pressure, so that the height of the hands depends on where the horse is carrying his head. Hands do not have to be held thumbs-up.

Some people believe that the saddle seat position is easier to learn than other styles because the rider's legs can be used to brace himself in the saddle, and also because gaited horses are comfortable to ride. The novice rider starts at the walk, when a slight motion in the saddle is permissible. Particular attention must be paid to the animal's head carriage, which is set by a combination of curb and snaffle bit pressure, but no sawing action should be used. The saddle seat riders post during the trot, and must learn to do so rapidly, in time to the gaited horse's animated leg action. The hips are kept under the body, so that there is no mechanical up-and-down motion nor a forward-and-backward swing. In the canter, 'the saddle should be polished' with the rider going with the horse, and this is easier to achieve on a Tennessee walking horse, which has a rocking chair canter.

The slow gait and rack are comfortable paces performed only by five-gaited horses, and require the rider to sit quietly. Intermittent calf pressure is permissible at the slow gait, when the legs are held straight down. In the rack, the legs can be held slightly further back.

A technique that takes practice to master is to make a saddle horse 'stretch' or extend his forelegs into the stance assumed while being judged for conformation.

The saddle seat used for showing three and five-gaited horses, and in this case Morgans. It differs from the classic seat as the main purpose is to show off rather than control the horse. As seen in the picture the legs are further away from the horse and the hands higher.

USE OF AIDS

'Aids' is the well-chosen word for the methods used by riders to communicate with the horse. They both control and direct the horse and in some instances instruct him in his work for man.

Throughout the ages the great horseman has sought to improve and refine his use of the aids until the communication between himself and his mount is such that they almost think as one. Even to come anywhere near this standard requires years of dedication and practice, but the aids used do not vary from those taught in any good riding school, and a high degree of proficiency is within the reach of most riders.

Natural and artificial aids

Aids are usually divided into two groups: the 'natural aids' are those given by means of the rider's body or voice; 'artificial aids' are those requiring some form of strap or gadget to achieve the right effect.

In the second group, only the whip and spurs have any part to play in the training of horses, but for practical purposes other things (such as martingales) may be advisable if horse or rider lacks experience.

The success or otherwise of using 'natural aids' is directly related to the ability of the rider to sit in the correct position in the saddle and to maintain the position under all circumstances: in other words, to be 'still' in relation to the movement of his horse. This is possible only if the rider is supple, relaxed and in command of all his muscular reactions. Involuntary or unco-ordinated movement on the part of the rider will either confuse the horse or, if repeated too frequently, cause him to 'stop listening'. This can easily turn a free, intelligent horse into a dull automaton. It is therefore up to the rider to ensure that he knows and uses the correct aids if he does not want his horse to become indifferent to them.

The legs

A horse's first line of defence is flight, and his immediate reaction to the pressure of the rider's legs is to move forward in an effort to escape. All riding is based on this reaction, and the horse's desire to move forward must never at any time be lost. Even in the most advanced dressage movements, impulsion must still be in a forward direction, although—in the piaffe, for example—he may be actually trotting on the spot. Once a horse learns that he can evade the rider's aids by going backwards or by conserving his energy, man is no longer master. Then the horse may develop such vices as rearing, napping or bucking, which make him a danger to

himself and to his rider who may be thrown.

If the rider wishes his horse to be 'light' to the aids he should use only enough pressure with his legs (in particular with the inside of the upper calves) to remind the horse to go forward. This pressure should never be a steady squeeze or a heavy thump with the leg and heel, but a quick vibrant action with both legs on or just behind the girth. If the rider is sitting correctly, his legs will automatically touch this spot. No leg aid should be prolonged; if it is ineffective, it should be repeated once more with greater firmness. Should the horse still not react it is wiser to use the whip, not as a punishment but to supplement the rider's legs. This is done by giving one short tap on the horse's ribs just behind the rider's leg. In other words, the rider asks the horse

once or twice to go forward to the leg, and then, if necessary, demands it. It should be remembered that frequent use of the whip can nullify its effect as an aid, so it should never be used unless the rider's natural aids have failed and then only as a refinement of that aid. The same can be said of the use of spurs, which must never be used as a punishment and are in any case not suitable for use on young horses or by inexperienced riders.

The leg is resting in the normal position—just touching the horse but it is perhaps a little tense. The legs should be so relaxed that the horse's breathing can be felt; they should enclose the horse, but gently. In this normal position the spur is not in contact.

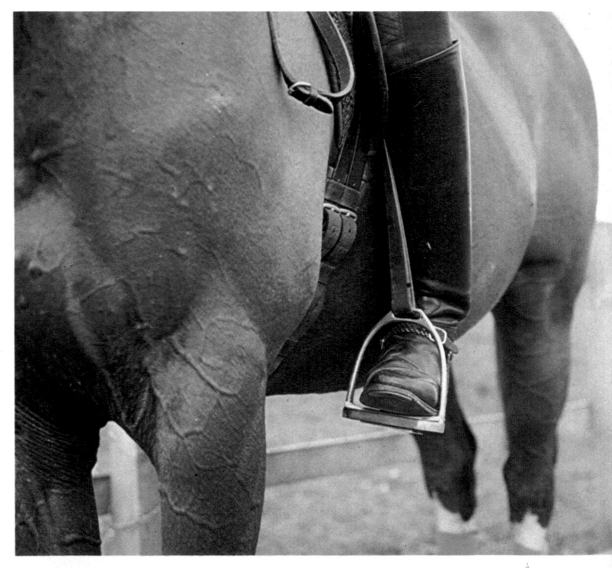

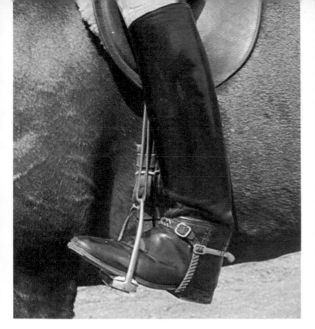

Far left: The leg is being applied on the girth when it is used to generate impulsion. The leg should be applied in a series of vibrations and not simply pushed against the horse.

Left: The leg is being applied behind the girth when it is used to ask for a lateral movement. When it is drawn back to this position it is used to indicate to the horse which leg he should lead on at the canter.

Below left: The spur is being gently brought into use. It is not being dug into the horse.

Below: The whip is the most useful of the artificial aids as the strength of its use can be varied. Only in extreme cases should it be for punishment; in general it reinforces the leg aid.

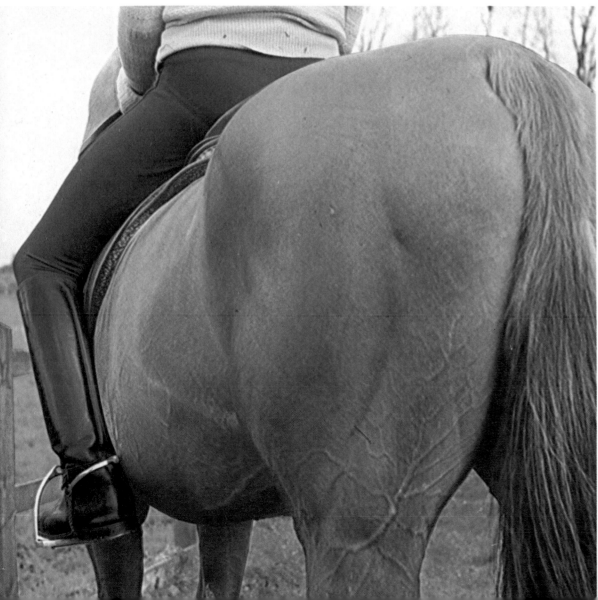

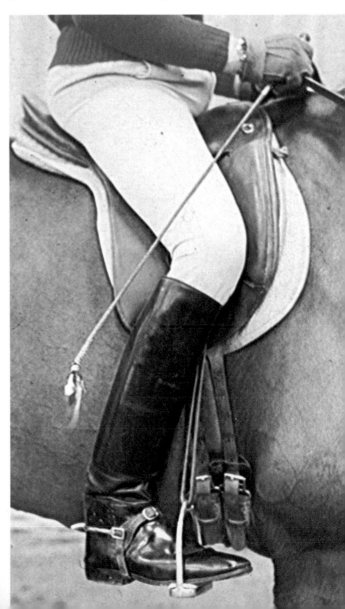

USE OF AIDS

The hands

Once the horse moves forward it is the rider's task to control and direct the energy created. This he does through the reins to the horse's mouth. Once again, unless his seat is secure and his hands and arms supple he will be unable to use his hands independently of the rest of his body.

Unless the horse feels that he can go forward and touch the bit without experiencing pain, he will try to withdraw from it by ceasing to go forward or (in an effort to escape) will pull against it. If, however, the rider's contact with the horse's mouth is both light and steady and if the flexion in his wrists follows the natural movement of the horse's head and neck, the animal will relax his mouth and accept the bit as an aid to control and understanding.

It should never be forgotten how easy it is to damage the sensitive bars in the horse's mouth and that this contact is the rider's closest link with the horse's brain.

Except in rare circumstances the reins should be held in both hands with the snaffle reins lying between the fourth and fifth finger of each hand or, in the case of a double bridle, outside the little finger while the bit (curb) rein takes the place of the snaffle rein. The slack can then be taken up through the palm of the hand and allowed to hang over the top of the first finger, with the thumb resting lightly on top of it. The reins should be held short enough to enable the rider to keep a steady but light contact with the horse's mouth. His fingers should be closed because an open hand leaves nothing to give to the horse when following the natural movement in his head and neck. The movement is most noticeable at the walk and trot, and the rider must always allow his hand to follow this without losing contact or allowing the rein to 'flap'. In this way, the rider's hands will be 'still' in relation to the horse's movement.

The reins should be used only to tell the horse either the speed or the direction at which he should proceed. At all other times they merely retain a steady but light contact. If, like the legs, they are used without thought—for instance, when the rider is talking to friends and not attending to his horse—the animal will soon stop listening and will no longer respond to the slightest change in the contact on the rein.

Thus it can be seen that the legs help to create forward impulsion and the hands decide how it should be used. This is done by varying the position and the degree to which these aids are used.

Below left: The snaffle rein held correctly with the thumbs pointing towards the sky and the hands close to, but not resting on the neck.

Below: Hands held this low are stiff and cannot move with the horse. The horse tends to resist this and does not bring his head lower.

Bottom: Hands held horizontal make the elbows come out and the arms become stiff. Unless the arms are relaxed they cannot adjust to the horse's movement and contact with the mouth will vary.

HOLDING THE REINS: SNAFFLE BRIDLE

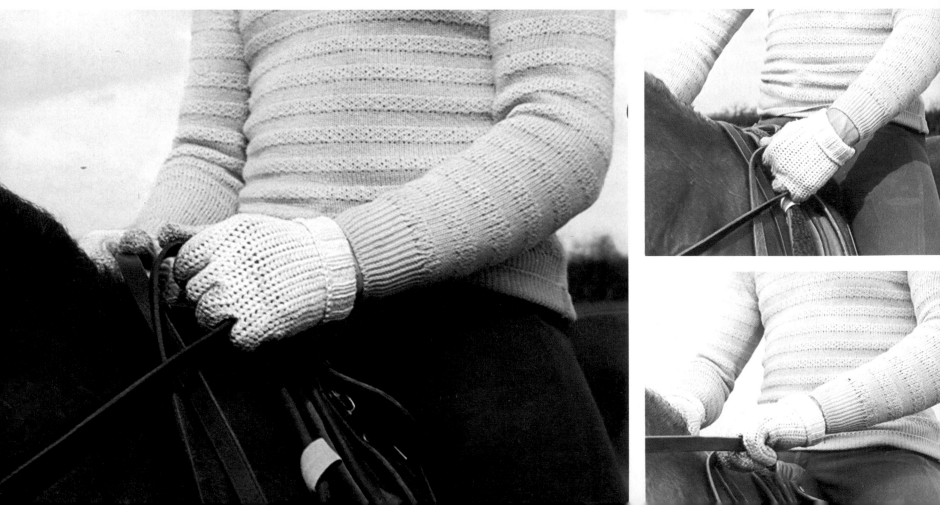

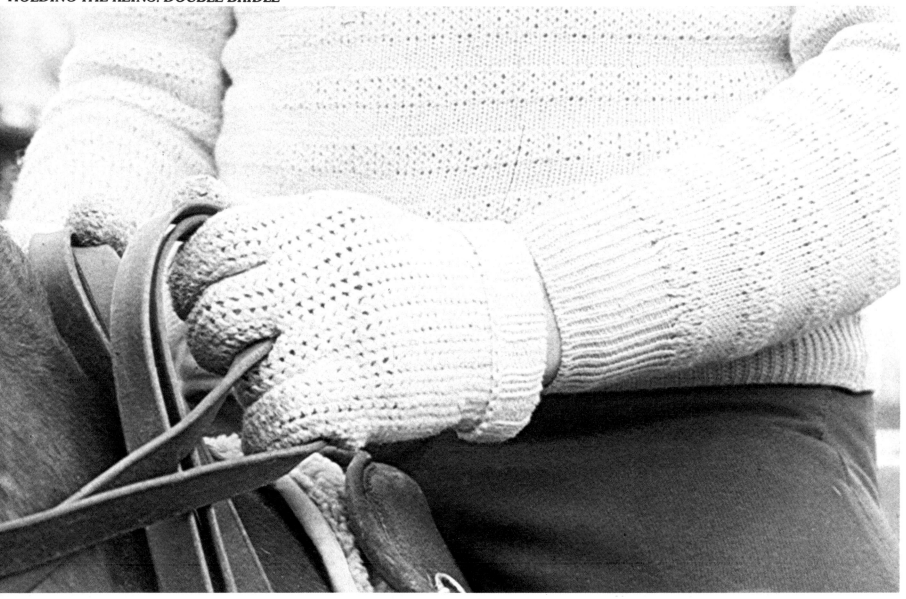

Above: The reins of a double bridle held in acceptable fashion with the bit rein around the outside of the little finger. Sometimes this same rein is held between the little and fourth finger.

Far left: With the hands unlevel the contact with the mouth is uneven and therefore incorrect. With the knuckles of the finger uppermost, as for the snaffle rein, the hands do become more rigid.

Left: With the hands so close to the body their movement is restricted and it will be impossible to keep a constant contact with the horse's mouth when he walks, trots or canters as there is then considerable movement in the head and neck.

USE OF AIDS

To turn a corner

The need to change the position of the leg and hand aids is partly to make a clear difference to the horse, who, having an amazing memory, will quickly associate that position with the required movements. The other reason is concerned with the way a horse actually moves. Once he knows that pressure of both the rider's legs is telling him to go forward, he will also move only one hind leg forward if he feels the increased pressure of that one of the rider's legs. On a circle the rider must apply his inside leg to ensure that the horse brings his inside hind leg not only well forward but also slightly under the weight of his body to maintain his balance while turning. Some of the impulsion created by this movement will then be carried diagonally forward towards the horse's outside shoulder. This impulsion is received and controlled by the outside rein: that is to say, the rider keeps a passive contact on this rein and, by closing his fingers, allows only sufficient of the impulsion to escape to maintain the required pace. At no time should this hand either lose contact or pull backwards. This is known as the passive outside rein controlling the pace while the rider's inside leg creates the impulsion.

At the same time the rider's outside leg should be very slightly behind the girth and ready to be applied if the horse tries to wing his quarters away from the pressure of the rider's inside leg. This is known as the outside leg holding or controlling the quarters. The role of the inside hand is to be very light and flexible and to ask for a slight bend in the direction of the circle.

When being ridden, a horse must either be going straight or turning, and these two basic positions and their appropriate aids apply from basic to advanced stages of training. The one thing that alters is the degree to which the aids are applied.

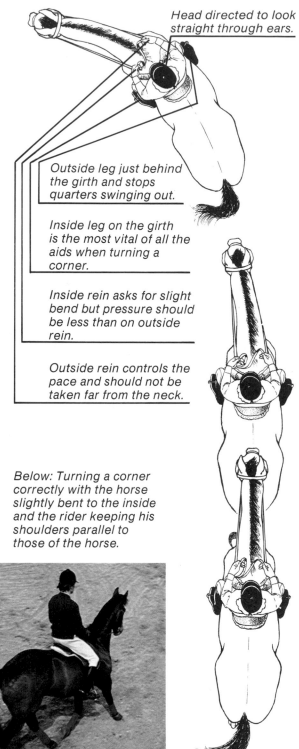

Head directed to look straight through ears.

Outside leg just behind the girth and stops quarters swinging out.

Inside leg on the girth is the most vital of all the aids when turning a corner.

Inside rein asks for slight bend but pressure should be less than on outside rein.

Outside rein controls the pace and should not be taken far from the neck.

Below: Turning a corner correctly with the horse slightly bent to the inside and the rider keeping his shoulders parallel to those of the horse.

To trot

This is a two-time gait with the horse's legs moving in diagonal pairs (see Gaits of the Horse). The rider has two alternatives; 'to sit' when his seat does not leave the saddle or 'to post' (to rise), when he sits in the saddle as one pair of the horse's diagonals come to the ground and rises out of it as this same pair of diagonals leave the ground. It is important that the horse is not made one sided by the rider always sitting for the same pair of diagonals. This is very easy to develop as every rider finds it more comfortable to sit to one particular diagonal pair. The rider must learn to change diagonals by sitting down in the saddle for an extra beat before starting to rise again. He should do this frequently when hacking, and when schooling should learn to sit to the outside diagonals (ie rise when the inside hind leg and outside foreleg come off the ground, and sit when this same pair return to the ground).

Right: The rider is rising from the saddle when one diagonal pair of legs is off the ground, and sitting for the other pair. In the large picture he returns to the saddle as the inside diagonals reach the ground. Above he sits as the outside diagonals are off the ground, and below rises (a little too high) when the inside diagonals come off the ground. The body is forward of the vertical.

THE SITTING TROT

The sitting trot in which the rider does not leave the saddle at all, but his lower back is used to absorb the horse's movement.

THE RISING TROT

If the horse's back is stiff this is difficult, and the tendency is for the rider to be thrown and to bounce in the saddle.

The bounces are painful to the horse who tries to escape them by hollowing his back and his head usually comes up, as in the picture.

When the horse and rider are not in harmony it is best to return to the rising trot until they both become more relaxed.

The rider sits to the trot and thinks about building up the impulsion. To do this he applies his inside leg and restrains the horse from going into a faster trot by holding (not pulling) on the reins (the outside one particularly).

The rider is drawing his outside leg back, to brush along the horse, but not to dig into him, in order to indicate to him to bring his outside (off hind) forward, and so strike off with the near foreleg leading.

In response to this the horse has brought his off hind much further forward than he did when trotting. Although in this case he is offering some resistance by opening his mouth.

The horse has struck off into the canter to lead with his near foreleg and the rider is returning his right leg to its position close to the girth. The rider will keep using his inside leg to generate impulsion.

To canter

The only other position the rider needs is that which tells his horse to change pace into the canter. At the canter (a three-time pace) the foreleg and hind leg on one side will be slightly in advance of the pair on the other side. Consequently it will be easier for the horse to describe a circle if the inside legs are leading. When the horse has learned to bring forward a hind leg in answer to a touch from the rider's leg, he can be asked to strike off on the required lead.

To induce him to strike off into the canter on the correct lead he should go into a corner slightly bent toward his leading foreleg. The rider's outside leg should be drawn back to tell him to move his outside hind leg forward. Then, according to the sequence of the canter (see Gaits of the Horse p138), the inside hind leg and outside foreleg will now move forward together and he will finally lead with the inside foreleg. Thus the rider's outside leg tells the horse to bring forward that hind leg. It should not be applied too strongly or it would then be asking the hindquarters to move sideways, thus causing confusion in the future when lateral work is taught. It is the rider's inside leg that asks for the forward impulsion, so it must be applied on the girth at the same time as the outside leg. Any reluctance or laziness to go into the canter should be remedied by stronger use of this inside (not outside) leg and if necessary a few taps with the stick on the inside.

Once the horse has struck off into the canter, both the rider's legs return to the correct position at the girth to keep up the impulsion. Should the rider wish to change the canter lead, he first brings the horse back to the walk or trot and then reverses his canter aids. Eventually, when both he and his horse are well-balanced and have sufficient collection, the change can be made during the short period of suspension in the canter pace that comes immediately after the leading foreleg hits the ground. The horse will then change the sequence of his stride while in the air. This, known as the flying change, is quite natural to the horse when unmounted, but it is very difficult to teach a horse to change both hind and fore leading legs (they usually just change in front) before he has mastered the medium standard movements of dressage. That is the horse is straight, performs lateral movements happily and is reasonably collected.

These demands, are made of dressage horses only, as show jumpers and polo ponies have to do flying changes and few are trained to medium dressage, but change automatically.

A SERIES OF FLYING CHANGES

The flying change takes place during the moment of suspension. Often the suspension time is prolonged to become a small jump enabling a clear change to take place.

This horse is performing advanced work and one stride later has changed to his near fore.

This is the moment of suspension coming after the leading leg has hit the ground. The rider has applied his leg to ask the horse to bring the inside right hind forward to lead with the off fore leg.

The horse has obliged, to lead with the off fore leg. The rider is then drawing his right leg back to ask for the horse to change to the outside leg as the off foreleg touches the ground and the moment of suspension occurs.

USE OF AIDS

The seat

So far this chapter has dealt only with the use of the hand and leg aids, but a correct and supple seat can play an immense part in training a horse. If the rider is sitting in the right position and is supple and relaxed, he has only to sink softly down in the saddle as the horse's hooves touch the ground to ensure that he and his mount rebound together. In this way, the rider will be in harmony with his horse and able to absorb the strong upward thrust of the horse's back through his own supple loins and thighs instead of being thrown off the saddle and falling stiffly back. The latter type of riding invariably causes the rider to start gripping in an effort to maintain his position and the horse to tense the muscles of his back in anticipation of the jar when the rider's seat returns to the saddle.

If, on the other hand, both are relaxed and the impulsion is being maintained, the deeper the rider sinks down with his horse the greater will be their joint recoil, and the horse's steps will become lighter and the stride more rounded and therefore shorter. This is the true way to obtain collection and has nothing to do with the false collection created when the horse's head and neck are positioned by the use of the reins or when he is merely slowed down to take shorter but less elevated strides. Neither method will produce the soft muscular roundness of outline with slightly lowered quarters that is the aim of collection. Few riders have the ability or the time to train their horses to achieve great collection, but once a rider has learned to appreciate the power that lies in the correct use of a supple seat he will find that all horses work much more freely and

willingly for him and that he can use almost invisible hand and leg aids. This applies whether he requires a collected or an extended pace. The latter is directly dependent on the first because unless there is spring and height in the collected paces there will be insufficient time in the air for each set of legs to lengthen the stride. A rider who tries to obtain extension from a pace that lacks impulsion or by the use of rough leg aids will achieve nothing but greater speed and hurried strides, whereas true extension should be performed in the same rhythm as the other working, medium or collected paces.

The rider is sitting well (apart from a little rounding of the shoulders) to produce this good collected trot with elevated stride—note how high the fore and hind legs are off the ground.

USE OF SEAT: COLLECTED TROT

EXTENDED TROT

Above: In these cases it appears that the rider's seat has been used too harshly. His body has come behind the vertical and the horse has reacted against it to hollow his back resulting in his hind legs not coming far enough under him and going above the bit.

Left: The rider is sitting deep using his seat to ask for this excellent extended trot yet he is relaxed enough to absorb the extra movement.

USE OF AIDS

The lateral aids

Once a horse is going freely forward and is 'straight', with the hind feet following in the track made by the fore feet, and once the rider is truly in control of the quarters, it is possible to start riding lateral movements. These are any movements where the quarters do not follow the same line as the horse's forehand and are often referred to as work on two tracks, encompassing such exercises as leg yielding, shoulder in, renvers, travers and half pass. All are used to increase the horse's balance and obedience, the suppleness of the quarters and the joints, and the freedom of the shoulders.

In all cases, the horse must be going forward well. Only leg-yielding can be performed in a working trot; all other lateral movements require a degree of collection whether carried out at a trot or at a canter. They do not, however, require the rider to use the legs in a different position from those he adopted when riding a turn or circle. By varying the degree of pressure of the leg just behind the girth, yet still maintaining impulsion by his seat and other leg at the girth, he will be able to move the quarters to left or right.

By riding straight forward while holding this position the horse will perform renvers (quarters out) or travers (quarters in). If the pressure on the outside leg (ie the one behind the girth) is increased, the horse will go forward and slightly to the side in half-pass. If, on the other hand, the horse is ridden forward as though to start a circle until the forehand has left the track and the pressure of the inside leg—which is at the girth—is increased while the rider's opposite hand prevents him from continuing in the circle, the movement will be shoulder-in. If this movement is correctly executed it should be possible at any time to return to the circle by slightly relaxing the pressure of the leg at the girth and the opposite hand, thus allowing the horse to move forward again on one track into the circle.

None of these lateral movements should be attempted until the rider is confident that he can produce enough forward impulsion and can ride a true circle at all paces. Then he will need only to vary the use of his individual leg and hand aids to master all lateral work. As there is so little natural impulsion in the walk, many advise against doing such exercises at this pace, because it can easily lose its regularity and sequence. It does, however, give the novice horse and/or rider a less hurried opportunity to understand the aids. Therefore as long as training at the walk is kept to a minimum and always followed immediately by some energetic movement straight forward, it can be beneficial. All lateral work can be done at the trot and eventually the canter.

Finally, whatever ambitions a rider may have, it cannot be stressed too strongly that if he and his horse are to reach their true potential every effort should be made to achieve the correct position in the saddle and to learn to use the aids effectively.

THE LEG YIELD

| Inside leg kept behind the girth to stop the hindquarters from swinging in | Inside rein near to the neck controls the pace | Outside rein away from the neck asks for the bend | Outside leg close to the girth asks for lateral movement |

THE SHOULDER IN

| Inside leg on the girth asking for lateral movement | Inside rein away from neck, asking for slight bend | Outside rein close to neck controlling pace | Outside leg just behind the girth to hold the quarters |

THE TRAVERS

Horse bent around rider's inside leg which is applied on the girth to maintain impulsion

Asking for bend with inside rein

Controlling pace with outside rein near to the neck

Asking for lateral movement with outside leg behind the girth

THE HALF PASS

Inside leg applied on girth and used to keep up impulsion

Inside hand asks for bend.

Head straight and looking forward

Outside hand near to the neck used to control pace

Outside leg applied behind girth asks for lateral movement

Learning to ride
JUMPING

Many people believe that jumping requires a different seat and aids from those used for riding on the flat. This is not the case. A jump is only a very elevated canter stride and the position when jumping is the same seat. All that has changed is that the rider has closed the angles at his hips, knees and ankles, enabling him to ride with shorter stirrup leathers, to lift his seat just clear of the saddle and to lean slightly forward over his horse's wither. The imaginary line that was discussed under the classical position would now go directly from the point of the rider's shoulder to his heel. In other words, although his weight remains over the horse's centre of gravity, his whole body is compressed like a spring. It is also important that the rider should not collapse at the waist or curve his back, which should at all times remain as flat as the natural line of his spine allows. The elbows may go rather further forward and the reins will be shorter, but there should still be a straight line through the rider's forearm and hand to the horse's mouth. As in the more upright position, all the rider's weight should be going down through his supple seat, thighs and knees.

In the jumping position it is not essential for the actual seat to touch the saddle. Some show-jumpers believe it is advantageous to bring the upper body into an upright position and to lower the seat into the saddle three or four strides in front of a fence. They feel that they can then use their seat to exert a greater influence over the horse. Show-jumping, however, is a very specialized sport and it is wiser for the less experienced rider to perfect a correct jumping position and to concentrate on maintaining that position while coming into a fence, going over it and landing. In this way he will be less likely to be left behind the horse's movement and to pull his horse in the mouth, and will also be in the correct position to go straight into the next stride after landing. Once his position is truly established he will be able to influence the length of the horse's stride by using his legs and seat and by controlling with steady hands, which are independent of the rest of his body.

THE JUMPING SEAT

The rider has a contact with the reins and is using her seat and legs to drive the horse's hindquarters under him to build up the power for the jump.

GETTING LEFT BEHIND

One of the most common faults amongst novice riders is to stiffen up and to get left behind the movement over the fence. It has happened to this rider which has meant her weight is restricting the action of the horse's back but she has avoided hanging on to the reins, which is a bad mistake.

JUMPING WITHOUT STIRRUPS

Jumping without stirrups is an excellent means of developing balance and muscles. This rider looks quite happy without them on the approach.

The rider is coming forward and allowing with her reins (but not losing contact), so that the horse can lower his head to look at the fence, and prepare himself to make a good bascule.

The rider has come forward, but just a little too much as she has lost contact with the reins and her legs have gone back. This fault is not as serious as getting left behind and holding the reins too tightly.

The rider is returning to her normal position, but a little late, perhaps due to her coming so far forward over the fence, and she will find it difficult to balance the horse.

On the take off stride the rider has been a little too anxious not to catch the horse in the mouth and has lost contact with the mouth which makes it more difficult for the horse to find his balance.

Her leg has remained in a good position throughout and she has re-established contact quite well, to balance the horse after the fence. Her hands are not level and her body is slightly twisted.

JUMPING

The position over the fence

Horses jump by dropping their weight on to their forelegs and bringing their hindquarters well under their centre of balance. As the forehand springs into the air the horse has time to tuck his forelegs under his chest before the hind legs hit the ground and propel his whole body over the fence. If the rider is sitting in a correct position and is supple and balanced, the less he moves or interferes with the horse the easier it will be for them both. As the horse's forehand rises, and the horse's hind legs come under the body, the withers will come closer to the rider's chest and the saddle will drop away from his seat. Relying on his balance and suppleness and, if necessary, gripping with his legs and particularly his knees against the saddle, the rider is ready to accept and go with the powerful forward thrust as the horse takes off. To make an efficient jump over the fence the horse has to round his back and to lower and stretch forward his neck and head. It is therefore necessary for the rider to give the horse sufficient length of rein to achieve this without actually losing contact. This he does by leaning forward, straightening his elbows and allowing his hands to go forward and down towards the horse's mouth. This must be done as the horse asks for the extra length of rein and not by throwing the rein forward and abandoning all contact, although this fault is better than causing the horse pain by getting left behind the movement and pulling on his mouth. This is serious because it soon causes a horse to lose confidence and to jump with a flat or hollow back. As the horse lands, the rider has only to rebend his elbows to maintain contact and to be in the correct position for the next stride.

Position on landing

If the rider has maintained the forward position while over the jump he will be able to absorb the jar of the horse's forelegs touching the ground through his supple loins and thighs. Because his seat is still just clear of the saddle it will be easier for the horse to bring his hind legs well forward and under his body on landing. Then both horse and rider will be in the correct position to go straight forward into the next stride.

The rider's task

The rider's task is principally to ensure that the horse is going forward to the fence in a calm balanced manner with sufficient impulsion in each stride to release power at the right moment and propel both of them over the fence. An experienced rider can also help the horse by controlling the length of the stride so that they are able to take off from the correct spot relative to the height and width of the fence. But it should never be forgotten that once this place has been reached it is the horse who has to jump, and the rider can best assist by staying 'still in relation to the horse's movements. Riders who throw themselves forward by straightening the knees or who practise other acrobatic feats are usually only compensating for the inadequacy of their own position or lack of suppleness, and rarely help the horse. All too often such riders rely on their horse's speed and courage and then have to use rough methods to control and/or go with him over a fence.

Learning to jump

The best way for a rider to learn to jump is to go to an instructor who understands the use of the cavaletti and related distances between fences. Cavaletti are used as a form of gymnastic training for both horse and rider. Early lessons are confined to walking and then trotting over a few heavy poles lying on the ground. The rider should be sitting in a correct jumping position, looking straight ahead between the horse's ears. The poles will set the rhythm of the horse's stride and it is the rider's task to feel this and maintain it after leaving the poles and until he turns to ride down them again. At no time should the rider try to check or interfere with the horse in front of the poles. All he should do is to make sure he is sitting in harmony with his horse and is maintaining the impulsion and rhythm. If the horse gets excited he should be ridden quietly in a circle before going down the poles.

Once this can be done with calmness, a small fence can be set up at the end of a line of trotting poles. When the horse is ridden down the line at the trot he will take one extra stride and be in the right place to pop over the little fence. The rider, having maintained his forward position over the poles, has only to bring his chest a little closer to the horse's withers and to allow his hands to go forward as the horse lowers his head and asks for more rein, to have achieved his first jump. Magnified many times and at a much faster pace, the same technique will stand a rider in good stead over a Grand Prix show-jumping course.

Gradually the number and size of the fences can be increased and the trotting poles reduced to one or two, but it is essential that the distances are always correctly measured. Not until both horse and rider are much more experienced should the fences exceed about 1m (3ft) in height.

Once the rider can sit still in relation to his horse and maintain rhythm and impulsion, he can start jumping more natural fences — small posts and rails, hedges, etc — but unless his 'eye' is well established it is wise to continue to ride into a fence at a trot, using a placing rail to put his horse into a canter. He will then take one stride and be in the correct place to jump the fence. As the rider becomes more experienced he can start jumping at an angle and through combinations of fences, but this should not be attempted until the rider's position is really established and he is able to control his horse by his seat and legs rather than his hands.

Then, if the groundwork has been thorough and unhurried, there need be no limit to his equestrian ambitions and achievements.

Right: Debbie Johnsey just a few years later and with world wide victories to her credit, competing at Hickstead.

Below: Debbie Johnsey, as a young rider jumping in junior competitions on her stallion Champ.

Bottom: Learning to jump at home over small natural fences which the pony enjoys.

For many centuries, Europeans have concentrated on the technique of riding, building up a large network of riding schools and developing a highly efficient system for producing trainers.

Europeans are still the leaders in the world of equestrian education but other countries are following suit and today riding schools and centres are mushrooming all over the world. The facilities they offer range from a few ancient, work-worn ponies to the immaculate stables, indoor schools and extensive outdoor facilities of most up-to-date equestrian centres. Before the novice chooses where to ride it pays to make a thorough investigation to decide which is the most suitable.

Riding Schools and Centres
In the UK there are some 4,000 licensed riding schools, and it is illegal for anyone to accept payment for giving riding lessons on his own horse without first obtaining a license from the local authority.

The classified pages of a telephone directory and advertisements in the local newspaper will yield the names of local riding schools; but such sources cannot tell an enquirer how good the schools may be. The British Horse Society and the Association of British Riding Schools both run approval schemes: any school approved by either body must conform to certain standards of stable management and instruction.

The BHS publishes an annual booklet, *Where to Ride,* which contains a list of riding schools in the UK. The riding schools are listed in three sections, 'approved' schools (in the BHS's opinion the best), 'recognized', or simply 'listed'.

The Association of British Riding Schools publishes its list of approved schools in a handbook, giving details of size, range of facilities and any specialities.

The UK's leading school is the National Equestrian Centre at Stoneleigh in Warwickshire. It was opened in 1967 with a view to making it a kind of university of the horse. A large number of different courses are run there and include refresher courses for qualified instructors to bring them up-to-date with new techniques and to ensure a high standard of instruction throughout the country. There are also training courses for selected young showjumpers and advanced courses taken by specialist instructors in dressage, jumping and combined training.

In Sweden there is one of the most picturesque and well-equipped equestrian centres in the world. It was the base of the Swedish cavalry from 1868 to 1968, a period during which Sweden won more Olympic equestrian gold medals than any other nation in the world. Today, Strömsholm is the national equestrian centre for civilians. Its stables hold 100 horses, ranging from unbroken youngsters to those that can tackle medium-level jumping or perform Olympic-standard dressage movements. There are specialized courses in jumping and dressage, and for instructors and grooms. The most important of these is the 'long course', which lasts six months and attracts students from all over the world.

In France the national school is at Saumur, the home of the Cadre Noir, a cavalry troop famous for its eminent equestrian competitors, instructors and authors over the past century. Today, the Cadre Noir still gives instruction to both nationals and foreigners, who can take courses for instructors or in dressage.

In Germany Warendorf in Westphalia contains both the Deutsche Reitschule, the national school for instructors (which also takes foreigners as working pupils), and the Olympic Committee (DOKR) equestrian centre. The DOKR runs impressive facilities, and the best riders can train there. The German national trainers in each of the three Olympic disciplines run courses at Warendorf.

In the south of Germany, at Karlsruhe, is the Reinstitut von Neindorff, where riders have exceptional opportunities to learn about dressage. There are more than 70 horses, many of which are trained to a high standard of dressage.

Austria boasts the most famous riding school in the world. People come from all lands to watch the High School movements performed by the members of the Spanish Riding School. For riders, this school is the ultimate in the world of training, but the only pupils regularly accepted are young Austrian citizens, who enter the school in their teens and serve a long apprenticeship. Occasionally, foreigners with outstanding ability are taken as pupils for periods lasting from six months to two years.

In Spain the Andalusian Riding School is the

A large group taking a lesson at the international riding school at Tata in Hungary. On the continent horses are used even for beginners.

creation of Alvaro Domecq Diaz. His purpose is to perpetuate Andalusian dressage, which blends the classical movements with traditional riding techniques of the region.

In the USA the American Horse Shows Association (AHSA) has set up a Riding Establishment Committee, which lays down standards to be met before a riding school can become a member of the AHSA.

In addition, state and regional Professional Horsemen Associations have member-establishments, although membership does not necessarily indicate quality of horses or instruction.

The USA's most famous centre is at Gladstone, New Jersey, which is the home of the United States Equestrian Team's show-jumping and dressage squads. The three-day event squad opened its own Facility in Hamilton, Massachusetts.

The Potomac Horse Center in Maryland has been designed for men and women of any age with some riding experience. Potomac is particularly well-known for its dressage work.

The Bit o'Luck Stables are one of the newest large centres, specializing in dressage, cross-country and stadium jumping. They have three centres, at Alachua, Florida; Buck Hill Falls, Pennsylvania; and Middleburg, Virginia.

In October 1974, the Walnut stud farm at Lexington, Kentucky, became the Kentucky State Horse Park, the first state park devoted to horses. It already had many of the necessary stables; show rings, cross-country courses, steeplechase courses and dressage arenas are now being built.

A number of colleges offer BSc degrees or BSc in Physical Education that include horsemanship programmes. Special summer courses are available at many of the schools and colleges that include horsemanship in their regular programmes.

In Australia riding schools providing facilities from hack-hiring to instruction in advanced equitation exist in every state. There is no official control over riding schools, apart from local Board of Health regulations and zoning regulations. Surveys of riding schools and equestrian centres are made and published by the magazine *Australian Horse & Rider.*

Becoming a professional instructor

Germany has won the largest number of equestrian Olympic medals and this success is mainly due to the quality of German trainers. The fully qualified trainer will have completed four stages. The pupil spends three years as a Groom before taking a six-week course and an examination to qualify as a Professional Rider. A further year, a three-month course and an examination entitle him to be a Riding Instructor. The Riding Instructor can then apply to become a Horse Master: to reach this stage, he must prove his ability to train horses and riders for top-level competitions.

In Sweden government support has been given to the training of riding instructors. There are two grades of instructors, I and II. Qualifications are obtained after courses at Strömsholm.

In France the Ministry of Youth and Sport sets the examinations, as it does for instructors in all other sports. There are three grades of riding instructor: the Monitor; the Instructor, who can qualify after a course at Saumur; and the Professor, who must be over the age of 25.

In the UK schools for instructors can be found all over the country. Students can enter on a working-pupil basis (ie, tuition in exchange for labour). Hazy definition of this status has led to abuse, however, and some students have been used as cheap labour, receiving little, if any, tuition. Most of the major schools run intensive courses as preparation for the examinations and, although this means paying fees, it is probably the most thorough education.

The British Horse Society (training and development department) arranges syllabuses and decides upon qualifications. There are four levels of professional qualification: the Assistant Instructor certificate (BHSAI); the Intermediate Instructor certificate; the Instructor's certificate (BHSI); and the British Horse Society Fellowship (FBHS).

In the USA, with no governing body equivalent to the British Horse Society, it is relatively easy to become a trainer. No examination or license is required.

In 1974 the Morven Park International Equestrian Institute was opened, and it is the world's only civilian institute of horsemanship and equestrian arts. Many of the students at the Institute attend Springfield College in Springfield, Massachusetts, and receive credits toward their BSc degrees while at Morven Park. The certificates of qualification awarded are Master and Assistant Master of the Horse, and Approved Instructor.

Members of the famous Spanish Riding School.

Early handling

From their earliest days horses must learn to accept but respect the human, for the establishment of this type of relationship will avoid many fights and misunderstandings in the future. It starts with getting the foal used to the touch of the hand in his first few days of life. He should be stroked and talked to, as long as this does not disturb the mother. Later, if the foal comes in at night, he can have daily handling sessions; if he is out at grass all the time, regular fondling may be more difficult to arrange and, if necessary, can wait until the animal is weaned, but no opportunity of talking to and handling him should be missed.

Remember that the fondling should not become spoiling. Too many tit-bits can turn a young horse into a biter. This or any other bad habit requires that he must be reprimanded, if possible the first time, with the voice and a gentle but firm slap on the neck.

Where handling sessions are possible, the foal should be taught to wear a headcollar (halter). This is most easily accomplished if one person approaches the foal from the nearside, puts his left arm around the foal's chest and holds the tail at the root with his right arm. With the foal thus securely held, a second person can put on the halter. A third helper should restrain the mare if necessary.

To teach a foal to lead, he should be pushed from behind and never pulled by the halter. At first it is best to lead the foal only when he is following his mother, but if he co-operates willingly then he can be taken on small independent circuits, though never too far from the mare. At all times the aim must be to establish some discipline without either frightening or hurting the foal. Force should be used only if all else fails, and only in the case of a deliberately wilful youngster.

Early handling sessions can also include an introduction to grooming, stroking his tail and picking up his feet.

After weaning he will no longer have his mother to follow when led, so at first it is best to have an older horse to accompany the foal. Later he can be taken off on his own. The important point is to keep up the handling, and never to leave him running wild without any contact with humans for too long. If he can become progressively more obedient and trusting, then breaking in should be an easy process.

When to break in a horse

The time for breaking in depends on the breed and future of the horse. Flat racehorses are 'backed' (broken) in the autumn as yearlings, and some small breeds are broken in at two. In general, however, three years is the best age. Big horses might have to be turned out to grass and rested after breaking, so that their large overgrown limbs can mature. Smaller, athletic horses can be kept in work, as long as it is carefully graduated and never too strenuous.

When deciding the exact date to start breaking in, the most important point to remember is that at least one hour every day for approximately six weeks must be available. Continuity of training is vital at the early stage.

Another important rule is to keep the horse manageable. A well-covered frame or a gleaming coat means little if the horse is uncontrollable. The best diet, therefore, is a low-energy one, using pellets/cubes rather than oats. If the youngster starts to get lazy, oats can be increased; one easily caught should be turned out to grass.

Tying up

When the horse is relaxed while being led around, it is time for him to learn to be tied up. A horse that runs back as soon as he feels the restrictions of a tethering rope is a nuisance; it is vital that the habit should not be allowed to develop. Some people, believing that the horse should never be frightened,

When moving a foal it is important not to pull him along by his headcollar. A stable rubber around his neck is used to stop him and an arm around the hindquarters to encourage him forward.

prefer to tie the rope to a piece of string, which will break if the horse pulls back. Generally, however, it is better to convince the horse that it is impossible to pull free. Use a wide-webbed headcollar, which will neither break nor cut, and tie the horse in his stall or stable. Leave him next to a haynet so that he can munch away; but remember to tie the haynet so that the foal cannot catch his foot in it. For the first time, leave him for only five minutes or so, watching carefully; then gradually extend the period.

Below: Foals should be fondled often so that they become used to humans.

Right: It is best to take the halter (headcollar) off the foal when turning him out.

LUNGEING

Lungeing is a vital part of a horse's education, and helps to establish balance, rhythm, and the ability to turn circles and to go forward, all without the encumbrance of a rider's weight. The exact amount of activity devoted to lungeing, however, varies enormously. In many countries it is used merely to teach the horse to understand commands and to get him used to saddlery before being ridden, and perhaps after breaking as a useful means of exercising the horse. In such disciplines as the Spanish Riding School, however, it is a vital part of training, and a horse may be lunged for three months prior to riding. At these schools the lunger is highly skilled at this difficult art.

Preparations

The equipment consists of a cavesson, a lunge whip with thong and a snaffle bridle with a bit that is kind (ie, with not too thin a mouthpiece) and that fits the horse. Some trainers prefer to use a special breaking bit. A well-padded roller that fits the horse is also needed, together with a breastplate (although a piece of string is equally effective).

The person lungeing a young horse must be experienced. First-timers should always practise with an older animal beforehand.

The first stage is to put on the cavesson in the stall taking care that the noseband is tight enough to prevent it from slipping round the cheek straps up to the eyes. Attach the lunge rein to the cavesson and coil it over your hand, starting with the free end, so that it will unwind smoothly. Lead the horse to an enclosed area with one hand on the lunge rein close to the cavesson, and the other holding the coil and the lunge whip.

Some trainers like to have an assistant to lead the horse, although an experienced lunger with reactions quick enough to estimate and prepare for the horse's next move is usually better on his own.

If the horse proves stupid or excitable, the main aim is to prevent him from panicking or hurting himself. Try therefore to keep him at a walk, and ensure that he does not get free: this is easier if he is kept in an enclosed area, using barrels and poles to form a temporary enclosure if necessary. If the animal proves very unmanageable, then lunge him for a short time on soft ground or sand, where he will get tired without injury.

The essential points when lungeing are never to take your eyes off the horse, even when bending down to pick up a whip; always to be behind the point of the horse's shoulder so that you are in a position to control the horse's hindquarters with the whip and his head with the rein; and always to keep your pupil on as large a circle as possible.

To achieve this, you should first halt the horse and move away from it. To circle left, hold the rein in the left hand and the coil and the whip in the right. Reverse this position for a right-handed circle. Cluck or click to him to move off, perhaps flicking at his hind legs with the whip. It should learn to associate a cluck or click from the voice with the need to go forward. Persuade him to walk around in a small circle, and as he gets the idea, gradually increase the diameter.

The aims of lungeing

These are to get a horse to move quietly in a circle of about 15m (49ft) in diameter (in the early stages, be content with a smaller circle); to make him walk, trot and halt on the lunge, on both hands (in these early stages, he is not ready to canter); and to make him responsive to the commands of the voice—'walk', 'trot', and 'whoa' (or 'halt'). The commands for an increased pace can be in a higher tone and accompanied by clucks. To slow, a low soothing voice is best.

When these goals have been achieved and the horse is relaxed but respects the commands of his trainer, the roller can be introduced.

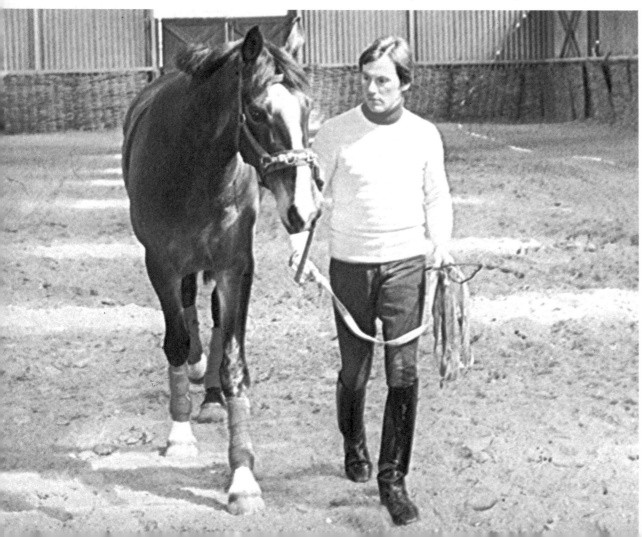

Left: The first stage is to get the horse confident when being led around. Using the lungeing cavesson is best as if the horse tries to get away it is stronger.

Above right: When the horse is first lunged it is best to keep him free of all but the essential tack—the cavesson. The lunger has a good contact with the lunge rein and the whip is ready for use in his right.

Right: The horse has shied and moved in towards the trainer. Contact has been lost reducing the trainer's control. He is correctly moving quickly, to use his whip to encourage the horse to move out, and to shorten the rein.

The trainer moves to stay level with the horse's barrel where he can control the hind quarters with the whip and the head with the rein.

LUNGEING AND LONG-REINING

To put on a roller it is best to be in an enclosed space, but it should be a good-sized stall or stable in case the horse starts to buck.

One of the most common problems is the roller slipping back, tickling the horse in a sensitive area and making him buck and frighten himself. The roller should therefore be fixed with a breastplate, or with a piece of string if a breastplate is not available. The roller can then be left quite loose so that there is no feeling of pressure around the horse's girth. Provided the horse does not freeze or misbehave, the roller can be tightened gradually, notch by notch, until it exerts a slight pressure. The horse can then be lunged with the roller in place; if the horse behaves well, the roller should be left on after the return to the stable. It is putting on and removing the roller that most disturbs a young horse. The first time it is worn, therefore, it is advisable to leave the roller on for two or three days. After this period it can be taken off and put on again each day.

To put on a bridle ensure that it is a little large, so that it will slip easily over the horse's ears. Then shorten it so that the bit is just about to cause wrinkles in the side of the mouth. It is important that the bit is neither too low nor too large, or the horse may develop the serious habit of putting his tongue over it.

Some people leave horses loose with the bridle on and the reins detached. It is very easy, however, for a horse to rub his head, catch the bit and frighten himself, so it is better to tie the animal up where he cannot get into trouble.

After a few days, the horse can be lunged with the bridle on. The cavesson is worn over it (*see picture*) with the lunge rein still attached to the cavesson. The lunge rein must not be attached to the bit, because its action would be to pull the bit through the horse's mouth.

To put on a saddle wait until the horse is quite relaxed when lunged in the roller. At first, a breastplate or piece of string should be worn so that the girth need be done up only loosely without any danger of the saddle slipping. A saddle can be worn during lungeing, with stirrup irons attached if the horse is sufficiently relaxed. The irons can be left hanging down, so that the horse grows used to being touched in the area where a rider's legs will be.

To put on side reins, make certain that they are not too tight (the head should never be behind the vertical) and are of equal length, so that they can effectively achieve their aim of helping to get the horse straight and teaching him to accept the bit and to achieve a good outline (the top line of the back and neck should be rounded, not hollow).

Side reins, which run from the rings of the bit to the saddle or roller, are often used but they can do great harm if attached too tightly. The lunger must be able, by tactful use of the whip and the voice, to drive the horse's hindquarters up so that he accepts the bit. It is all too easy for the equine pupil to evade the contact of the reins by tucking his head in and stiffening his back.

Long-reining

When the pupil has learnt the commands of the voice and moves forward freely, some trainers advocate long-reining to prepare him for riding. Long-reining is essential if the horse is to be driven. The practice entails attaching long reins, which should be as light as possible, to the bit, and running them back through rings on the roller to the trainer, who stands about 2m (6-7ft) away at the rear.

To use long reins successfully the trainer must have sensitive, light hands, because the length of the reins and their consequent weight exaggerates the action. He must never hang on or pull on them, only squeeze and play with them as when riding. He must be agile on his feet and quick to react with his hands if he is to follow the horse and not get in a muddle with the reins, which could easily frighten the horse. Consequently the art of long-reining must be learnt on an older animal, and practised on youngsters only when the trainer is confident of his ability to do more good than harm.

The trainer positions himself to the rear of his horse with a long schooling whip in one hand, and the reins held as for riding in each hand. He can either walk directly behind the horse or stand to the inside so that the pupil can circle around him. An assistant should hold the animal's head until he relaxes, as he may not understand what is required of him, and become frightened. If at any time the reins start to tangle, the trainer should release the outer one and get the pupil to circle him, as in lungeing.

The first stage is to get the horse walking forward,

and changing direction when the trainer asks, at the same time as lifting both reins up so that they clear the hindquarters in the change. If the pupil remains calm and obedient, and the trainer is proficient, then variations can be introduced—trotting in circles around the trainer, figures-of-eight at the walk and trot, and a little extension and collection of the trot.

It is possible to use long reins to teach or improve advanced dressage movements. Many experts use it for working at the piaffe. When breaking in, however, the important point is not to ask too much; the work should be kept to the walk and trot, and only as the horse strengthens up (rarely in less than two months) should cantering be started.

Left: Lungeing the young horse with a roller on. A piece of padding has been placed underneath it in order to prevent any rubbing, and breast girth used to ensure it cannot slip back, which might alarm the horse.

Below: Lungeing with a saddle. The stirrups have been rolled up but when the horse becomes relaxed they can be left loose to get him used to pressure where the legs of the rider will come.

Top right: Skilled trainers can use side reins running from the bit to the saddle or roller. These are a good length as they are coming into effect, but if any shorter the horse's head would come behind the vertical.

Bottom right: Long reining at the trot needs an active trainer. A saddle can be used instead of a roller but it is inadvisable with young horses in case of damage.

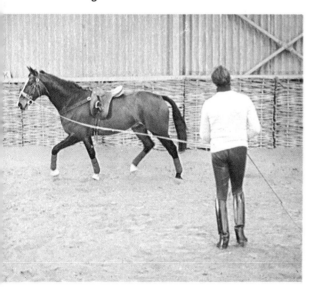

BACKING

Lying across the horse

Two people are needed for this exercise, the rider and the person who has been breaking in the horse (the trainer), to whose voice the horse should by now be obedient. The trainer holds the lunge rein with the left hand and boosts ('legs up') the rider with his right, so that the latter can lie with his stomach on the saddle (see picture). The trainer holds both the horse and the leg of the rider for he can then feel what each is about to do. For example, if he senses that the horse is about to run off, he can tell the rider to jump down.

Most horses freeze when they first feel a rider's weight, so as soon as the rider jumps off, the horse should be moved forward. This encourages the horse not to leap forward from a locked position when it is later asked to move off with the rider on his back.

While the rider lies across him, the horse should be patted around the neck and every effort should be made to make him relax. As soon as he starts to do so, he should be led forward at the walk with the rider resting across the saddle, but with the trainer still holding his leg.

Riding

Once the horse shows understanding and is relaxed when the rider lies across the saddle, riding can begin. In the first stage, the trainer (the man on the ground) is in charge: the rider is passive and the only purpose of the reins is to raise the horse's head if he starts to lower it to buck. It is advisable to use a neck strap for the rider to hold in case of trouble.

The rider is given a leg up and the horse is asked to walk forward. He can be led around the school, with the trainer using his voice and the lunge rein for control.

The next stage is to start lungeing the horse at the trot. Towards the end of the lesson on the second or third day, or when the horse is relaxed, the lunge rein can be removed. It is wise, however, to act as if the horse were still being lunged; the trainer should remain in the centre of the ring, using his voice, while the horse moves in a circle around him.

After two or three days, barring problems, the rider can start to walk and trot around the ring on his own. As soon as he becomes confident of his mount, the rider can start taking the young horse on hacks, provided that there are suitable bridle paths in the area and that the horse can have the reassurance of another horse and rider.

The great advantage of trail riding (hacking out), rather than working in an arena, is that the young horse will find a host of things to interest him. His

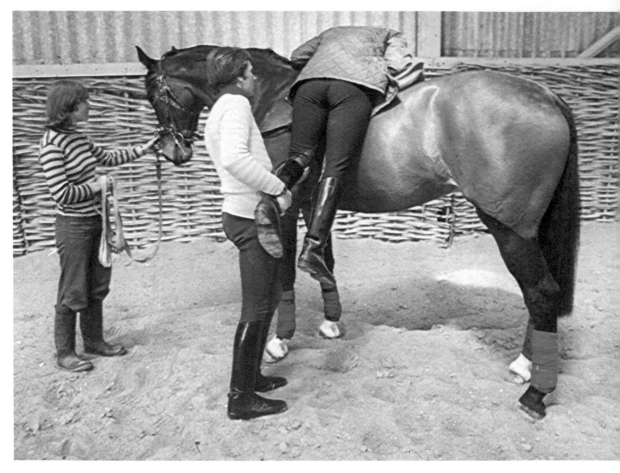

mind is taken off the novelty of being ridden, and the rider can start to replace vocal instructions with those from the leg without disturbing the horse unduly. Before going out on a hack, the horse should be lunged daily. After a time, however, the periods of lungeing should be reduced, and stopped completely as soon as the rider is confident of the horse's behaviour.

Some people believe that a young horse should be ridden on a loose rein. In the end, however, the rider must make contact with the mouth, and it therefore seems advisable to introduce him to this practice early, rather than attempt to convert him later. So, on these early hacks, a gentle contact can be taken on the reins and the horse quietly introduced to the idea of being ridden on the bit.

Potential problems of breaking in

The aim, of course, is to avoid creating problems in the first place, not to frighten the horse into misbehaving or realizing that it is stronger than his rider. No stage should be tackled until a previous

one has been mastered in a relaxed fashion; for instance, the horse should be lunged sufficiently before he is ridden to ensure that he does not disobey out of freshness. The following problems, therefore, should rarely arise.

Rearing is a bad vice, but young horses rarely rear without a reason. Ensure that his mouth is not too tightly held, that his teeth are not hurting and that the bit is not pinching him. If the horse does rear, the rider should get his weight forward and loosen the reins: otherwise he can easily pull his mount over backwards. The horse should be ridden forward with determination as soon as his forelegs touch the ground.

Bucking can be caused by too tight a girth, a saddle that has slipped back, or an excess of freshness. If a horse starts to buck, keep his head up with short, lifting jerks on the rein and urge him forward.

Running away cannot be prevented by strength alone. A horse that is really running away should be turned in ever-decreasing circles, using only the inside rein with varying pressure.

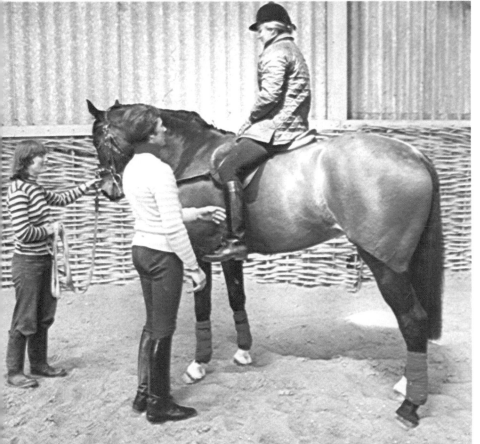

Top left: At first the rider gets the horse used to her weight by lying across him. The trainer is keeping hold of her leg so that he can help her down if the horse gets worried and starts to misbehave.

Above: The rider has been let down into the saddle. With the two people helping it is easier to prevent problems. It is important the horse is patted and talked to all the time in order to keep him calm.

Top right: When moving off for the first time the horse will be likely to hump and stiffen his back. The rider must try not to stiffen against this. The horse relaxes quickest if everybody is relaxed and confident.

Right: Before horse and rider go on their own it is best to do a little lungeing, which the horse already knows about, with the added reassurance of the trainer he has been working with. This rider is brave and has no neckstrap to catch hold of if the horse should suddenly decide to buck.

CHAPTER THREE/BASIC SCHOOLING

The aim of schooling is to teach a horse to understand, respect and gain confidence in his rider and to make him more supple, balanced and relaxed. Schooling will help the horse to use his ability to the full, whatever field he is to specialize in. He might have been able to jump high fences before training, but he will be able to do so for many more years and more successfully if he can work in a relaxed, efficient way, accepting help from his rider rather than fighting and relying on its agility to get out of difficulties. Impatient riders may try to by-pass the flat work in their haste to get on with the action; but a little patience pays dividends, extending a horse's working life and making the animal more pleasurable and successful to ride whether in racing, jumping, hunting, eventing or merely hacking around.

For the best results, good basic training is needed. This involves getting the horse to go forward rhythmically, straight and relaxed, with the hindquarters engaged and the rider maintaining a light elastic contact with the bit. To achieve this, the programme must be varied according to the horse's temperament, conformation and natural ability.

A suitable programme for an average young horse would start with 20 minutes' work in an arena, ridden or lunged, before being taken for a hack, and on the sixth day having a longer hack. This would not suit all temperaments or types, however. Weak, lazy horses need hacking to give them some excitement, including if possible plenty of hill work to build up the muscles. On the other hand, a neurotic horse would be more relaxed with longer periods of steady work in the arena. A nappy one must not be given an opportunity to misbehave: he should always go hacking with another horse, and should never be worked until bored in an arena. The trainer can experiment and must be alert and flexible so as to work out a constructive programme that will develop the horse's strong points and overcome his weaknesses.

It is important to devise activities that are not too difficult for the stage of training and maturity that the horse has reached. Otherwise he may become crotchety, resisting if the work is beyond him. At the same time enough must be asked of the horse to keep him alert and attentive to the rider.

The aim of basic schooling is to make the horse understand the aids of the rider and to make him more supple, balanced and relaxed. This will make everything more fun for horse and rider and enable the horse to do things better, even hacking across country as in the picture.

THE PACES

The movements

The walk can be easily ruined, because an untrained horse tends to tense up against the rider, losing the rhythm of the four hoof-beats. It is advisable to do no more than get the horse walking with a light contact on the bit until he is truly relaxed.

The trot requires a pronounced rhythm, and should be carried out at sufficient speed to make the strides both high and active. If too high, the trot may look pretty but the hock action will tend to be straight. If there is too much activity and speed, the trot will become rather flat and hurried.

At first the rider should post (rise) at the trot, only sitting for a few strides when the horse improves. If the horse does not lose his rhythm or go hollow in the back, and the rider is not thrown around, then he can sit for longer and longer periods. It is much easier to control the horse from a sitting trot but if this is attempted too early the horse will become very stiff in the back.

The trot is usually the best pace at which to work a young horse, for the walk may make him tense and the canter is rarely sufficiently balanced. At the canter, it is more difficult to vary direction frequently because the leading leg has to be changed.

The canter should have a definite three-time hoof-beat and the danger is that it can easily turn into a four-time pace. It is important therefore that the horse must be kept going forward freely at all times.

Another danger is a disunited canter. The horse's inside foreleg and hind leg should be in advance of the outside pair (leading with the inside legs). If he canters disunited (leading with the near foreleg and off hind leg or vice versa), the rider will feel uncomfortable and the horse will be unbalanced. He should be brought back to the trot immediately and the true canter re-established.

The most likely time for him to become disunited is if he strikes off into the canter on the wrong leg (with the outside legs leading, or counter canter). This will make it difficult to negotiate a corner and the horse will try to change. A young horse usually manages this only with the foreleg and thus becomes disunited. Always try to establish the correct lead from the start, by asking him to canter out of a circle. The animal should already be bending correctly, which will make it easier to strike off on the inside legs.

Turning a corner/circle may cause a young horse to want to change rhythm. This must not be allowed.

THE TROT

Keeping a contact at the walk can cause resistance and this horse is overbending.

Although two hoof beats later he is no longer behind the vertical he is still tense.

If a horse resists at the walk it is very easy for him to lose the rhythm of the four hoof beats.

THE WALK

A good trot in which the outside diagonals are moving as a pair and just about to hit the ground.

The outside diagonals are just coming off the ground. The hocks could be better engaged.

The outside diagonals have come off the ground and are about to reach their highest level.

THE CANTER

The canter to the right in which the leading foreleg is about to come off the ground. This is followed by the short period of suspension when all the legs are off the ground. It is during this period of suspension that a flying change is made.

Less than one stride later, all the legs have returned to the ground. It is the outside hind leg, however, that is the first to get there and it is about to leave the ground in the picture.

This is the moment following the period of suspension when the outside hind has returned to the ground. It will be followed by the pair (the inside hind and the outside foreleg). In a bad canter, a four time version, the pair's hoof beat is not simultaneous.

This is the same moment as, above, but one stride later. It is interesting that at this point the horse's head comes behind the vertical and returns to a good position for the remainder of the canter stride. In the canter there is considerable movement of the horse's head and neck.

TURNING AND TRANSITIONS

Aim to keep the head slightly bent to the inside, with fore and hind legs moving on the same track, so that the hind legs do not swing outward or come inward. To achieve this the rider has to co-ordinate his hands and legs (see Chapter 1). It is also important to prevent the horse from falling in to the inside of the circle (a very common fault), achieved by using the inside leg on the girth (further behind would push the quarter out). Avoid neck reining with the inside rein (a natural reaction) because, although this might stop the horse falling in, it will give him the wrong bend and make him stiff through his back.

Remember that in changing direction the bend in the neck should be altered to the inside.

Transitions from a slower to a faster pace The aim is to keep the rein contact and the outline of the horse the same, so the rider must not lean forward and let the horse go faster, but sit upright and urge him forward with his seat and legs. The first step of the new pace should be high and upward, ie, the horse should not be pushed forward on to his forehand. From the walk to the trot both legs of the rider should close on the horse. From the trot to the canter the inside leg is applied with a series of nudges on the girth. This is better than one hard one, which might startle the horse and lead to a change of outline. The outside leg is applied behind the girth: gently, if the horse tends to swing his quarters in; more strongly if they come outward.

Transitions from a faster to a slower pace Here, the aim is not to pull the horse backwards (the horse usually resists this by going above the bit), but simply not to allow him to go on at a faster pace. The rider sits deep in the saddle and applies the legs, pushing the horse to a resistant hand. From the canter to the trot, the rider sits deep in the saddle, while his hands resist the forward draw instead of following the movement of the canter. At the first step of the trot the horse must be ridden forward to ensure the hindquarters are engaged. The same principle is followed when moving from the trot to the walk, and into a halt.

As the horse learns to relax during the transitions, he can be asked to go directly from the canter to the walk. Do not attempt this too early, however, or he will be too stiff in the back, will be unable to lower his hindquarters and will either go heavy on the hands, falling onto his shoulder, or resist by going above the bit and becoming hollow in the back. With this more demanding transition, extra encouragement from the rider's seat and legs is needed to get the horse to place his hindquarters well underneath. Make the transition progressive and not too abrupt as this produces resistances.

In the first picture (right) the horse is going straight but by the second the rider has asked for a bend with the inside rein. As the horse starts to turn the rider twists his shoulders to keep them parallel with those of his horse. Most of the rider's action cannot be seen for it is his inside leg that is working on the girth to keep up the impulsion and around which the horse is bent. His outside leg can be seen resting against the horse, brought into play if the hindquarters swing out. The other vital aid is the outside rein which is used to regulate the pace. Many beginners use it to stop the horse turning too sharply and by pulling on it bend the horse to the outside. This offbalances him and care must be taken that the outside hand does not move.

CAVALETTI WORK

Training should bring out the best in the horse, by building up his confidence and agility through progressive work. In jumping, this means starting with poles and cavaletti so that the period between not jumping and jumping is so short that the horse is not aware of it. Try to ensure that the progress is never forced so that the horse can remain relaxed.

The cavaletti

The cavaletti consists of a pole 3m (10ft) in length that is bolted to a cross piece at either end so that it can be used at three heights simply by turning it over on to different sides. The longer the sections of the cross piece, the higher these heights will be, but the normal measurements are a 92cm (3ft)

cross piece so the bar can be 25cm (10in), 38cm (15in) or 48cm (19in) high.

No training stable should be without cavaletti, which are easy to make, carry and adjust in height. When walking or trotting over them, the horse has to lift his legs high, which flexes the joints and teaches him to concentrate and to co-ordinate his limbs. By placing the cavaletti at equal distances apart, the horse will develop rhythm; and putting them at a set distance in front of a fence ensures that the horse will take the right length of stride before take-off, without learning to accelerate and flatten.

To start with, use poles on the ground. As with all other obstacles, the horse should be shown them first. As long as the horse has time to look at them

and sniff them, he has no excuse for stopping in fright. The rider, too, knows that he must ride firmly.

Start with one pole and then add more progressively (up to eight) at 1.2m (4ft) to 1.5m (5ft) intervals depending upon the size of the horse's stride. During all jumping training, it helps to have an assistant who can give advice, move poles and adjust distances.

As soon as the pupil has learned first to walk and then to trot over the poles calmly and without losing rhythm, then cavaletti can be introduced. They should be at the lowest height at first and the rider should aim at developing a springy rhythmical trot over them.

By introducing variations, the rider can teach his

CANTERING OVER CAVALETTI

TROTTING POLES LEADING TO A HOG'S BACK

mount to lengthen or shorten his stride. When he is taking one stride at the trot between each cavaletti the distance between them can be extended to 3m (10ft) or more or less, according to the pupil. The distances should be shortened or lengthened by a few inches at a time, eventually introducing two short distances followed by two long ones (but never vice versa).

The horse can then be taught to canter over cavaletti, popping straight in and out (2-3m (6-10ft) apart). At the end of the line a parallel or hog's back could be placed (see picture) at either 3m (10ft) or 6m (20ft) from the last single cavaletti.

Another excellent exercise is to put the cavaletti in a circle with a diameter of about 20m (65ft) placing them either 1.5m (5ft) apart for trotting or 2.5-3m (8-10ft) for cantering. Alternatively, cavaletti can be scattered around, so that the horse can be trotted over them out of turns, on angles or in succession.

At all times the horse should trot or canter over the cavaletti with rhythm, balance and calmness. The rider must approach them as if there were nothing there. Tensing up, which spoils the horse's rhythm, can be overcome by breathing deeply or by shutting the eyes when on a straight line for the cavaletti.

The exercises may be carried out at the sitting or posting (rising) trot. More control and greater activity of the hindquarters is achieved at the sitting trot and it is therefore preferable unless the horse is too weak and stiff in the back to accept the rider's continual weight, or unless the rider has an insecure or heavy seat and finds it difficult to sit softly.

The distances mentioned are not standard. Horses and ponies have different lengths of stride, and sloping ground or heavy going (such as sand) also affect the length of stride. Trainers must use their common sense, and if in doubt experiment with the cavaletti at their lowest. If the distance appears wrong, change it immediately and do not persevere under the illusion that it ought to be right—there are no hard-and-fast measurements.

If the horse gets in a muddle because either the exercise was too difficult for it or a mistake had been made in the distance, go back to a simpler exercise.

Jumping a series of cavaletti at the canter. These have been positioned at their highest point, ie the pole on top. They have been placed 3m (10ft) apart which is an easy distance so that the average horse has neither to lengthen nor shorten his stride, and the rider is at all times remaining forward with a light and at times loose rein contact, not interfering with the horse at all.

Three trotting poles 1.2m-1.5m (4-5ft) apart have been placed in front of a hogs back made out of cavaletti. The poles make the horse flex his hocks, see the first two pictures in the series; by the third however, he has broken into the canter. The poles also position him in a good place for take off. In this case the last pole is 3m (10ft) from the hogs back but as the horse has stood off quite far (last picture) the distance could be shortened to make him bascule more.

Basic schooling
JUMPING

A horse's jumping is difficult to improve but easy to spoil. Consequently it is vital to have an ideal to aim for, to keep a check on progress and, if the horse is failing to keep up the standard, to seek advice from an expert. Ideally, the horse should approach the fence in a balanced, calm manner, listening to the rider and with a rhythmic stride. He should then jump the fence with a bascule (lowering his head and neck and rounding his back so that it forms an arc), because this is the most efficient way of clearing a fence. On landing, he should re-establish the balanced, calm, rhythmical pace of the approach. Jumping in this way calls for relatively little mental and physical effort.

It is easy to hinder or destroy a horse's natural ability by getting him over-excited or allowing him to jump very flat or to refuse to jump. With few exceptions, these problems arise because rider and horse are advancing too fast, so that the horse fails to understand what is expected of him, finds jumping difficult and loses confidence. If this happens, the horse must immediately be taken back to the early stages and given some more work— some on the flat to get him obedient, and some over poles and cavaletti to help restore his rhythm and agility. The rate of progress will depend not only on the horse's natural ability but also on that of the rider. If they are both learning together then great patience and thoughtful training are needed.

Jumping without a rider
Most trainers believe that a horse should be without a rider when he is introduced to fences. It is wise to extend this stage if the rider has had little experience of teaching horses to jump. Jumping loose forces the horse to think for himself and relieves him of the anxiety of carrying a rider. It can take place on the lunge, or in an indoor or fenced school, or down a chute (enclosed lane) of fences. Riders lacking the latter facilities will have to make do with lungeing, and this is just as effective if the lunger works carefully.

In lungeing it is important, as always, to ask for only a little improvement at a time. Start with a pole on the ground before progressing to cavaletti and after a few days a fence. Remember to show the horse each obstacle before asking him to go over it, and position the animal so that he arrives at the middle of the obstacle, and has two or three straight strides before having to take off. This means that the lunger will have to be very active, moving quickly to get his pupil in the right place.

When the fence is introduced always place wings or sloping poles on either side to discourage the

horse from running out, and ensure that the wings are low so that the lunge rein cannot get caught in them. When the horse is in the air, see that he has freedom to lower his head (the lunge rein must not be tight and the horse should not wear side reins). Finally, do not ask too much by starting jumping before he has warmed up with at least ten minutes at the trot and canter on the flat. Do not jump the horse for more than two or three consecutive circuits, but give him regular breaks of three or four circuits on the flat.

If the horse is to be jumped free in an enclosed school, start with a low fence, built with very large wings to prevent him from running out. Two or more assistants are needed to cover the school so that the pupil can be quietly but firmly encouraged

The red and white pole acts as a wing and prevents the lunge rein catching on the cavaletti. In the first picture the trainer has a good contact for control and is behind the horse to enable her to use the whip. On take off she loosens the contact so he can lower his head.

(with the voice and cracking whips) to keep going around the outside of the school, and straight toward the fences.

Training a horse loose is invaluable as long as he is not excited through confused controls and does not discover, through incompetent or hesitant handling, that it is easier to go around the outside than over the top of the fence.

JUMPING

Jumping with the rider

When the horse has learned while free how to clear a fence in a relaxed manner, then the rider can take over. It is, however, an excellent idea to continue giving him occasional lessons free. The variety is good for him, and so is the opportunity to jump without relying on the rider.

The best way of introducing a fence is by extending the cavaletti lesson. For a 16hh horse, a 61cm (2ft) post and rails can be placed 6m (20ft) away from the last of three trotting poles or cavaletti at 1.5m (5ft) apart. In this way, as long as the rider helps the horse to keep up the rhythm and impulsion, he will arrive in a good place for take-off.

The rider is a vital aid in getting the horse to go calmly and confidently toward the fences. As he rides toward the fence he must reassure the animal that he is there to help, not to hinder. The reassurance comes largely from the rider's legs, which should feel as if they were enclosing the horse, and the tightening of the seat and legs on the approach encourages forward momentum. Some trainers like to give their horses a loose rein so that they learn to look after themselves and there is no risk of interference to the mouth from the rider. For competent riders, however, maintaining a light contact on the mouth (but no hooking or pulling)

makes it easier to keep up the rhythm and to activate the hind legs. Choose one method or the other and stick to it. It is disturbing for the horse to expect a contact and lose it in the stride before take-off. Unfortunately, this is a common fault among riders, which makes it difficult for the animal to keep balanced, and can even ruin his confidence.

For the rider, the take-off can be tricky. At the trot it is difficult to judge the exact moment of take-off and the rider must be relaxed and have a good enough seat to be able to follow the horse's movements. If he anticipates the take-off he will unbalance his pupil; if he gets left behind, he may jab him in the mouth, which will make the horse fearful of using his head and neck. Unless the rider is confident of being able to follow the horse, it is best to jump on a loose rein and to put one hand on a neck strap.

Gridwork

Although most trainers prefer to introduce the early obstacles by setting them up after one or more cavaletti, opinions differ over the next stage of training. Some like to continue over single fences, others over grids (a line of fences with none, one or two strides between each). The danger of the grid is that unless distances are set correctly and measured

A SINGLE FENCE

Trotting into a single fence. All looks well at this stage although the hocks are a little far out to give him the power to spring.

A GRID

The two cavaletti help both to engage the hindquarters and to place him in the right place to take off, so avoiding the mistakes in the top sequence.

The horse is rounding himself well, the rider is sitting quietly just keeping him balanced but not interfering.

The horse is sizing up the upright poles which lie one stride ahead for him to jump, and has not jumped high over the cavaletti.

The stride later he has decided not to jump. The rider has anticipated to the take off, coming off the saddle and cannot use her seat to push him into and over the fence.

He slides into the fence. The difficulty arose because for the first time that day there was no cavaletti before the fence to help him judge the right point for take off.

The horse is in the middle of his non-jumping stride. It is a good one with the hocks engaged, head lowered and back rounded.

The horse is about to take off, quite close to the fence which will make him bascule. The rider has let the reins go which could unbalance him.

The rider is in a very good position. The horse is putting in a good leap although he will have to tuck his hind legs up well to clear the fence.

Upon landing note how the pasterns are bent. The rider is in a good position to balance him correctly.

59

frequently to ensure that fences have not been moved, they can create traps, perhaps causing a horse to crash into a fence. This could damage the horse's confidence, and it is best not to use grids unless there is an assistant to monitor their measurements.

A correctly measured grid builds up a horse's confidence, as the animal will always arrive at an easy take-off position. The rider can sit quietly without having to pull him back or push him forward, and this helps the animal to keep his balance and rhythm. Most important, however, the distances between the grid fences can be intentionally altered. A shorter distance teaches the horse to take shorter strides, to get close to the obstacles for take-off and to bascule to clear them. A greater distance encourages him to extend his stride, to take off further back and to stretch himself in the air. The grids are thus excellent gymnastic exercises.

It is best always to start the grid line with one or two cavaletti or poles, as this helps to relax both horse and rider. The next fence can be 6m (20ft) away and the following 7.5m (23ft) apart for one stride or 10.5m (33ft) for two. The longer distance allows the horse to break into a canter. The fences can be between 61cm (2ft) and 1.07m (3ft 6in) high, and if a parallel is introduced the distance should be measured from the centre of the two poles.

Single fences

At first, single fences should be very low, between 61cm and 92cm (2-3ft), and it is best to jump them from the trot because the slower pace forces the horse to bascule in order to clear them. Here again, it is important to keep up a rhythm, so if the animal darts toward a fence, act as if not intending to jump it, and circle the horse quietly to one side. Re-establish the rhythm and try again. Remember not to haul the horse out at the last moment, as this might get him into the habit of running out or stopping.

Try to build a variety of fences to jump. At first, they should not be too alarming or painful to the horse if he knocks them down. Later, however, the fences should be made more imposing to encourage a horse to put in a better jump. A fairly solid fence will teach an animal that it is wiser to try to clear them.

A horse that can approach a 92cm (3ft) fence with a good outline at a rhythmical, balanced trot and jump it with a good bascule can be considered to have completed his basic schooling both on the flat and over fences. He should now be ready to specialize in the chosen field.

FURTHER GRIDWORK

A grid of cavaletti followed by a single pole and a parallel. With no groundlines it is more difficult for the horse, but he should bascule better.

The horse is lowering his head and appears about to bascule well.

The horse is lowering his head well to look at the second pole of the parallel. The rider has come rather far forward which will make it difficult to keep a steady rein contact.

He does jump a little flat, however, and has not folded his legs, perhaps because he is too interested in the next fence.

Upon landing the rider is in a good position to keep him balanced as she has a light contact with the reins and has her legs on his sides.

The stride between the two fences is quite a long one and the horse is having to stretch out in order to reach a good place for take off.

The jump is a little disappointing for such a good take off. His back is rather straight, he is not using his head and neck very much, and his legs are left dangling, not tucked up.

The landing with the rider timing her return to the saddle well. Any sooner and she could have restricted his use of hindquarters. Any later and she would have found it difficult to balance him correctly after landing, which would have made an approach to a subsequent fence awkward.

GETTING A HORSE IN CONDITION

Whatever work a horse has to do, he must be fit enough to cope with it without placing undue strain on limbs, wind and heart. This degree of condition (fitness) cannot be acquired quickly. The process must be progressive so that, almost imperceptibly, the animal ceases to be round, sloppy, soft and lazy, and becomes hard-muscled, tough, strong and clear-winded.

The transformation is achieved by a balanced programme of feeding and exercise. The feed supplies the proteins and carbohydrates needed to build up energy and muscle. Exercise strengthens the animal, develops the muscles, gets rid of surplus fat, hardens up the legs and clears the wind.

Right amounts of feed and exercise
The type of horse governs the length of the fitness programme. Native breeds are naturally tough and keep themselves strong even at grass. Consequently more work can be asked of them in a shorter time than of the more delicate breeds. Most ponies, therefore, can by-pass weeks one and two on the fitness chart.

The stage of conditioning (fitness) already reached determines the point at which the programme should be started. A horse that has been at grass for more than two months must start at week one of the chart. A horse returning to work after leg trouble should stay on week one for up to one month. If he has been rested for two to three weeks, he can start at week two or three. There are no hard-and-fast rules. The programme should be eased if the horse shows signs of puffiness in the legs, sweating a great deal, distress when breathing or not eating his feed.

The proposed work governs the degree of condition (fitness) required. A horse kept for rallies and hacking does not need to be very fit, whereas an eventer must be hard and lean enough to stand up to the rigours of endurance work.

In drawing up a suitable programme, first consider the date by which the horse must be fit and then work backwards, taking into account the factors given above. This will tell you when to start work, and determine the number of weeks needed to bring the horse to the required fitness and what should be done each week.

Types of conditioning work
Roadwork at the walk is time-consuming but very beneficial, because the hard surface strengthens the legs without jarring them, and the horse is never under strain. Trotting should be introduced progressively but not too fast as this can be jarring, and the rider should change diagonals frequently (see Chapter 1), to keep his weight distributed evenly. The best roadwork for getting fit is going up and down hills. Again this must be progressive, but walking and eventually trotting up hills develops muscles, makes the horse work and helps to clear his wind. In all roadwork it is important not to slop along, for this means that the horse is not working hard enough and can easily slip and hurt his knees (many stables insist on knee caps being worn as a precaution).

Lungeing is less time-consuming but should be only a supplement to roadwork. Start at the walk.

Galloping must be left until the horse is very fit, for the extra speed means he is at greater risk of damaging himself. It is important therefore to gallop only on good going, ideally on a racehorse trainer's gallops if permission can be obtained.

Schoolwork tunes up the muscles once the early part of the programme has hardened the horse. Again, the introduction must be gradual. A jumper should start over cavaletti and progress to the height of the obstacles that he will compete over. The

THE FEEDING AND EXERCISE PROGRAMME

Week	Oat and hay ration	Exercise
1	Worm on bringing in 1.8kg (4lb) oats 8kg (18lb) hay	Walking on the roads for ¾ hour
2	1.8kg (4lb) oats 8kg (18lb) hay	Walking on roads 1 hour, alternated with 1 or 2 days lungeing for ½ hour
3	2.3kg (5lb) oats 7.7kg (17lb) hay	On roads 1 hour with short periods of trotting alternated with 1 or 2 days lungeing for up to ¾ hour
4	2.3kg (5lb) oats 7.7kg (17lb) hay	Start a little schooling, which should be continued in all the weeks ahead: it can be before roadwork or alternated with it
5	2.7kg (6lb) oats 6.8kg (15lb) hay	Increase roadwork to about 1 hour 20 min
6	3.2-3.6 (7-8lb) oats 6.4kg (14lb) hay	On roads 1½ hours Start canters over about 0.8km (½mi)
7	3.6-4.5 (8-10lb) oats 5.9kg (13lb) hay	Roadwork up to 1¾ hours 2 canters during week
8	3.6-4.5kg (8-10lb) oats 5.9kg (13lb) hay	Roadwork of 2 hours 3 canters during week
9	4.5-5.4kg (10-12lb) oats 5.4kg (12lb) hay	Roadwork 2 hours 1 gallop of up to 1.2km (¾mi) at half speed
10	4.5-5.4kg (10-12lb) oats 5.4kg (12lb) hay	Roadwork 2¼ hours 2 gallops at ¾ speed
11	5.4-7.3kg (12-16lb) oats 4.5-5.0kg (10-11lb) hay	Roadwork up to 2¼ hours 2 gallops at ¾ speed
12	5.4-7.3kg (12-16lb) oats 4.5-5.0kg (10-11lb) hay	Roadwork 2½ hours 2 gallops at ¾ speed

dressage horse has to become a gymnast, but must start work with simple exercises for short periods. **Cantering** should not be begun until the horse has been in work for a few weeks, and again must be progressive. Some riders canter in straight lines and up and down hills, others in circles (which must be on both reins), and the choice depends largely on the facilities available. Cantering must be carried out on a good surface. If the only suitable area is a sand arena, circling is a necessity.

The chart left, is for an event horse ready to go in a one-day event. The hunter should be ready by the end of week nine, the show-jumper after week seven, the pony for rallies (who generally starts at week three) should be fit enough by week five. For these latter horses gallops are unnecessary. The amount of food should be adjusted according to the size of the horse.

Right: A horse being ridden for the first time after a long rest. He has a big belly and no muscles on the back or neck.

Below: Walking on roads is excellent for getting a horse fit.

THE PONY CLUB

There are Pony Clubs all over the English-speaking world, and even in places where English is not the principal language. Pony Club members may ride Arab horses on sun-baked desert sand, rangy Whalers in the Australian outback, Quarter-horses in Western America, Cape ponies in South Africa or genuine, home-grown native ponies in the British Isles, but the basic aims of the Pony Club are the same everywhere, and the rallies of the members follow much the same format.

This is not really surprising because all the Pony Clubs sprang from one society for young riders that was founded in England in 1929. The object of the society was to teach children how to care for their ponies and how to become better riders. There were — and still are — further objectives dealing with sportsmanship, citizenship and other lofty ideals, but the most important is still the care and improvement of horse and rider.

The activities

The working rally is the main means of achieving this end. Most Pony Club branches arrange various activities for their members, all of whom have to be under 20 years of age, but the working rally is the only one that they are expected to attend regularly. At most working rallies, children are given a period of mounted instruction by qualified instructors, followed perhaps by a short course of jumping or basic dressage. In this way, bad habits can be dealt with before they have time to become established and problems can be ironed out quickly and effectively.

If this makes the working rally sound a solemn, even boring occasion, it is not meant to. Most children, in fact, thoroughly enjoy the working rally, appreciating the chance to learn from an expert how to school their horses and teach them to become responsive, well-mannered rides. After all, a well-schooled horse enhances every form of riding, from a gentle hack to a day with hounds.

Although records of membership are kept at the headquarters of the Pony Club in every country or state, the actual organization of the rallies is in the hands of local branch officials, all of whom work voluntarily. Each rally, therefore, is geared to the needs of the children in that area, based on the organizers' personal knowledge of the riding standards and horses of their members. Large branches, with 300 members or more, are usually divided into sub-branches, and advanced instruction can be arranged for those children who are capable of attaining an exceptionally high standard. At the other end of the scale are very small branches with fewer than 20 members and here, of course, the

opportunity for individual instruction is great. Although the method of teaching riding may not vary much, the type of instruction is tailored to individual needs. For example, there would be no point in building a show-jumping course if all the members were mounted on Shetlands (not such an impossibility as it sounds: when the Orkney branch started in 1963, all five of its members rode Shetlands and arrived at the first rally with only two saddles and three bridles between them).

Rallies are usually held during school holidays, although here again flexibility is possible, some small branches meeting as often as once a fortnight throughout the year.

Apart from the working rally, all branches organize other forms of activity, from mock hunts, gymkhanas and hunter trials to dismounted rallies such as lectures, film shows and special outings. The activities vary from branch to branch; trail rides and bush walks are popular in Western America and Australia, cross-country rides and orienteering in some parts of Great Britain. In hot countries, members often take their horses swimming.

At dismounted rallies, children learn such things as stable management and first aid, shoeing and the importance of well-kept feet, and the principles of lungeing and bitting. Some gatherings, such as dances and barbecues, are purely social; bus trips whisk children off to major horse shows (as spectators) or on visits to racehorse training stables and leading stud farms.

Right: Pony Clubs arrange many competitions for their members and this young rider is taking part in one of their jumping classes.

Below: Even though this girl is very young it is part of Pony Club policy that she be entirely responsible for her mount.

THE PONY CLUB

The promotion of hunting is an important aim in the Pony Club. Many branches have close links with their local hound pack and members may be allowed to hunt on certain days at reduced fees. At special children's meets, much effort is given to teaching children what hunting is all about, the habits of foxes and how hounds work. It is rare for a hunt not to co-operate with the Pony Club branch or branches in its country; older hunt members are well aware that the future of their sport depends on encouraging the young, and many Pony Club children grow up to take an active part in their local pack.

The highlight of many a Pony Club member's year is the annual camp, which usually lasts a week. The horses are accommodated in stables or on horse lines, while the children sleep under canvas or in barns. If sleeping accommodation is difficult to arrange, the children attend daily. The advantages of camp are numerous: seven days' concentrated teaching inevitably improves the skills of both rider

and mount; children get to know and to make friends with other members; teams for inter-branch competitions can be selected and the training begun.

Inter-branch competitions have been held at a national level since soon after World War II. More recently, exchange visits have been arranged between members in different countries. All Pony Club branches, wherever they exist, follow a system of testing children in horsemanship at various levels. The tests are optional but most children volunteer to take at least the lower standards. Only a few are capable of reaching the very high level of the A Test, and those who do so usually go on to a career with horses. Most attain their C Test certificates and a large number of these progress to B Test standard. The lowest standard, the D Test, is designed to encourage younger members. Periphery tests include those in hunting, country lore, road sense and horsemanship.

The greatest value of the Pony Club is that it has

something to offer every child, whatever his skill as a rider or the quality of his horse. At a rally, no child will be asked to do more than he and his mount are capable of achieving.

Preparation for a rally

The organizers do not expect hard-muscled fitness from a horse kept wholly at grass; rallies are not endurance tests. They do, however, expect that a horse will be properly prepared, within the limits imposed by circumstances.

This means that he will be brought to the rally well turned out, with tack clean, mane and tail clear of tangles, and coat free from superficial dirt and mud. His feet should be shod with shoes in good condition, securely fixed, or (if habitually left unshod) the hooves should have been recently trimmed and tidied. Bridles and saddles should fit.

Preparation for a rally, therefore, must begin well in advance. The work expected of the pony will not be particularly hard, but may be more than he is accustomed to, and a feed of concentrates to suplement his normal grass diet, given the night before and on the morning of the rally, will provide the animal with the extra energy he requires.

A rally is not an occasion for stay-a-beds. Even if the animal is being transported to the rally by vehicle, unhurried preparation is always best. The animal must have time to digest his food before setting out. Grooming should be more than a lick and a promise.

It is even more important to leave plenty of time if the rider is hacking to the rally. The instructor will not take kindly to a member whose mount arrives puffed and sweating because he has had to canter most of the way.

At all times, Pony Clubs are at pains to instil in members a sense of caring for their animals. So many of the children who ride today are first-generation riders. For them and their non-horsey parents, the Pony Club is a ready and willing source of information and advice.

Left: A Pony Club show where many types of classes are held for members and include Best Rider, jumping and gymkhana events.

Right: A Pony Club camp where the ponies stay for anything up to a week in stables or on tethering lines, and the children live in tents or dormitories. The children look after their ponies and competitions are often run to judge who does this the best.

GYMKHANAS

It is a well-known fact that converts make the best fanatics. When the British Army in India in the last century adopted the Indian practice of organizing gymkhanas or mounted games, their enthusiasm soon outdid that of their Indian hosts. Gymkhanas became a regular feature of life under the British Raj, and donkeys, mules, even camels were pressed into service for the occasion.

These light-hearted gatherings had many underlying advantages. They helped to cement regimental loyalty by bringing together officers and men in an atmosphere of relaxation and laughter. Women were also permitted to take part, and gymkhanas provided entertainment for the wives and daughters of all ranks. Most important of all, they served to keep soldiers and horses alike in a state of suppleness and fitness, and made a welcome change from route marches and drilling.

In recent years, there has been a revival of interest in gymkhanas for adults, and many riding clubs hold such frolics for their members. This is not surprising, because gymkhanas are first and foremost great fun, with much to offer the not-so-skilled. At the same time, the element of competition gives a bite to the proceedings, making mounted games immensely popular with those who lack the opportunity and finance to take part in adult competitive sports. Organizers of gymkhanas, though, should remember that it is a kindness to limit some classes to adults only. It can be embarrassing for an adult on a 16hh hunter to be beaten by a shrimp of a girl on a Shetland!

When gymkhanas were introduced to Britain by soldiers returned from service in India, the sport found a whole new band of eager participants among children, whose small, agile, sure-footed animals were so admirably suited to the demands of mounted games. Today, it is largely children who take part in gymkhanas, not only in Britain but throughout the riding world.

Types of events
The events themselves are a testimonial to human inventiveness. At one time, most of the competitions were tests of speed, with perhaps a few sheep hurdles introduced as jumps. Today, a gymkhana entrant may have to peg out a line of washing, throw potatoes into a bucket, sew on buttons, ride pillion through a line of obstacles, dress up (or undress), carry flags/buckets/shopping baskets/waste paper from one end of the arena to the other, burst balloons, snatch apples with his teeth; anything, in short, except stand on his head while cantering around the ring, and even that may come in time.

Speed is no longer the criterion; deftness, agility and suppleness carry a far greater premium.

Ponies, with their manoeuvrability and their cat-like cunning, tend to make better gymkhana mounts than horses. Indeed, many a wily old gymkhana pony knows the rules better than his rider and is capable of completing the course whether there is a child on his back or not. It is a remarkable sight to see a skilled pony negotiate a line of bending posts at a canter, executing a series of flying changes as he zigzags between the posts and curving his body closely around the final post before zigzagging back.

Preparation for gymkhanas
A top-class gymkhana pony has to be as fit and hard-muscled as a polo pony, and it helps if the rider can be likewise. But the vast majority of those who take part in gymkhanas are nowhere near that standard of fitness, and such is the infinite variety of mounted games that there is no necessity to attain it. In any case, most competitors are mounted on grass-fed animals, who are perfectly capable of taking part in a series of gymkhana events, say, once a week during the holidays without suffering any ill effects.

Practice, however, is a different matter. Practising such exercises as bending, turning, stopping and starting all help to make a pony agile, provided they are carried out for no more than 20-30 minutes a day. Ponies can be trained to stand still near a bucket, and not to buck or shy if a balloon bursts or a plastic bag flaps close by. Even a highly strung animal can, with patience and rewards for good behaviour, learn to regard most gymkhana activities with equanimity.

Right: Chase Me Charlie, where competitors follow each other over a single fence that is gradually raised.

Below: This is one of the favourite gymkhana events, a bending race where the competitors race their way in and out of a line of poles.

SHOW-JUMPING

Show-jumping has become the most popular form of equestrian competition, probably because the rules are easy to understand. A competitor gets penalized for certain easily recognizable mistakes, and the winner is the competitor who incurs the least number of penalties, returns the fastest time or gains the highest number of points, depending on the type of competition.

Types of Competition

Every country bases its national rules on those of the international equestrian organization the Federation Equestre Internationale, (FEI). Although titles may vary, there are three basic categories of competitions:

Table A is a competition in which the entrants jump a course and are faulted for the following mistakes:

First disobedience	3 faults
Obstacle knocked down	4 faults
Second disobedience	6 faults
Fall of horse or rider	8 faults
Third disobedience	elimination

The winner is the one with the least faults, but in the case of equality of faults between two or more of the competitors there can be a division or a jump-off, or the competitor who has recorded the fastest time is the winner. The conditions of the competition state whether time will decide in the first round, or the first, second, third or fourth jump-off.

Table B is a competition in which the entrant jumps a course and each fault is penalized by adding ten seconds to the time for the round. The winner is the competitor who has recorded the fastest time.

Table C is similar to Table B except that the penalty seconds added vary according to the length of the course and the number of fences.

The element of speed has been introduced to many competitions as an additional test. A horse that can jump a course fast (which entails both going at speed and cutting the corners into a fence) must be responsive to his rider, balanced and well trained. The speed element has thus made it necessary to school horses, and makes a class more exciting and interesting for spectators.

The time of a competitor is taken from the moment he rides through the start until he reaches the finishing line. It is recorded either by a stop-watch, or by breaking a ray at the starting point which completes a circuit and sets a clock going in the judges' box. This stops as the competitor passes through the finish, breaking another ray.

The time allowed is the time in which the competitor should have completed the course. It is

calculated on the speed laid down for a competition (350m per minute is the norm) and the length of the course. If a competitor exceeds the time allowed, penalties are incurred. The time limit is twice the time allowed. If a competitor exceeds this, he is eliminated.

The basic rules

The judge's signal is a bell, whistle or hooter and the competitor will be eliminated if he starts before this is given. It can also be used to stop and re-start a competitor during a round.

A knockdown occurs if any element of the fence (wing, flag, pole, brick, etc) is lowered in height. The only exception is if a pole lower than the top pole, but in the same vertical plane, falls.

Disobediences include: a circle causing a competitor to cross his tracks before jumping the next obstacle; a refusal (ie, stopping in front of a fence), but a horse that does a standing jump without reining back has not refused; a run-out (when the horse swerves past the fence it is supposed to jump, or jumps to the outside of the flags marking the edges of the fence); a resistance (if the horse stops, naps, goes backwards or turns around.

Combination fences are doubles, trebles or multiples (two, three or more fences with no more than

These mistakes all incur penalties.

Above: Tony Newberry on Snaffles makes a very definite refusal (three faults).

Above right: Although this competitor is demolishing the fence, it will only be four faults.

Below right: Eight faults as Graham Fletcher takes a fall—the horse's shoulders and hindquarters are on the ground.

two non-jumping strides between each). In cases of a refusal or a fall in the middle of a combination, the competitor must start at the first part again.

Flags mark the extremities of the fences, red to the right, white to the left. If one is knocked down the competitor is penalized four faults.

Unauthorized assistance is forbidden during a round. Shouts from the ringside to get the horse to go forward, or to remind the competitor of the course, result in elimination.

Elimination is incurred for: three refusals; taking the wrong course; starting before the bell; showing an obstacle to a horse before starting or after a refusal, a resistance lasting more than 60 seconds.

A fall occurs when the rider is separated from the horse so that he has to remount, or the horse's shoulders and hindquarters touch the ground.

The upright straight fence is built so that its entire structure is perpendicular to the ground and each element is placed one above the other in the same plane.

The spread fence is built so that the structure has width as well as height.

The ground line helps the horse to arrive at the best place to take off. The easiest take-off point at a fence is usually a distance away from it that is 1 to 1½ times its height, and the essence of successful show-jumping is to get the horse to take off within this zone.

The horse judges the point for take-off by looking at the bottom of the fence, which is known as the ground line. If there is no ground line (eg a single pole) the horse will find it difficult to judge where to take off and will have to rely on his rider. For this reason it is best for the rider to learn to judge the take-off point not from the base, but from a higher section of the obstacle. Even more difficult is a false ground line when a brush or wall is placed behind the poles. If the animal judges its distance from the brush or wall, he is likely to get too close.

A ground line slightly out on the approach side makes the easiest fence of all and is used for novices, as the first fence, and when trying to make the horse jump as high as possible.

Distances between fences

The distance between fences is another factor in making it easier or more difficult to arrive at the best take-off point ('right') for the fence. The distance can be set so that the average horse taking normal strides will arrive right. On the other hand, it can be made so that the horse will have to lengthen or shorten his strides in order to arrive right, and this tests his obedience.

The distance between doubles and combinations can also be made more or less difficult, but the rider can help the horse to take the required length of stride either by approaching the first element slowly if it is a short distance, or fast if it is a long distance, and/or by checking for a short distance, or pushing on on landing for a long distance.

The optimum distance will vary according to the type of fence (upright or spread), and the rider can get a rough idea of the number and length of the strides by measuring centre to centre. The optimum distance is about 8m (26ft) for one non-jumping stride and 11m (36ft) for two. When deciding how to approach the double or combination the rider must take into account the going, the slope of the ground, the types and height of the fences and, most important of all, the length of his horse's stride.

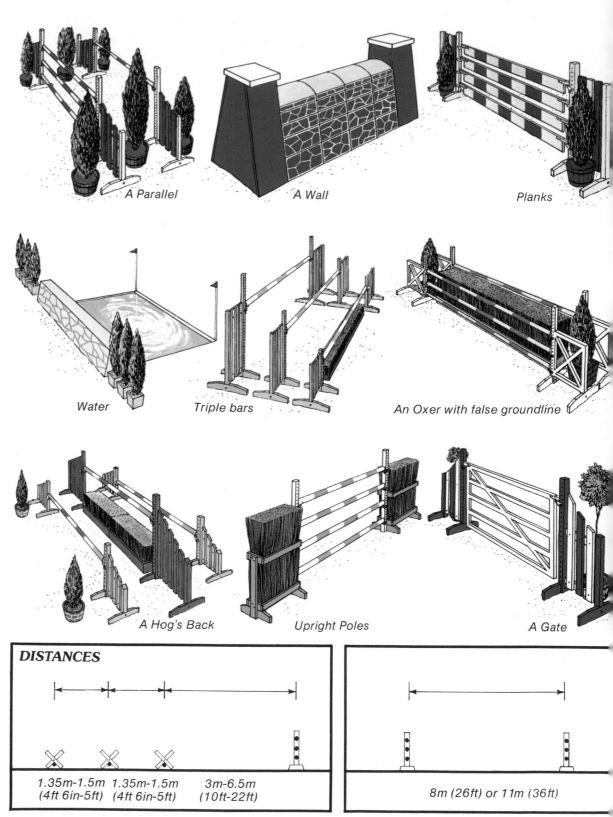

A Parallel   A Wall   Planks

Water   Triple bars   An Oxer with false groundline

A Hog's Back   Upright Poles   A Gate

DISTANCES

1.35m-1.5m (4ft 6in-5ft)	1.35m-1.5m (4ft 6in-5ft)	3m-6.5m (10ft-22ft)

8m (26ft) or 11m (36ft)

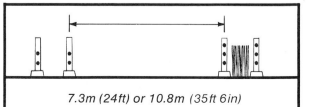
A well built parallel suitable for the novice class in which this army officer is jumping at the Royal Windsor Horse Show.

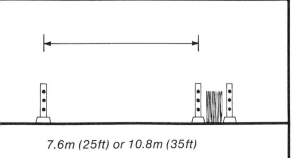
7.6m (25ft) or 10.8m (35ft)

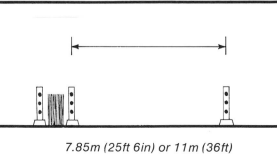
7.85m (25ft 6in) or 11m (36ft)

7.3m (24ft) or 10.8m (35ft 6in)

SHOW-JUMPING

The horse should first and foremost suit the rider, who must decide whether he gets on best with excitable or lazy horses, wicked or easy ones. Most great riders prefer horses with some temperament, as they have to be a little devilish to enjoy jumping enormous fences. The novice rider needs above all a sensible, bold horse, who might not manage an international course but will be less likely to object to inexpert riding, confusing aids and a beginner's mistakes.

Conformation should be good, because this will make the animal easier to train, as there are fewer weaknesses to overcome. All jumpers should have strong hindquarters, as this is the source of power.

Today's leading horses tend to be 'blood' animals who can jump wide fences and go fast. The heavier, cob-like horses, so popular in the past, do not have the scope to tackle today's formidable courses. For the beginner, however, the latter might be a wiser selection. Less easily upset, their shorter stride makes it easier to arrive right at a fence.

Ability is the most important factor of all. The only common feature of all good jumpers is that they jump high poles and wide ones without effort.

This is a good fence for training as a single pole encourages a horse to bascule, and the tyres introduce him to something strange. The rider however should be wearing a hat.

JUMPING A DOUBLE

Training the show-jumper

A greater variety of methods is used in the training of show-jumpers than for any other sport, but the classical method is the most sensible, as the unorthodox ones tend to rely on the natural talent of the rider. It is, therefore, best to develop a good style as long as style does not become an end in itself—to clear the fence must always be that.

Elementary dressage helps to establish these aims, and so does practical work. Opening gates aids obedience and teaches the horse to move sideways. Going up and down hills mobilizes the shoulders and develops the vital back muscles. Hunting stimulates impulsion and the ability of the horse to look after himself, and increases his confidence over unusual fences. The trainer must weigh up the personality and physique of the novice horse, and decide what work he needs and whether he needs to be stimulated or calmed down.

In classic training the horse learns to approach a fence calmly, rhythmically, with balance, obedient to his rider and collected like a spring, so that he is ready to leap high and wide. In the air he should arch his head, neck and back (bascule). In this way he will use up less physical and mental energy, but to achieve this takes time and hard work, mainly on the flat.

Flat work has as its primary aim to get the horse obedient to the leg and always waiting to go forward. The canter should be springy and rhythmic and the animal should be able to shorten and extend its stride easily. The other important aim is to turn smoothly so that the horse can come out of a corner with the balance and impulsion to jump a fence immediately.

A double of parallels is one of the most tricky obstacles as impulsion is needed to clear the spreads, yet this must be combined with precision to clear the first bar of the parallel.

The horse is taking off a little far back and the rider has taken him off on his mouth (pulled on the reins). This is only advisable in emergencies to encourage extra effort.

The rider knows the horse will need his help and is returning into the saddle as quickly as possible without interfering with the hindquarters clearing the fence.

The competitor is riding very hard to get his horse to extend his stride enough to reach the fence and to gather impulsion for the spread. The rein contact is good.

The horse is springing well, although the back is straight, probably due to being taken off on the mouth. The hands resting on the neck prevent them following any head movement and so hinder basculing.

In mid-air the horse is clearing the big parallels easily, although he would not have to spring so high with a better bascule. It cannot be stressed too often that there is no substitute for basic gridwork and classic training to encourage a horse to bascule correctly.

SHOW-JUMPING

Elementary dressage helps to establish these aims, and so does practical work. Opening gates aids obedience and teaches the horse to move sideways. Going up and down hills mobilizes the shoulders and develops the vital back muscles. Hunting stimulates impulsion and the ability of the horse to look after himself, and increases his confidence over unusual fences. The trainer must decide what work the novice horse needs.

Training over jumps must maintain confidence at all times. Problems can be avoided, particularly refusals, by being patient. When the fences are small it is usually best for the rider to interfere as little as possible. He can sit quietly, concentrating on keeping the horse balanced and in a rhythmic stride.

As the horse progresses, many riders start to interfere. To do this requires a good eye, which all great riders have, enabling them to judge when to ask the horse to extend or lengthen his stride so that the animal arrives right for the take-off. Such riders demand that their horses respond immediately to their checks or leg aids, but those who are less talented are better advised to train their horse to

look after himself. Without a good eye there are bound to be occasions when a rider cannot see where to take off and keeps checking desperately, mistakenly hoping that this might get his horse into a good take-off position. All the checks will do is to reduce impulsion and make it even more difficult for the horse to get out of trouble. The normal rider should keep a balanced, rhythmic approach with plenty of impulsion and let the horse look after itself.

Work over fences is progressive (see Chapter 3). After the basic work, the horse must be made familiar with all the fences met in the ring, which should be introduced at a low height. The rider must be firm and determined to get over the fence, although patient and calm.

The most frightening obstacles for many horses are doubles and combinations. Here, it is important to ensure the distances between the obstacles are correct and to keep the jumps low until confidence has been built up.

When nearly ready to enter competitions, or even after a few have been attempted, speed jumping may be practised at home. The horse must learn to

take fences at angles, to cut corners so that there are only one or two straight strides before the fence, and to ensure that fences can be jumped cleanly at a fast pace. The last, however, should not be practised too often for fear that the horse will start to flatten.

Flattening (not basculing) is one of the commonest faults among show-jumpers but it can be improved by gridwork and jumping low, wide parallels. The other common fault is for horses to slow up in to the fence and to take off too close. The excitement of hunting can help here, so can good ground lines and the use of grids where the distance is gradually made longer so that horses learn to extend their stride.

Training a show-jumper does not end at home. Competitive experience is essential. A horse's first sight of different obstacles and of the colour, noise and atmosphere of a horse show can be startling. If the animal has formed an understanding with his rider, however, he is likely to cope with these strange events more willingly and will try harder to give of his best. Forming a sympathetic partnership is the central aim of training a show-jumper.

Left: An inviting fence for training.

Above: Johan Heins (Holland), the 1977 European Champion gets his horse to fold his legs and bascule well.

Right: Aachen, West Germany, one of the most famous show jumping arenas in the world.

Competing

Walking the course provides a vital opportunity to decide what the problems are and how to tackle them. First, find out and memorize the route, then look for possible problems. Each fence should be studied and its approach planned. Flimsy uprights will need a collected approach and accurate placing of the horse to clear them. Spreads need impulsion and greater speed to enable the animal to jump wide enough. Spooky fences (ditches and novelty types) may cause a horse to stop, so the rider must be prepared for this, and ready to give encouragement with his legs, seat, voice and whip (if necessary).

Decide where to turn into a fence, bearing in mind that it is easiest to jump a fence from a straight approach giving the horse time to prepare himself. Novice riders all too often tend to cut into fences too quickly. Distances in combinations and between related fences should be measured so that the rider knows whether he has to push on for a longer stride or check for a shorter one.

In speed competitions the rider has to clear obstacles as quickly as possible. There are two ways of cutting time. The first is to cover the course at a good pace. When walking a course, decide which fences are solid enough to approach fast and which ones are set with shorter distances and are flimsy in appearance, thus demanding more care. The second way is to take the shortest possible route (cutting corners). Decide which fences are easy enough not to need a long approach. Some can be jumped at angles but this is risky if the fence is a spread because it means clearing an even greater width.

For those fortunate enough not to be early in the jumping order, watching others tackle the course is a useful aid. Many problems may be unforeseen, such as shadows obscuring fences or dips in the ground upsetting balance. For problems already noted, it is easier to decide how to tackle them after seeing how others do it.

Warming-up in the last important minutes before a competition the rider helps to get his horse supple, obedient, jumping boldly and cleanly; and himself seeing a good stride (judging the correct place for take-off).

The essence of making wise use of the warming-up time is for the rider to know himself and his horse: to know whether he needs to jump many practice fences to get his eye in, or whether it is possible to jump high, wide fences—only a strong rider with good judgement can do this safely without making errors, crashing the fences and upsetting the animal. On the other hand, a stylish rider who does not interfere but leaves the horse free to make its own adjustments may usefully spend the time on jumping grids with a loose rein, as this encourages the horse to bascule and to think for himself.

Character and ability of the horse are important in planning a warming-up session. Lazy ones need short bursts at a fast canter, a good waking-up, and probably not too much work. Excitable ones usually need plenty of work, carried out quietly and calmly. This is the fascination of jumping, in which the ability and character of both horse and rider have to be analyzed and understood if they are to be used to full advantage.

Right: Warming up over a practice fence.

Below: Turning quickly after a fence to save time.

SHOW-JUMPING

Jumping the round is the climax to the warming-up, and the animal should be feeling responsive, supple and ready to try hard over the fences. Lazy horses can be galloped into the arena, excitable ones walked. There are a few vital minutes before the judge's bell rings, when by trotting and cantering between the fences the horse can be acclimatized to the arena and the atmosphere.

The bell signals the start of the action: a good balanced rhythmic approach toward the first fence is needed, and the rider must be ready for anything, as the horse is rarely settled. If he slows up, the rider must give him confidence and push him on.

Upon landing, balance, rhythm and collection must be re-established in the first stride. Ahead lies one problem after another, some anticipated, others unexpected. A show-jumper has to react quickly to problems and to have a good eye for a stride and the knack of getting horses to go for him.

Top left: A young competitor who may one day become as successful as these top riders.

Below left: Gerd Wildfang from Germany, renowned for his sympathetic hands.

Top: Kevin Bacon (Australia) whose unorthodox style on Chichester has won them many prizes.

Above: One of the greatest horsemen in the world is Frank Chapot from America.

Right: One of the most stylish riders—Bill Steinkraus (USA) here winning the Olympic Gold.

DRESSAGE

Dressage trains a horse to be more agile, supple, responsive and powerful to ride; more light, free and loose in his movements; and more beautiful to look at. Most riders of dressage horses grow fascinated by the challenge of turning rigid, disobedient animals into ones with which they can be in close harmony. It is not instant conversion. Short cuts through the use of gadgets and force may mean the horse will do the work 'for' his rider but never 'with' him. The horse is likely to be tense, and the great pleasure of being on a horse who enjoys his work and trusts his rider will never be felt.

Riders have enjoyed dressage for centuries. High School (advanced dressage) enjoyed a great vogue in the courts of Europe during the Baroque era. To ride a horse well was considered an essential attribute for the nobleman. Musical rides were organized to entertain onlookers and to give riders the challenge of producing performances of a higher standard.

These musical performances on horseback are still one of the most popular aspects of dressage. The principal classical exponents are the Spanish Riding School in Vienna and the Cadre Noir of Saumur in France. Then there are the more circus-like and unconventional performers: Peralta, for instance, who fights bulls on horseback, Nuno Oliveira of Portugal and Los Caballos Andaluces, but it is the competition side of dressage that has shown the greatest boom in recent years. From the Olympic arena to Pony Club level, the number and quality of dressage riders has increased.

Competitions

Competitions take the form of a dressage test, which ranges from the very simple, when a horse is asked only to walk, trot, canter and halt, to the international tests, of which the most difficult is the Grand Prix. For this, the test used in the Olympic Games, it takes four years or more to train a talented horse.

The tests consist of a number of sections containing movements and transitions, and for each section a maximum of ten marks can be awarded. The mark given signifies a standard of which the scale is as follows:

10 excellent, 9 very good, 8 good, 7 fairly good, 6 satisfactory, 5 sufficient, 4 insufficient, 3 fairly bad, 2 bad, 1 very bad, 0 not performed

NB In some tests (eg FEI Three-Day Event Test) a scale of 6 is used.

At the end of the test, marks are given for the general impression of the horse, for which there are normally sections covering impulsion, paces, and

submission. There is also a section covering the rider's position and seat and the correct application of aids.

The judge has a writer who takes down the mark given for each movement on the test sheet (one for each horse). There is also a space for remarks about the performance.

The movements

The walk is a marching pace and the four hoof-beats should be regular and maintained in all work.

The trot is a two-time pace on alternate diagonals separated by a moment's suspension. It should show elasticity, rhythm, impulsion and cadence (springiness of step).

The canter is a three-time pace that should be united, light, regular and cadenced.

Collected paces entail taking higher and shorter steps than those of ordinary paces. The hindquarters are lowered, resulting in greater impulsion in a forward and upward direction. The neck is raised and the head perpendicular to the poll. The more advanced the work the greater the amount of collection asked for.

Extended paces have longer, flatter steps, but not quicker ones, as at all times the same rhythm must be kept up.

Medium paces have steps that are between those for the extended and collected paces. They are

THE EXTENDED TROT

Left: An extravagant extended trot in which the hind legs are working well to come as high as the forelegs. Ideally the neck should have lengthened more as the head is just behind the vertical.

THE REIN BACK

Right: The rein back which the rider has asked for by applying his legs behind the girth. Restraining any forward movement by using the reins, but not by pulling on them, and by putting his body fractionally forward of the vertical.

THE HALT

Below: A good square halt in which the legs are correctly placed, the hinds are well under the body and the horse is remaining on the bit waiting for the aids to move off.

rounder than the extended, but longer than the collected.

The rein-back is the movement in which the feet are raised and move backwards in diagonal pairs, almost simultaneously, with the horse remaining in the same position, staying on the bit and taking equal strides backwards.

The halt is achieved when the horse is motionless but standing with his legs forming the four corners of a rectangle. He remains on the bit and is ready to move off when asked by the rider.

The counter canter is when the horse canters on a circle or curve with the outside leg leading, and is bent to the leading leg.

DRESSAGE

Simple change of leg is a change of leading leg by bringing the horse back from the canter to the walk; after one or two well-defined steps, he moves off into the canter on the other leg.

The flying change of leg is when the horse changes the leading leg at the canter. The change of the fore and hind lead should be made simultaneously. Flying changes can be single ones, or in series at every fourth, third, second and, eventually, single stride. The aim is to maintain straightness, impulsion and rhythm during the changes.

The pirouette is a small circle on two tracks with a radius of the length of the horse, the forehand moving around the hindquarters. Pirouettes can be performed at the walk and the canter, and are either half pirouettes (180°) or whole pirouettes (360°). The aim is to maintain impulsion and rhythm, and to keep the horse on the bit while bent slightly in the direction of the turn.

The turn on the forehand is when the horse pivots around one foreleg. The other foreleg turns a small circle and the hind legs describe a larger outer circle.

The transitions are changes of pace and speed and must be made smoothly, with the horse remaining light in the hand and in the same position.

The lateral movements entail the horse stepping sideways as well as forward.

The leg yield is the simplest of the lateral work, with the animal moving sideways straight, except for a slight bend at the poll away from the direction of the movement.

Top: The simple change in which the horse is brought back smoothly from the canter to the walk (first three pictures). Note how the rider is using his seat and legs in the first picture to push not pull the horse into a slower pace. After he has made one or two walk steps the aids are applied for a strike off to lead on the opposite leg (note in pictures 3 and 4 the rider's inside leg being applied on the girth). In the last picture the canter has been re-established.

Right: The leg yield which is the simplest of the lateral movements. It is probably the best exercise to use to teach the young horse about lateral work but is very rarely included as part of dressage tests in the arena. The third picture shows the crossing of the hind legs, and the fourth just moments later the crossing of the forelegs. In the last the horse is starting to go straight forward but he is still slightly bent in his neck.

THE SIMPLE CHANGE

THE LEG YIELD

DRESSAGE

The shoulder-in is when the forehand of the horse is brought in to move on a different track from the hindlegs, which continue on the original track. The horse is slightly bent around the inside leg of the rider and away from the direction of the movement.

The travers is when the outside legs step over and in front of the inside ones, with the horse bent around the inside leg of the rider and looking in the direction in which it is moving.

The renvers is an inverted travers, ie he is still bent around the rider's inside leg but his head is away from not towards the outside of the arena.

The half pass involves the horse moving on two tracks on a diagonal that is as close as possible parallel to the wall. The outside foreleg and hind leg step over and in front of the inside ones, with the horse slightly bent around the inside leg and looking in the direction of the movement.

The piaffe is a very cadenced, elevated and collected trot on the spot.

The passage is a very collected, very elevated and very cadenced trot, in which the moment of suspension is longer than for any other form of trot.

The figures
The volte is a circle of 6m (19½ft) in diameter.

The serpentine is a series of loops, which may be to either side of the arena or a specified distance on either side of the centre line.

The figure of eight consists of two voltes or circles of equal size performed on opposite reins.

THE TRAVERS
Below left: The travers is usually performed along a wall or a fence to which the horse's head is turned but bent a little to the inside.

THE SHOULDER IN
Below: The shoulder in differs from the travers in that the hind legs remain on the original track and only the forelegs cross. This horse has not taken his forelegs far enough off the track.

THE HALF PASS

A good half pass in which the horse is bent around the rider's inside leg. However a more advanced dressage horse should have a little more bend in the body. This is not possible for young horse who has not learnt to use, or made supple the necessary muscles.

The horse is almost parallel to the track with the head just in the lead. It is important that the hindquarters should never lead and therefore when starting the half pass the forehand comes off the track before the rider applies his outside leg to ask for lateral movement.

The horse is crossing over well and taking good sized strides. To make this possible it is important to keep up the impulsion. The rider does this by giving aids with his inside leg on the girth, and keeping his weight to the inside.

Another important point in the half pass is to keep up the rhythm. This is helped if the rider applies his outside leg, to ask for the lateral movement, in rythmical nudges and not by using a continuous pressure to try and push him over.

DRESSAGE

The arena

Dressage tests are performed in arenas of two sizes. From the novice to the middle grades it is normal to use one 20m by 40m (22yd by 44yd), and above these grades one 20m by 60m (22yd by 65yd). Both should be bordered by a low fence about 30cm (1ft) high. The surface must be level; it may be grass, but sand is more usual for important events.

The rider

Dressage entails the pursuit of perfection. In jumping and racing, dash and courage can offset poor technique and lack of knowledge. In dressage, however, the wrong distribution of weight or a rough hand can hinder the horse's use of his body and prevent him from performing a movement correctly, if at all. Attention to detail is basic to success.

The FEI recommends that all movements should be obtained without 'apparent effort of the rider. He should be well balanced, with his loins and hips supple, thighs and legs steady and well stretched downwards. The upper part of the body easy, free and erect, with the hands low and close together without, however, touching either each other or the horse and with the thumb the highest point; the elbows and arms close to the body, enabling the rider to follow the movements of the horse smoothly and freely and to apply his aids imperceptibly. This is the only position making it possible for the rider to school his horse progressively and correctly'.

A rider with a 'feel for the horse' (a natural ability to anticipate a horse's action and apply any necessary correction before a problem arises) can achieve these standards more easily. All riders, however, need some form of instruction.

Instruction is becoming more easily available in every country in the world. Many governments now subsidize equestrian education. In general, the Pony Club and the Riding Club provide relatively inexpensive tuition from increasingly expert advisers. There are also riding schools and freelance independent trainers. Parents and friends are often helpful assistants. Finally, there is the horse: the experience gained by riding a variety of horses, and by riding a trained horse that can do the movements, can be as valuable as human instruction.

The horse

Conformation must be good, because the dressage horse is a gymnast, and the advanced movements demand the maximum use of the body. Any weaknesses in shape will make this difficult.

Paces should be free, regular and straight, in which the hindquarters are active and able to create impulsion.

Temperament must be equable, for the horse must willingly enjoy the work and not be nappy or stupid. A horse with these virtues can be very expensive; every equestrian, whether he specializes in racing, in jumping or in eventing, seeks such a type. For those who are not rich, 'the most practical way of acquiring a quality dressage horse is by breeding (from carefully selected mates); by purchasing as a foal or yearling; or by searching for a horse that has some defect (eg, touched in the wind, weaknesses in the tendons) that prevents him from competing in the more arduous equestrian sports.

Riders taking up dressage, however, cannot expect to rise to the most advanced levels immediately. Up to medium level, a horse with a sensible temperament and straight active paces is more than adequate for dressage.

Training the dressage horse

In training a dressage horse the rider must know what he wants, be able to ask the horse clearly and be certain that the horse is physically capable of doing it. The 'school of dressage' has a logical programme in which the movements and exercises become progressively more difficult. Each supples a further part of the body and asks for more collection, culminating in the ultimate test of competition dressage, the piaffe and the passage. Although it is possible occasionally to try out more difficult exercises, the earlier stages must be returned to and constantly improved. Skipping out on a stage leads to weaknesses that reveal themselves as more advanced work is asked for.

The first stages of dressage training have been discussed in Chapter 3 and the following outline of movements used in tests up to and including medium standards can point out only some of the more important factors.

The extension or collection of a pace must be achieved without changing the rhythm. When asked for longer strides (extension) or shorter strides (collection) the horse must not quicken into a faster rhythm, or drag his hind legs into a slower one. The

Our demonstrator David Hunt competing.

change must be eased from the animal quietly; collection comes not by pulling on the reins but by using the seat and legs to engage the hind legs further under the horse's body, and extension not by leaning forward and letting go of the reins but by building up the impulsion and asking with strong leg, back and seat aids. The horse is usually best taught to collect his strides before being taught to extend, and during the early stages the rider should be satisfied with just a few strides of either.

The counter canter must maintain the same rhythm, outline and bend as in the true canter. It should be introduced gradually by taking the horse off the track of the arena/school in a small loop. The rider must keep his legs firmly around the horse in the position that asks for the required leading leg. If the horse does not change behind and/or in front, the loop can be deepened in the days that follow and eventually a circle can be tried. This has excellent suppling effects, but only if the horse does not change leads.

The turn on the forehand should be taught by halting alongside a hedge or wall and, to turn to the right, by asking for a slight right bend. Ease the right leg back behind the girths to ask the horse to step over his near hind leg with his offside one. The rider's left leg should remain on the girth to prevent the horse stepping backwards and to ensure that he pivots around his forelegs. The animal should not step forward. To turn to the left, reverse the aids.

The pirouette at the walk starts by collecting the horse, bringing the forehand off the track with both hands, with the inside leg on the girth to keep up the impulsion and the outside leg behind the girth to stop the hindquarters swinging out. At first it is best for the pirouette to be a small circle to prevent the horse from pivoting on his hind legs instead of keeping them moving in the same rhythm of the walk, and to stop him stepping backwards.

Lateral work is when the horse's forehand and hindquarters are on two different tracks. For novice riders who are not certain of the aids and aims, it is best to start at the walk, as soon as the horse has established a rhythm to all its paces. The angle should never be more than 30° (less at the start), for the aim must always be to have the feeling of going forward more than sideways, otherwise impulsion is lost and resistances build up.

The shoulder-in should start with a small circle (ie, bringing the forehand off the track), but the rider must stop the horse from going forward into it by building up the pressure on the outside rein and increasing the pressure of the inside leg on the girth.

Harry Boldt (Germany) 1976 Olympic individual silver medallist applies his left leg behind the girth and turns his shoulders to the right to ask for a flying change to the right.

The horse should then step along the track of the school with his hind legs and forehand just off it. The quarters should be stopped from falling off the track by keeping and, if necessary, using the outside leg behind the girth.

The travers is excellent training for the half pass, for a wall, or a hedge or fence, can be used to keep the animal in position. Come out of the corner and, instead of going straight, build up the pressure on the inside rein and outside leg so that the horse moves sideways bent around the rider's inside leg, his head to the outside of the arena.

The half pass can be introduced by turning down the centre line and returning to the side while

HRH Princess Anne who is particularly talented at dressage taking part in the dressage phase of an event. She is about to turn a corner at the canter.

keeping the bend of the turn, but not asking for lateral strides. Once this is understood, then the rider's outside leg can ask for lateral movement. It can help, too, to come into the half pass out of shoulder-in, and to go back into shoulder-in at any time when the rhythm is lost in the half pass.

The rein-back should not be taught too early, or used too often, for it is very easy for a horse to become resistant and to anticipate backing whenever in the halt. The aim is not to pull the horse back, but to come to a halt by closing both legs. Then increase the pressure of the seat and leg aids while the hands restrict the forward movement; then the only way for the horse to move is backwards.

Equally important is the intention of the course-builder. Course-building is a subtle art; the course-builder needs flair, imagination and the ability to foresee the consequences of the problems he sets. Big, straightforward fences on open ground—parallel bars, hedges, sleeper or picnic tables, etc—are not generally alarming to horses, though they may well be frightening to the rider, especially if he approaches them on the wrong stride. It is the number and type of 'problem' fences that most test

Left: Drop fences when the horse lands at a much lower level than he takes off are included in most cross country courses. In some cases he cannot see the landing so it appears to the horse as if he is taking off into space. This takes great courage and in all cases he must be well balanced to absorb the impact of landing from a great height.

Below: Bruce Davidson on Irish Cap in the 1974 World Championships where they were the individual gold medallists and helped their American team to achieve the same placing.

Eventing—also referred to as horse trials or combined training—is the all-round test of horse and rider. The competition has three phases: dressage, cross-country and show-jumping: in order to do well, the rider must be proficient in all three branches of riding, and the horse must combine obedience, agility, speed, stamina and jumping ability. There are competitions at different levels ranging from varying standards of one-day events (all the tests on one day) to the three-day event where the phases are not only more severe but include additional endurance tests (roads and tracks, and steeplechase phases).

Dressage
This is the first of the three phases and the test has to be ridden from memory. The standard of the test varies from very simple to medium (with lateral work). These dressage tests are judged by the same values as for pure dressage: ie, the horse should be active, using his hindquarters and wanting to go forward with rhythmic, regular paces. He must be straight in body, and appear to obey willingly.

Speed and endurance (cross-country)
The tests of the second phase—known as speed and endurance—vary in duration and in the size of the fences, and this dictates the calibre of the competition. A total distance of up to 24km (15 miles) has to be covered in the Olympics, when it is divided into sections: (A) roads and tracks, (B) steeplechase, (C) further roads and tracks and (D) cross-country.

In many horse trials, especially at the lower levels, only (D) the cross-country is included.

Roads and tracks can be of various lengths: at the Munich Olympics, phase (C) was 15.1km (9½ miles). The speed average required is 240m (262yd) per minute, a very fast trot; penalties for exceeding the time are given at the rate of one per second.

The steeplechase course is between 3km and 4km (2-2½ miles) long and the speed needed to avoid penalties is 690m (755yd) per minute, or nearly 40kph (25mph). For many horses, this is nearly flat out. After the second roads and tracks phase, there is a compulsory ten-minute recuperative halt before the cross-country.

The cross-country phase is the centrepiece of a horse trial. The course for a three-day event can be anything between 3km and 8km (2-5 miles). A speed of 570m (623yd) per minute is required; penalty points are given at the rate of 0.8 for each second over the time allowed. There can be up to 40 obstacles.

The fences vary from event to event. Natural features—hedges, ditches, banks, hills and type of terrain—play their part in dictating the type of course.

the courage and ability of the horse and the skill of the rider; problem fences may often be deceptive, appearing far less formidable than straightforward ones.

The average horse may be unsettled by deep and dark ditches; landing where he suspects a drop but cannot see it; or jumping into water. He may find physically difficult such things as jumping two fences in succession when there is no room for a non-jumping stride; or a combination of fences set at an awkward distance apart, so that he has to take exceptionally long or short strides.

The coffin now features in some form on most courses and consists of three elements, a fence followed by a ditch, then another fence. The coffin is always tricky and frequently causes a large number of refusals. In addition to the difficulties of jumping any combination of three closely spaced obstacles, the horse tends either to concentrate on the ditch when approaching, or to see it at the last minute, and so find it difficult to jump the first fence. The higher the fences, the closer they seem to be to the ditch; and the wider and spookier the ditch, the trickier the obstacle is to judge correctly.

The water jump is also a feature of most courses. Although some horses are quite happy to jump into water, many more have to be persuaded to overcome their natural reluctance and schooled to build up a trust in their rider.

The essence of the cross-country is a partnership between horse and rider. The rider has to convince the horse that what lies ahead is negotiable, and has to set the animal at the obstacle in such a way as to make it as easy as possible for the horse to jump it. For example, if the fence ahead is a huge hedge with a gaping ditch in front, the rider will have to encourage his horse and make him have a cut at it; if the horse goes into it in a labouring way, a much greater effort will be needed to jump it. On the other hand, any coffin-type fence, or a quarry, or a short striding combination, requires a much slower approach, with the horse collected together and the rider judging the take-off point.

Show-jumping

In three-day events, the horses have to pass a veterinary inspection on the final day before embarking upon the last stage, the show-jumping. Show-jumping is rarely demanding in itself; according to the rules, the object of the examination is 'to prove that, on the day after a severe test of endurance, horses have retained the suppleness, energy and obedience necessary for them to continue'. A clear round is often vital on the last day; a fence down may change the final order.

The rider

The three-day event demands much of the rider and it is essential that he should be fit. He need not have the accurate eye for a stride that is the show-jumper's stock-in-trade, but he should be brave and confident of his ability. He must have the sensitivity and coolness to time his riding-in for the dressage correctly, and to cajole his supremely fit horse into producing his best performance in an atmosphere of tension and anticipation. In a three-day event the rider has to time precisely his progress on the roads and tracks and in the steeplechase, and in every event he must inspire his horse with the courage to negotiate—as fast as is safely possible—a series of awesome and solid obstacles, many of them especially designed to daunt both horse and rider. In the show-jumping he has to return to the cold-blooded accuracy of the show-jumping ring and persuade his stiff and battle-scarred horse to jump clear. If by this time he is among the leaders, the pressure will be particularly great.

The horse

Good event horses come in all shapes and sizes; and although Thoroughbred horses usually find it easier to get through the ardours of the endurance test, many good eventers are not Thoroughbred. Eventers must have stamina, however. They have to gallop fast enough for the steeplechase and maintain a steady gallop for up to 18 minutes for the cross-country. Above all, they must be sound, for the necessary fitness work as well as the competition imposes great physical strain.

Horses with character are more likely to have the combination of courage and stamina the cross-country calls for, but they must also be sufficiently level-headed for the dressage.

They must enjoy jumping and find it easy to jump big fences out of a galloping stride; they must respect the fences. The full scope of a show-jumper is not necessary, but can be reassuring; for the rider, when faced with an intimidating log pile at the top of a steep hill, likes to think that the horse has something in reserve.

Training the event horse

Dressage has aims and methods similar to pure dressage. The major difference is that it is only one part of the training programme and cannot take up the entire exercise time. Depending largely on the horse's temperament and standard of dressage, riders either school for about 20 minutes each day before going out on conditioning work or have a longer session two or three times a week. The condition work, however, can include some dressage for transitions, establishing rhythmic cadenced paces, and even lateral work can be practised along tracks and in fields. Another difference is that the test has to be performed on a horse fit enough to gallop for miles. In such a state the animal is likely to be on the verge of exploding in an arena, and the rider must learn how to handle this: whether he must be ridden forcefully or sensitively; whether he needs to be worked in for hours, or if this just gets the horse more excited and it is best to do only relaxing work before a test.

Show-jumping requires similar training to that of a show-jumper except that the eventer will never be expected to jump so high. Consequently, carefulness is the important goal rather than an ability to jump **Cross-country** calls for boldness and cleverness, high or wide fences.
both essential assets when jumping across country,

The most essential factor in training a horse to go across country is to make him confident. Of all the obstacles he must be taught to tackle, jumping into water is one of the most frightening, and it is best to start by splashing around so that he finds out it is not very deep or alarming.

and it is through giving a horse confidence that these are gradually built up. One of the most pleasant and efficient ways of achieving this is to take the young horse hunting.

The cross-country courses, however, have become increasingly sophisticated, with a greater variety of fences than are ever found in a single hunting country. The horse must be introduced to ditches, drop fences, coffins and water over and into which he has to jump. Because it is best to keep them small, many hazards can be constructed at home. Most countries also have centres where riders can practise over a wide range of cross-country fences. Competitions themselves can form part of the training programme. It is usually possible to introduce a horse to competitions where the fences are very low, in hunter trials or club one-day events. The competitor can start by riding steadily, only aiming for the speeds needed for victory when confidence has been built up.

Endurance is not emphasized for novices, but it is still vital to get them fit enough not to tire in the cross-

country section. Otherwise it is easy for falls to occur and for muscles, joints, tendons or ligaments to be strained. As the standard of the event rises, so does the importance of the endurance aspect. Consequently, although a novice is asked to go little more than 1½km (1 mile) at a speed of 31kph (19mph) over the cross-country fences in a three-day event, he must steeplechase over a course at 42kph (26mph), and he must cover around 16km (10 miles) of roads and tracks at about 14½kph (9mph), then 6½km (4 miles) of obstacles at 31kph (19mph). To endure this he must be as fit as a racehorse.

A horse cannot remain at peak fitness for long and in most countries it is usual to divide the eventing year into two seasons with one long rest and one shorter one in between. Preparing a horse for a one-day event takes about three months (see Getting a horse fit) and for a three-day event an extra month. Although a typical programme was outlined above, it must vary according to the horse. Some are stuffy and difficult to get fit, so they need longer and faster work; others might muscle up quickly but because they are excitable it is best to do this over longer distances at a slow speed. Much depends on the length of rest a horse has had. One that has been let down for only three weeks or so will need less initial roadwork and galloping than one that has been resting for months. Finally, there is the soundness of the horse to consider: one with weak legs needs slow up-hill work rather than numerous long gallops to become fit.

Stable management, if properly carried out, keeps a horse sound and feeling well. Rigorous tests put him under strain and the maintenance of his health is a vital aspect of training an eventer.

Feeding is important, but although advanced horses need large quantities of energy and protein foodstuff, these are not essential for the novice. If high spirited, he can be fed largely on cubes (pellets).

In the medical field the stable manager must be alert. Precautions, such as always wearing brushing boots or bandages in work, should help to avoid problems, but it is important to know the weaknesses of an individual animal. Immediate attention to such warning signs as a horse going off his feed, or heat in the tendons, can save serious difficulties later.

Competition work can be used as a means of advancing the eventer in countries where there are many events (UK and USA). The horse's strength and soundness can be analyzed to determine how many events the animal can stand up to, and his mental approach and ability should be considered when deciding how much competitive experience he needs. The type of course should be analysed to ensure that the competition does not ask either too much or too little for the gradual advancement of the eventer. A galloping course with large straight-forward fences might help some, but others could benefit more from a tricky hilly course. The ultimate goal must be decided on. This could be the Pony Club or the European Championships, and the timing of the events must be arranged so that the eventer is at the peak of fitness at the time of his highlight of the year.

A competition will provide most horses with the best experience of tackling cross-country fences. If weaknesses are shown in either the jumping or the dressage phases, novice jumping competitions or elementary dressage tests can be added to the competition programme. The best approach to training an eventer, or any other type of competition horse, is to establish a clear idea of what is needed at the proposed standard of the competition, to seek out any weaknesses that might prevent the horse from achieving the standard and to set about overcoming them.

Below left: Combinations of fences with one stride or none in between are difficult, especially this one with a drop followed by a rail and ditch.

Below: Jumping into water is tricky as the water slows the horse down so rapidly that many (not this one) nose dive and jettison their riders.

Bottom: The largest and most solid fences are often the easiest, and this competitor is putting in a great jump over an enormous log pile.

DRIVING

The new sport of combined driving was established in 1969 when a meeting of the FEI in Switzerland drew up the first set of rules for a three-day event on wheels. Since then it has become an increasingly popular sport for both competitors and spectators. The traditional competitive form of driving, private driving (showing), which calls for an elegant and eye-catching turnout, has also benefitted from the resurgence of interest in driving.

Private driving
Many more shows now hold private driving events, usually divided into classes for singles, pairs and tandems. If it is a large show, these will be subdivided again into height limits (ie, 14.2hh and under, and over 14.2hh).

Preparation
The accent is on spit and polish and meticulous attention to detail. The harness must fit well and be made partly of patent leather. The whip should be made of holly and the thong like a shepherd's crook. The ideal horse has manners, presence, and good conformation and moves well, although he can show more knee action than the ridden show horse.

Driving techniques
The driver of a horse-drawn vehicle is known as 'the whip'. He should sit upright and straight on the box seat, with feet planted firmly together and a knee rug wrapped around the waist. The reins are held in the left hand with the nearside (left) rein over the index finger and the offside rein under the second finger. The reins must be level, and the whip carried in the right hand (see photograph).

When driving a pair, the right hand assists the left. It is important that the hands should be held near to each other, so that there is no slack rein between them.

The pace, whether a walk or a trot, must be kept even at all times.

The show-ring
The competitor is required to circle the ring at a working trot, and to change direction when directed. After the judges have examined harness, carriage and horses, each competitor is usually asked to make a short solo performance in each direction and to halt followed by a rein-back.

Combined driving
There are three sections in combined driving: (A) presentation and dressage; (B) marathon; and (C) obstacle driving.

Presentation and dressage
Presentation is an inspection of the turnout at close quarters to assess the cleanliness of its components, the horse's condition, the driver's and passenger's correctness, and general smartness. One quarter of the marks for this phase are allotted to presentation, and the remainder to the dressage, a ten-minute series of movements driven in an arena of 100m by 40m (110yd by 44yd). The standard of the tests ranges from novice to advanced, and in the latter the movements to be shown include the collected, working and extended trots, the walk on the bit, and the halt, with ten seconds immobility followed by a rein-back, also figure-of-eight and serpentine movements, and deviation from the track with the reins in one hand, with good definition of paces.

Left: Holding a team (four horses). The near leader between thumb and first finger, two wheelers between first and second, and the off leader between second and third fingers.

Right: A team being driven in a dressage test. The whip is holding his reins Hungarian style with the horses on the left and right in his left and right hands.

Below: Holding a pair or single. For all driving the right hand is used in front of the left to influence horses individually or in pairs, and behind the left to pull the reins through.

DRIVING

The marathon

The marathon covers up to 18 miles, and is split into five sections: a steady trot (A), followed by a short walk (B), and then a ten-minute rest, a strong trot (C), another walk and rest (D), and finally a steady trot (E). A bogey time is set for each section. The fast central section is generally run at between 16 and 18kph (10-11mph) and contains at least five hazards, combining the natural hazards of tree, gradient and water with strategically placed stakes, logs and fences. Each hazard is surrounded by a penalty zone and must be completed within its set time; penalties are also incurred for knocking down one of the elements and if the groom or driver dismounts. The negotiation of this section calls for anticipation and a confident manoeuvring skill on the part of the driver, and courage and handiness on that of the horse, which must be fit and sound enough to endure a long drive over rough and undulating terrain, while remaining supple and responsive.

Obstacle driving

This final phase requires an obedient horse or horses and an accurate driver who has to steer the vehicle between a course of about 18 pairs of synthetic cones. The width between the cones is altered according to the size of the vehicle, and, depending on the conditions of the competition, will be 40cm (15in) more than the distance between the two wheel rims. The slightest touch from the vehicle dislodges a rubber ball poised on top of the cone, and incurs ten penalties. Penalties can also be given for failing to complete the course within the time allowed.

At the smaller combined driving events the presentation section may be omitted, together with sections D and E from the marathon.

The horse

With some experience and schooling, a good sort of family horse may excel in driving trials. The best animal is one that has a free and active stride but is not too finely built, and is responsive and willing yet sensible and unflappable. His conformation need be only good enough to comply with these requirements. A straightish shoulder is no fault in a harness horse, for it enables the weight of the vehicle to be evenly distributed throughout the collar. A pair or team of horses should be matched in stride, height, type and, ideally, colour. For those just beginning the sport of driving, it is wiser to start with a single horse or pony which is easier to handle and less expensive to maintain.

The equipment

The carriage must be in sound condition, and expert advice should be sought before buying one. Woodworm, for example, can be disguised with paint and filler. A gig or country cart is best for a single horse, a dog cart or wagonette for a pair.

Secondhand harness can be found but this too should be in good condition. In the long run it is probably wiser to buy a new set from an established maker, who will measure the horse to ensure a good fit, so that it looks better and is more comfortable.

Below left: In the obstacle phase this competitor takes his team between the cones. If hit, the tennis balls perched on top fall for penalties.

Below: Greisen from Denmark drives his team through a very deep water hazard.

Above right: The obstacle phase has a tight time limit and this competitor is having to hurry.

Far right: A single with a young whip going through the lake at Hickstead.

Below right: As it is easier and less expensive to drive a single most whips start with them.

TRAIL RIDING

Trail riding, and long-distance riding, testing the horse's and rider's ability to cover long distances over natural country, are undoubtedly growing sports. They are well suited to the times, as they do not necessarily require an expensive horse, nor do they entail the construction of costly cross-country or show-jumping courses.

Long-distance riding in the UK

In the UK, the British Horse Society has formed a Long-distance Riding Group with its own executive committee to administer it. Membership is open to any one who is already a member of the British Horse Society and who owns a horse of 14hh or over. Horses also have to be registered before they can compete in any official ride. These take the form of simple pleasure rides and team relay rides of 16-32km (10-20 miles), and the more serious qualifying rides of 64km (40 miles) and over. They have been found necessary because of the demand for entry in the national championship of long-distance riding known as the Golden Horse Shoe Ride. This takes place annually over 121km (75 miles) of the Exmoor National Park. It is a great test of stamina, as the country is very wild and hilly, with frequent gradients of 1 in 4. Nevertheless, like all long-distance rides, it is a friendly affair and competitors, officials and their horses all spend three or four happy days in the ancient village of Exford.

In all rides the care of the horse has first priority, and none takes place without the presence of veterinary surgeons who, in the longer rides, not only decide whether a horse is fit to start but during the ride can either eliminate or deduct marks from any animal that has not maintained his condition. This strict veterinary surveillance puts a great onus on the competitors to get themselves and their horses really fit. Nowadays, most succeed admirably and it is more often bad luck than bad horsemastership that eliminates riders. Nevertheless, the official stewards at any ride are empowered to deduct marks and even to eliminate competitors should they consider that not enough care has been given to their horses' welfare.

Under BHS rules there is no element of racing, as there is no individual winner. All riders compete against a standard—Gold, Silver or Bronze—which is defined by the average speed obtained and the number of marks deducted, if any.

The BHS Long-distance Riding Committee are represented on the Veterinary Scientific Sub-Committee, and group members are able to attend conferences and courses where such matters as the actual training and riding of long-distance horses are thoroughly discussed.

Probably one of the great attractions of all forms of long-distance riding is that it is well within the

Many riders go trail riding purely for pleasure and not to win prizes. This party, mounted on sturdy ponies, is getting some wonderful views across the Highlands of Scotland.

compass of any rider of any age on any type of horse. It seems particularly suited to the larger native breeds such as Welsh Cobs, Connemaras and New Forest ponies, and most animals with Arab blood find such distances comparatively easy. It is of interest that since 1968, when the first Golden Horse Shoe Ride took place, a particular type of horse has emerged as the most successful one to ride: a small, good-quality animal between 14 and 15.2hh, usually a native pony with Thoroughbred or Arab blood. Such horses have the speed, stamina, courage and temperament required for this sport.

Distance Riding in North America

A rapidly growing form of trail riding is known generically as Distance Riding, of which there are two types of events. A competitive ride requires contestants to cover a certain distance within a stipulated time. Arriving too soon or too late results in penalty points. An endurance ride is a race, with prizes awarded according to the order of finishing. In addition, the horse that arrives in the best condition is also given a prize. Distances for both competitive and endurance rides vary, anywhere from 20 to several hundred miles across varied terrain. The time in which it must be covered ranges from several hours to a week, but most events require coverage of 50 or 100 miles in as little as 24 hours.

There are no restrictions on the breed or type of horses that may be used. Arabs, Morgans, and Thoroughbred crossbreds tend to do well in Distance Riding, as do Quarter-horses. Whichever breed or type of horse is ridden, the animal must be at least five years of age.

Getting a distance horse into peak condition is essential. Stamina is gradually built up through increasing distances when exercising, and special attention must be paid to the animal's health. Teams of veterinarians and lay judges assess each horse at several stages of a distance ride; they give penalty points and can eliminate any animal in less than excellent condition.

There are more than 500 distance rides in the United States and Canada. Among the most famous are the Tevis Cup, 161km (100 miles) across California's Sierra Mountains; the Old Dominion 100-Mile Endurance Ride in Virginia, and the Green Mountain Ride in Vermont.

The Rockies in Canada provide spectacular scenery for trail riders, and also some interesting obstacles such as the river they are about to cross.

POLO

Polo was played in Persia as far back as 600 BC. Today, however, it is more popular in Western countries, with Argentina as the greatest polo nation. The USA comes second, and in the UK, France, Italy, Spain, Australia and New Zealand its popularity is on an upswing. The only major decline has been in India, which was one of the great polo nations of the inter-war years.

The game

The game is played with a ball that is not more than 8cm (3in) in diameter and 119-126g (4¼-4½oz) in weight. This is hit with the long side of the head of a polo stick, which is made of cane, varying in length from 1.2m to 1.4m (48-54in) according to the needs of the player, and with a cylindrical head 20-23cm (8-9in) long.

The game is quite rough, and protective gear is needed for both horse and rider. This includes a helmet and knee pads for the rider and bandages or boots for the horse.

The game is played between teams of four players. Number one plays the role similar to a centre forward in football as he hustles and bustles the opposing defense, creating a path for his team mates. Number two has to be particularly well mounted, as he governs the speed of play and probably covers 40 percent more distance than any of his companions. Number three is usually the highest handicap player and also the captain. He is the pivot upon which his side's attack and defense moves turn and he endeavours to use the opponents' play to his team's advantage. Number four should provide a solid and reliable defense and be a big hitter.

A match consists of between four and eight chukkers, each chukker lasting for seven minutes. The rules are designed to avoid dangerous collisions and the most important are those governing right of way. Basically, a player following the line of the ball has the right of way and any opponent who crosses his line or path will be penalized. It is also forbidden for a player to hold his stick in his left hand as mixed hands could be very dangerous. But a player is allowed to ride alongside an opponent and 'ride him off', when by deliberately bumping him he may be able to push him out of the way and get enough room to strike a ball. He is also allowed to hook an opponent's stick as he is about to strike the ball.

The rules are enforced by two mounted umpires. If they disagree, the final decision is made by the

Eduardo Moore (Argentina) about to hit the ball but Lord Vestey (UK) holds his stick in the way.

referee, who sits in a central position on the side of the ground.

Penalties are imposed by the umpires if a foul has been committed. These vary from penalizing the offenders with a goal and a free strike, to a free strike taken from a point assigned by the umpires.

Handicaps are based on a player's goal-scoring potential and range from 10 (the highest) to 0, or in some countries −2. Each team's handicaps are totalled, the one is subtracted from the other, and the difference is the number of goals recorded on the scoreboard at the start of the match to the lower handicapped team. Normally, the difference is multiplied by the number of chukkers to be played in the match, and divided by eight (the number of chukkers on which each player's handicap is based).

Training

A player must be able to hit the ball in all directions. He has therefore to learn a number of basic strokes: the offside forward, the offside backhand, the offside under the pony's neck, the nearside forward (similar to a tennis backhand), the nearside back-hand, the nearside under the pony's neck, the near- and offside back shots under the pony's tail. These shots are best practised at first on a wooden horse (a base with a saddle and bridle) placed in an enclosed pit where the sides are sloped so that the ball returns to the wooden horse after being hit.

At first the shots should be practised without a ball. When they have become natural and rhythmic, a ball can be introduced. For the forehand and backhand shots it is best to hit the ball when it is level with the stirrup.

Different grips of the stick are used with the backhand and forehand shots. For the latter the thumb is bent around the handle below the first finger; for the former the thumb is placed along the rearside of the handle.

The rider must stand in the stirrups to hit the ball so that, with the hips acting as a pivot, he gets the maximum range of movement. He should lean toward the ball, trying to get his head over it, at the same time as he swings arm and stick down in the same line, to hit the ball with the maximum momentum (aided by a flick of the wrist). He then follows through, back to the carrying position. This is when the stick is vertical with the hand and forearm horizontal.

The newcomer should learn both in the polo pit and by riding and practising the shots on his own. When this is going well he should arrange to take part in some slow chukkers organized by most polo clubs.

Assets of a good polo player are an eye for the ball, physical strength, courage, fitness and mental alertness. Horsemanship is of less importance than in any other equestrian sport.

The ponies are on average about 15.1hh, and a large number of the best come from Argentina, where they breed particularly tough and active animals. There the riders and grooms (gauchos) are highly skilled, turning ponies that start by working the cattle into high-class polo animals. They, and the players who train their own mounts, aim to make them manoeuvrable, obedient, quick to accelerate and stop, and willing to ride alongside and bump other animals (riding off is a vital part of the polo game).

BASIC POLO STROKES

1. Offside under the tail backhander

2. Nearside backhander

3. Offside backhander

4. Forehander

5. Nearside forehander

6. offside under neck

Below: The grip for a polo stick

HUNTING

Hunting became a sport when it was no longer necessary to provide food for the larder. It is consequently the oldest equestrian sport, but killing the quarry is not now the basic aim.

Stag hunting has the earliest origins; it is practised today by only a few packs in the British Isles, but in France it is still very popular. In English-speaking countries, fox hunting has the largest number of packs and followers, but, in areas where fox hunting is difficult, drag hunting, where the hounds follow a scent laid with a drag over prepared country, is gaining popularity. Coyote, wild boar, hares, rabbits and even humans (but by blood-hounds) are hunted from horseback. Whatever the quarry, the etiquette, preparation and procedure for hunt-followers is similar, based on traditions that have grown up over hundreds of years.

The horse
The stamp of horse required for hunting will vary enormously. Much depends on the weight and ability of the rider and on the local terrain. Some areas need horses that can gallop and jump, so the best hunters are those with Thoroughbred blood; but where there are hills and heavy going, a cob is better. As long, however, as the rider can recognize the limitations of his horse and not demand too much of it, then almost any type of horse can be hunted.

Preparation of the hunter
Although the greater part of the training is done by tactful riding in the hunting field, some preparations are essential before going hunting. The horse must be fit enough to stand up to the rigours of the day. He must be controllable (runaway horses endanger both their own riders and other followers). If there is likely to be much jumping (with some packs, especially stag hounds, it is rare) the horse must be introduced beforehand to the types of obstacles he will meet. This means finding out about the local country and, where appropriate, training over small dykes, banks, ditches, hedges, walls, and post and rails. Finally hunting is strenuous and horses with heavy coats will sweat, so in the interests of their well-being and turnout they should be clipped or partly clipped.

A day's hunting
Hunting is done at the invitation (and often expense) of the local farmers and landowners, so hunt-followers are their guests. Permission is needed to hunt and this is obtained through the Master or Secretary of a pack, who can grant it either for a day

upon payment of a 'cap', or for a season upon payment of a subscription, plus for each day's hunting a small amount known as field money or wire fund.

Once permission to hunt has been obtained, it is best to arrive at the meet about 15 minutes before the hounds are due to move off. This provides time to get accustomed to the exciting atmosphere, to pay the dues to the Secretary and to find out who the various officers are. These officers are the Master, or Joint Masters, the leaders of the hunt; the Field Master (often a Master), who controls the hunt-followers during the hunt; the Huntsman, who manages the hounds in the hunting field; and the Whippers-in, who help the Huntsman. These officers of the hunt may be greeted with 'Good Morning' but should not be engaged in conversation, as they need concentration to make the best use of the day's hunting. If they have to get past in a hurry, and there is a shout of 'Huntsman/Master please', it is important to give them room to do so.

After the hounds have moved off they usually proceed to a nearby covert (an enclosure of trees, bushes or scrub). Hounds are put into the covert in the hopes of 'finding' (picking up the scent of) the quarry. Once a hound has found, he will 'speak', and this will encourage the rest of the pack to take

up the scent. Once the quarry breaks covert, the hounds can follow, and while they are on the line then the 'field' (all the hunt-followers) can join them, as long as they are far enough behind not to interfere with the hounds' working. Riders must take care to remain behind the Master and the hounds at all times.

Any newcomer is safest fairly near the back of the field and should try to find a more experienced member of the hunt to follow. Only when confident of his horse's good behaviour should he make his way forward.

A kicking horse is a great danger in the hunting field, so a rider should keep his horse's hindquarters turned away from hounds, and should not put himself in danger by riding too close to other followers.

Do not ride a horse across a field of seeds; even when a field is grass, try to keep to the edges. Cattle and sheep should not be disturbed by riding through their midst, and gates must be shut so that the stock cannot escape.

Hunting is an exciting sport, with an atmosphere that affects even the horses, encouraging them to keep going when exhausted. Riders should remember the future and refrain from asking too much of the horse that gives such a lot.

Left: In the UK Boxing Day meets draw enormous numbers of spectators. Note the red ribbon on the dun pony to warn that he kicks.

Top: The field (hunting terminology for followers) streams down a valley in the USA.

Above: In the USA where wire fences predominate chicken coups are put as hunt fences and are not too difficult to jump.

Right: A meet of Goschen's Foxhounds on a crisp clear autumn day.

SHOW PONIES (UK)

Proven show ponies can be expensive animals, as the show pony world is highly prestigious and has become very professional. Many children and their parents find that they get far more fun out of owning a working pony, which not only has to look pretty but is asked to perform as well, by jumping a few, fairly natural fences.

Show ponies are required to walk, trot and canter, with a short, sharp gallop, and occasionally may be asked to give an additional show. Those with attractive conformation may also be highly strung, and are therefore suitable only for very experienced riders. For the average child, they do not come into the category of 'fun' animals.

Buying a show pony

The best way to acquire both show and working hunter animals is to go to a reliable dealer or breeder, tell him what is required and the amount to be spent and leave the rest to him. Unless there are unlimited funds available, it is no use hoping to become the proud owner of a champion show horse. The 'going' price for a pony which might hope to stand champion at Royal Windsor or the Royal International is around £10,000, perhaps more. Even then, he would have to be produced and ridden by professionals, at further expense.

The top working ponies are usually professionally produced as well, but the competent amateur, provided that he or she rides well enough to show the pony to his advantage, can be reasonably successful by learning how to turn out a pony properly, with a nicely pulled tail and a neatly braided (plaited) mane. Working ponies are less glamorous and more utilitarian than show ponies, and therefore a good deal less expensive.

The working pony, which has more bone and substance than the show pony, also has more uses, such as hunting, Pony Clubbing, one-day eventing, hunter trials—in short, any activities that a child and a pony enjoy doing together. Working classes, which originated in the USA, spread to Europe in the 1950s, providing an interest for children who found the show classes too professional and monopolized by those who seldom seemed to go to school during the summer months.

Show ponies at their best are lovely miniature Thoroughbreds, with beautiful movement, excellent conformation, proportion and symmetry, with an impeccable temperament and perfect manners.

A flashy appearance, however, should be viewed with caution. To the inexpert eye, it can hide such defects as weediness, shortage of bone and substance, bad limbs, stilted movement, crooked action

and hysteria. This sort of mount may be totally unsuitable for a child to ride unless an adult has 'ridden him in' for an hour or so beforehand. It might be that, in the pursuit of quality, breeders have in some cases sacrificed the pony temperament that is so vital to impart confidence to the young rider.

The height divisions

The smallest division has a height limit of 12.2 hands, to be ridden by children of 12 years old or less. These animals are usually grand types, with depth and substance, bred up from Welsh or sometimes Dartmoor foundation stock, and their good temperament makes them eminently suitable for children who can ride and want to go on.

The next division, for animals not exceeding 13.2

hands, seems to produce most of the champions. Basically, they have had more quality grafted on to the foundation, which has been achieved without losing the invaluable pony characteristic and type. This size is for children aged from 12 to 14 years.

There is more variety in type in the 14.2 hands division than in any other, and with this size of animal, pony type is sometimes harder to retain. Some of them look like small Arabs, others like small hacks, a few like small hunters. The rider, at 14 to 16 years, will graduate to a small horse after outgrowing the 14.2 hands high pony.

Height limits for working ponies are 13, 14 and 15 hands, which means that a pony which has grown too big for certain showing classes has a possible future if it jumps well—and many ponies do—in the working classes.

Left: Ready for the class, and the turn out is good, finished off by the thoughtful touch of a red buttonhole to match the browband.

Above: This pony Coed Coch Puff is a winner at one of the most prestigious shows of the year—the Royal International.

Right: One of the most attractive classes is for pairs of ponies when similarity and turnout play as important a part as conformation.

Britain is fortunate indeed in having nine native breeds of pony, most of which are excellent foundation mares when crossed with a small Thoroughbred, Anglo-Arab or polo pony sire to breed show and working ponies.

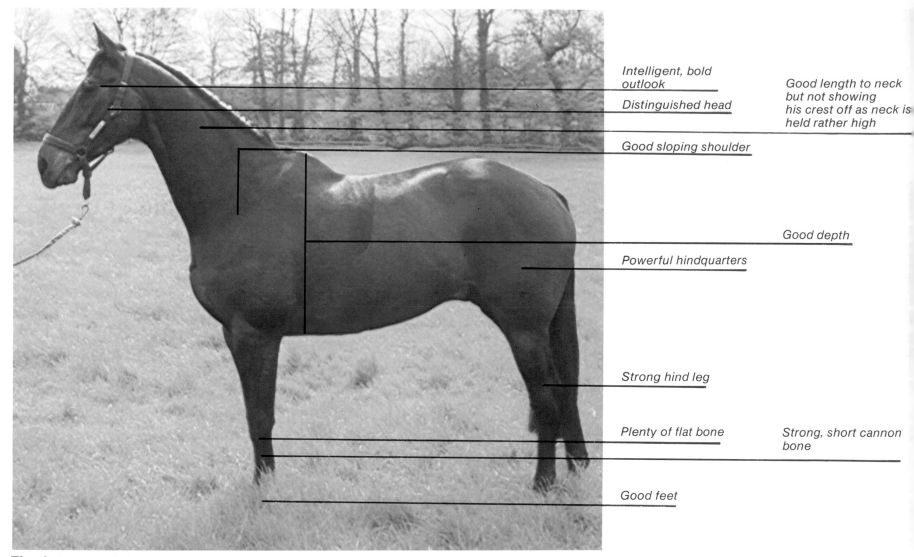

Intelligent, bold outlook

Distinguished head

Good length to neck but not showing his crest off as neck is held rather high

Good sloping shoulder

Good depth

Powerful hindquarters

Strong hind leg

Plenty of flat bone

Strong, short cannon bone

Good feet

The divisions of show hunters

Show hunters are divided by weight-carrying capacity into heavyweight, middleweight and lightweight, each capacity being assessed by the amount of bone below the knee (measured by its circumference) and the type of such bone, and by the depth and substance of the horse generally. The depth is measured behind the forelegs, in the areas where the girth lies, right around the barrel. All else being equal, the most valuable hunters are those that combine the maximum weight-carrying capacity with the greatest quality. Thus a Thoroughbred horse capable of carrying 95-100kg (15 or 16st) could be a very valuable animal indeed.

A middleweight horse must be up to 90kg (14st), and a lightweight horse 75-80kg (12 or 13st). There are also ladies' hunters (to be ridden sidesaddle), small hunters (which must not exceed 15.2 hands high), and working hunters (which are judged on their conformation and ride plus their ability to jump a course of mainly natural fences). The big shows also hold classes for four-year-olds under saddle and for novices who have not won a prize over a certain value by the time that the entries closed.

Showing the hunter

There is a great deal of enjoyment to be had from showing a hunter. It is possible to spend most of the summer at one show or another, for the big shows start in May and continue until September, and they all—but particularly the agricultural shows—boast an extensive classification for hunters.

Showing a hunter successfully is a considerable art. The object of the exercise is to ensure that the horse is looking and going at its best the entire time, but particularly during those all-important seconds when the judges are watching. The experienced showman knows just when this is likely to be, and keeps an eye on the judges at all times, in order to ensure that his horse will make a favourable impression when it really matters.

Unlike the hack or the pony, the hunter is not asked to give an individual show. Walk, trot, canter and gallop are the paces that the judge wants to see, and the gallop is a very important part of the proceedings. It demands good horsemanship and judgement on the part of the rider, and the ability to control the horse. Some of the worst falls have been

Above: Mr. Tom Hunnable's Langton Orchid who has been one of the best middleweight hunters in the UK, at the Royal Windsor Horse Show.

Right: Dublin is a Mecca for show hunters and this horse—Kilbegnet was a prizewinner in the Ladies' Hunter Class.

occasioned by slipping up on the flat. The walk is also important, for a free, swinging walk generally denotes the ability to gallop. The judge does not merely look at the hunter, however, but also rides him to feel how he goes. It is therefore essential for the hunter to be a good ride.

Like the hunting field, the hunter show-ring is a place where tradition dies hard and innovation is unwelcome. Clothes should be as conventional as possible, and the turnout of the horse must be absolutely conservative. Coloured brow bands, nylon girths, loudly checked coats, and hunting caps or bowler hats of any other colour than black or navy blue are out of place in the hunter class.

Buying the show hunter

As with every other category of show horse, the show hunter is best acquired from a reputable dealer, from the breeder or, if the horse already has some form, directly from the owner. The show and working hunter both have another outlet, in hunter trials and one-day events, given jumping ability. The good performer, with quality, good conformation and youth, will not be cheap to buy, but a four-year-old that is still green should become more valuable, and a hunter in its prime, say six or over, will have many useful years ahead of him.

Those wishing to win championships would do best to acquire a top middleweight horse, for a really good 90kg (14st) hunter takes a great deal of beating. The ambitious owner should send him to one of the leading professionals, rather than attempt to show him himself, because an unknown horse with a reputation to be made or marred needs the expertise of the professional showman. Later in the season, when the horse has perhaps won a few good classes, the owner can decide whether to risk taking over the showing himself, or to play safe and leave the riding arrangements as they are.

SHOW HACKS (UK)

The show hack is an elegant riding horse with outstanding conformation, perfect symmetry and natural balance, and unfailing good manners. He is Thoroughbred or nearly so, and a thing of beauty, and he must have presence—the undefinable quality that makes the observer look, and keep on looking.

In the last century there were covert hacks, on which hunting men and women rode to the meet in the days before the motor horse-box; and park hacks, on which ladies and gentlemen disported themselves among others of fashion in Rotten Row.

The show hack is more highly trained than the hunter, and more finely drawn, for he is not required to go across country or to jump fences out of heavy ground. Nor does he require the same rugged courage, which is by no means essential—or even desirable—in a horse that is often ridden before breakfast. Ideally, he must trot fast—pointing his toe—and canter slowly. The true hack canter is a delightful pace, the acme of comfort and elegance, accompanied by lightness in hand.

The hack is one of the best types of show animal for an amateur to produce. True, the horses that win championships are generally professionally produced, but an amateur who rides adequately can still have a good deal of enjoyment by competing in hack classes, either by buying a ready-made show hack or by acquiring the raw material and training it himself. Basically, the requirements are simple—walk, trot and canter. More advanced work can be produced in the individual show that each rider hack or by acquiring the raw material and training him

discouraged and the judges are really looking for a well-trained, obedient horse that will change legs when cantering a figure of eight, rein back and stand still, and they do not want anything in the nature of elementary dressage.

The divisions of a show hack

Hacks are judged half on their conformation, presence and movement and half on their ride, manners and training. There are three categories: the small hack, which must not exceed 15 hands; the large hack, with an upper limit of 15.3 hands; and the ladies' hack, to be ridden side-saddle, a most elegant sight. In addition, the London shows sometimes put on a class for pairs of hacks, one ridden by a lady, one by a gentleman. Here the way in which horses go together and how well they match one another are also taken into account.

In each class the horses walk, trot and canter around the ring, give their individual show, and are finally ridden by the judges. Then each one is stripped of his saddle and run up in hand before the judges, who are concerned with whether the horse moves straight. The horses are saddled up, remounted, sent out to circle the judges at a walk, and finally pulled into line in the order in which they have been placed.

Buying a hack

Some of the best show hacks in the past have come from the racecourse but they are often difficult to settle after being raced, and many of the most likely

prospects in terms of conformation, quality and type have problems of temperament that are by no means easy to resolve.

Hacks are probably best bought from a reputable dealer or a professional shower of hacks, most of whom have some that are surplus to requirements and are kept to sell on. It is no bad idea to spend a week or so under instruction from a professional, who will ensure that the novice is riding correctly and will take an interest in his or her progress in the show-ring thereafter. Professional advice is freely given, and of very real help. Those who make a living out of showing are the first to help newcomers to the show-ring to do things correctly and to enjoy their initiation.

Below left: An important part of the hack class is when saddles are removed and the horses' conformation examined minutely. After this they walk away and trot back, and the hack should lead willingly to show off his paces to best advantage. This can be taught at home when an assistant encourages the horse from behind.

Below: Turnout is a vital part of showing a hack. A horse that gleams, has well oiled feet, a neatly plaited main, a well brushed and trimmed tail, is much more impressive. Many showmen comb patterns onto the hindquarters. First dampen them, then draw a fine comb of the same size as the squares required against the lie of the hair to create a pattern.

FEATURES OF THE BODY

Pretty, elegant head with alert outlook, good presence

Good length to the neck and should get more of a crest on maturing

Excellent deep sloping shoulder

Enough bone, but not heavy or coarse

Lacking a little depth

Strong hindquarters that make possible a light ride

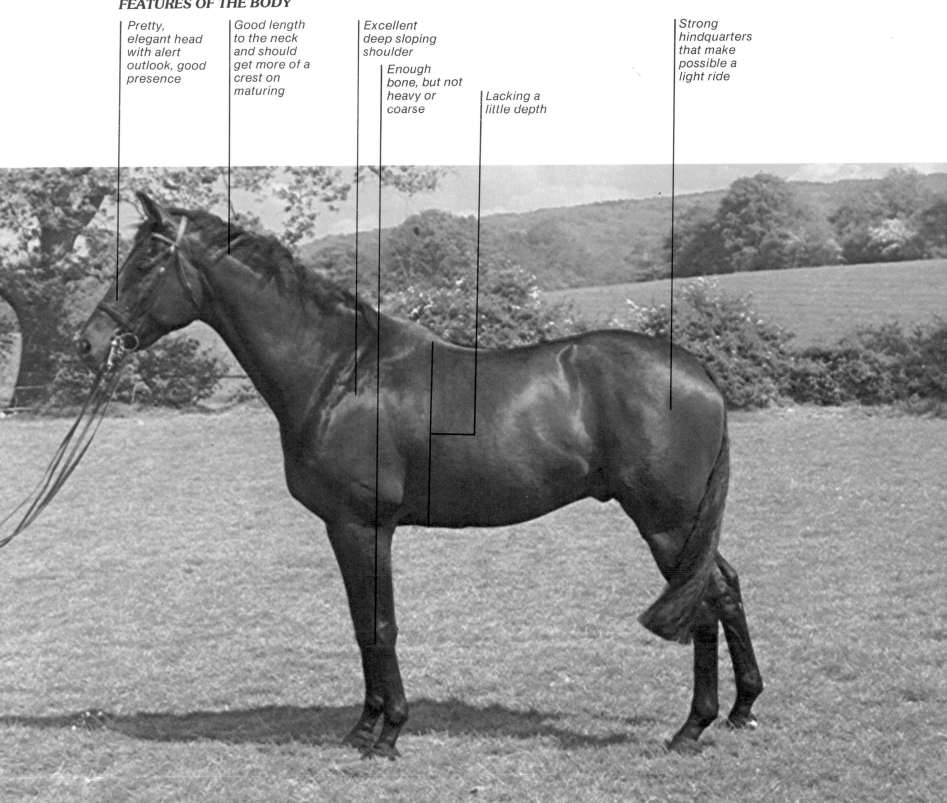

SADDLE HORSES (USA)

Think of the phrase 'saddle horse', and the image of any equine capable of carrying a rider comes to mind. Not so in the United States horse show world. The Saddle-horse Division is the province of the American saddlebred or Saddle-horse, the breed originally created to provide Southern plantation owners and their families with a flashy but comfortable ride.

The divisions of the saddle-horse

Saddle-horses are exhibited as three-gaited, five-gaited, or fine harness animals. Three-gaited horses perform at the walk, trot and canter in classes that include those for amateurs, ladies and juniors, and (with regard to the animals themselves) for stallions, mares and geldings.

Five-gaited horses are shown at the walk, trot, canter, and two other gaits, the slow gait (or singlefoot) and the rack. The slow gait is something of a broken pace in which each foot strikes the ground individually, and the rack is similar but faster. Both are artificial, in the sense that horses must be taught them, although American Saddlebreds inherit an ability to slow gait and rack. Five-gaited classes are similar to the three-gaited events, and include model conformation classes and a combination class in which horses are shown first in harness and then under saddle.

Fine harness horses pull light buggies at the walk, trot and park gait (the last is a slightly more animated trot). Good manners, including the ability to stand quietly, are of the utmost importance; fussy or unruly animals will be penalized, especially when driven by women.

Training

Saddle-horses in competition are seldom taken out of their stalls for any purpose other than to be schooled or exhibited, because hacking a gaited show horse may lead to injury or cosmetic blemishes. Training consists of encouraging the animal to achieve its distinctive high leg action. Toward that goal, a variety of leg boots, chains, and rattles are used.

The turnout

Much attention is paid to a Saddle-horse's appearance. Tail cartilages are nicked and reset to achieve high tail carriage, and wigs are often blended into the horse's own tail hairs to give an appearance of greater fullness. Three-gaited horses are shown with roached (hogged) manes and docked tails, whereas their five-gaited and fine harness cousins sport long manes and tails. When not being exhibited or schooled, most saddle horses have their tails bound up or kept in bags to guard against soiling.

Riders and drivers are also well turned out. Gaited riders wear saddle suits with bell-bottomed Kentucky jodhpurs topped by a derby (bowler) or high hat of the same colour, and women drivers are outfitted in long skirts or formal gowns.

The class

A gaited or harness class begins when all entrants are in the ring. The judge indicates via the ringmaster or show announcer the gaits to be performed and in which direction of the arena. Saddle-horses seem to thrive on audience reaction, and spectators are encouraged to applaud as their favourite contestant passes in front of the judge. In five-gaited classes the command to 'Rack-on!' is traditionally greeted by whoops and shouts, to which the horses respond by greater speed and animation.

If the judge has difficulty in selecting a winner, he may ask two or more entrants to perform longer than others. Finally, competitors line up in the centre of the arena, stretching their horses into the classic gaited horse extended pose while the judge walks down the line to inspect them. Where conformation is a factor, grooms race into the ring to help remove saddles, wipe away sweat marks, and attract the animal's attention to enhance its pose. Finally, riders remount and retire to one end of the arena to await the judge's results.

The top saddle-seat equitation title in the United States is known as 'Good Hands'. Regional qualifiers vie for the award at New York City's National Horse Show finals. After being viewed in a group, competitors go through tests on an individual basis, which may involve cantering in small circles, trotting a designated number of strides, halting, and performing rein-backs.

Horse shows in America range in type and cover the spectrum from hunters, jumpers, junior hunters, saddle-horses (both three-and five-gaited), fine harness, Western stock and pleasure to the breed divisions such as Morgan, Appaloosa and Welsh. There are also driving classes, gymkhana and equitation classes.
Below left: This eye-catching combination has just won a prize at Madison Square Gardens which is the most important American show.

Right: Saddle horses are also put into harness and this one is showing himself off well at the park gait which is a rather animated trot.

Below: Turnout is very important in the Saddle horse classes and this young lady's matching brown coat and Kentucky jodhpurs go well with the colour of her horse. The strain these animated paces put on the horse is shown by the amount this horse's pasterns are bent.

'Western riding' encompasses activities involving stock (from 'livestock') equestrian techniques, evolved from strictly functional beginnings: the working of herds of cattle on the ranges and plains of the American West.

The stirrups are considerably longer than in hunt seat or dressage, so that riders can brace themselves during the quick bursts of speed, rapid turns, and sudden halts needed to pursue and control cattle. The rider uses loose reins and carries them in one hand, enabling him to employ a lasso rope, or to gesture with his hat to attract a steer's attention.

The Tack

Traditional Western tack consists of Mexican-derived items. Simple bridles with only curb bits are used or perhaps a horse may wear a bitless hackamore or bosal (pronounced 'bo-sal'), which exerts controlling pressure on the animal's nose. Stock saddles, which may weigh up to 13kg (30lb), are marked by a high pommel (the 'horn' around which one end of a lasso is wrapped when used for calf roping) and cantle for the rider's comfort and security, and heavy leather stirrup fenders and rear skirts. Wool or synthetic saddle blankets cushion the weight of the saddle, which will also have thongs or hooks by which ropes and raingear can be attached. Parade saddles, which are used in showing classes, are more ornate, often studded or inlaid with gold and silver decoration.

The horses

There are particular breeds and types of horses that are most closely associated with Western riding. Although Quarter-horses came from the East, they quickly proved themselves well suited for ranch work. Appaloosas, the spotted breed developed by Nez Perce Indians of Idaho and Montana, are likewise widely used. Cowboys have always liked brightly coloured Palominos and Pintos, but Arabs and Morgans have been a more recent introduction to stock seat, ranch and pleasure riding.

Training

Contemporary training is a far cry from the bronco-busting methods of the Old West. Now, after a young horse has been made to accept a rider's weight and authority, emphasis is placed on learning to neck-rein, whereby he will change direction after receiving indirect rein cues; a horse will turn left when his rider 'drapes' the reins across his neck by reaching across to the left. The Western riding horse must also be taught to execute flying changes of lead at the canter (Westeners call that gait the 'lope') and to work 'off his hocks' in order to have the balance to respond instantaneously to any command. A good stock horse must be calm and learn not to react adversely to potentially frightening situations, such as having a steer turn in his direction; he must also be willing to stand quietly in the middle of a herd of cattle.

Although jeeps, helicopters, railroads, and trucks have replaced many of the older functions of stock horses on the ranch, horses are still used. The reason is that in quite a few situations horses can do what mechanized forms of transportation cannot, and besides they are wanted more and more for the increasingly popular Western riding sports.

Below left: A bronc being ridden with a snaffle bit, tight bit guard and draw reins.

Below: Dave Jones training his horse to do a slide. The horse is equipped with a spade bit, rawhide reins and a romal.

Rodeoing

The sport of rodeoing is an outgrowth of actual ranch work. Beginning as impromptu competitions among cowboys who vied with each other to see who was best, the events began to attract spectators and cash prizes and, in addition, money was wagered by participants and onlookers. In the USA there are now more than 500 rodeos sanctioned by the Rodeo Cowboys' Association (the professional sport's governing body) annually, to which must be added rodeos put on by organizations of which pre-teenage, high school and college cowboys and cowgirls are members, as well as events in which amateurs and dude ranch vacationers participate. In Australia, the Australian Rough Riders Association (ARRA) has more than 12,000 members and conducts a circuit of rodeos held in all the states. In the summer they are staged in the south, and as the weather gets colder the activities move further north.

Calf-roping

Of the five classic rodeo events — calf-roping, saddle bronc-riding, bronc-riding, bull-riding and steer-wrestling — only the first has contemporary application to ranch work. Calf-roping begins when a young steer or heifer is released from a chute and given a head start of several seconds. The cowboy gallops in pursuit and tries to lasso the animal. When he does, his horse slides to a halt, then backs up to maintain tension on the rope tied around the saddle horn so that the calf cannot elude the cowboy. Now on foot, the cowboy races to the calf, flips it onto its side, and ties any three of its legs together. The fastest time from start to finish wins, but no points are scored if the calf slips out of the 'piggin' string' around its legs. A good calf-roping horse is essential, and ropers usually give a portion of their winnings to the owners of such horses that they have borrowed.

Steer-wrestling

Steer-wrestling, also known as bulldogging, is another event that is scored against time. It starts when a steer is made to run down the length of the arena. A cowboy gallops alongside and leaps from the saddle. While locking his arms around the steer's head and horns, he digs his boots into the ground to slow the animal and then tries to wrestle it to the ground. The time ends when the steer is lying on its side, and the fastest time wins.

A contestant set to lasso his calf at a rodeo in Canada, the only rodeo skill still used in modern ranch work.

The contestant has roped his calf and his horse stands still keeping the rope taught.

Bronc-riding

Bronc- and bull-riding are exhibitions of strength and balance. In saddle bronc-riding a cowboy sits on a modified stock saddle and attempts to stay there for at least ten seconds, holding on with one hand to a halter rope. A surcingle strap with a leather handhold replaces the saddle in bareback bronc-riding, and the required time is eight seconds. Eight seconds is also the period that a cowboy must stay on board in bull-riding. He can use both hands to hold the rigging's (surcingle's) handhold. Scoring in all three events is according to the assessment of two judges, each of whom awards up to 25 points for a rider's style and a like amount for an animal's ferocity. No points are given, however, if a cowboy is thrown before the requisite time limit or if, in the case of bronc-riding, he touches the horse or saddle with his free hand or fails to spur the horse on its shoulders on the first leap out of the chute. (Additional and aggressive spurring during a ride will win higher scores.)

Clowns, pick-up riders and hazers

Contestants and their mounts or quarries are not the only people and animals involved at a rodeo. Clowns provide spectator entertainment, and also divert a bronc's or bull's attention away from a fallen rider. Pick-up riders move up to cowboys who have outlasted the time limit in bronc- and bull-riding to help them off their mounts. Hazers gallop alongside steers in wrestling events to make sure that bulls run in a reasonably straight line.

Barrel racing and other events

Women riders are in the spotlight when there is a barrel race. They run their horses individually around three barrels set in a triangular pattern, and the cowgirl who clocks the fastest cloverleaf is the winner. Other rodeo events include team roping (a pair of cowboys lasso a calf around its head and hind legs), trick riding, and wild horse, chuck wagon, and chariot races. Youngsters riding in junior contests may be asked to capture a goat or a greased pig.

The rewards of professional rodeoing can be great, with total annual earnings for overall and all-round champions in the USA in the range of $100,000 (£60,000). But expenses can be high. Rodeo participants pay their own entry fees and travelling and lodging costs, which can amount to many thousands of dollars a year. Equally demanding are the miles they must drive between rodeos, and they must become accustomed and impervious to injuries suffered along the way. A bandage, a shot

Trail of pain-killing drugs, and back in the saddle again;
The T no wonder the route to and from top fixtures is
carryii known as the Suicide Circuit.
kind o
cross-(### Cutting horses
the wa Cutting horses compete in their own events as well
reasor as being part of rodeo classes. It requires very
rider r special skills and not every horse is capable of
close learning to single out a calf from a herd, then to
over keep it isolated so that the animal is unable to rejoin
obstac the others. An innate sense of the job to be done is
side. essential in any prospective cutting horse, a talent
   Jud that will become evident when the horse is first
(60%) asked to work a herd of cattle. Some horses will
confo instinctively position themselves in the right place

Pleas *Exciting moments in bronc-riding. Below left, the*
The P *pickup riders move in to rescue a contestant.*
ances
versior
There

and almost anticipate their cues. Further training involves working on fast starts, halts, and turns in both directions. Of particular importance is that a horse learns to work off his hocks, in much the same way that a defensive football player remains in complete balance ready to move in any direction.

The ultimate aim is for the horse to participate in cutting horse events. Their riders appear to be mere passengers in the saddle, sitting back and holding a loose rein after indicating which calf is to be singled out. Then the horse takes over the work, interposing itself between the calf and the herd until the judge is satisfied that the calf has indeed been stymied. Cutting horse entries compete individually, and the fastest time wins.

These cutting horse competitions are a popular part of horse shows in the West and South est of North America, where the prize money can be very

high. In Australia it is a growing sport and the National Cutting Horse Association was formed in 1972 to supervise and formalize events.

Distance riding

Distance riding contests take place all over the United States and Canada, and in the USA they are dominated by those who adopt the Western style of riding. Their antecedents can be found in trail driving (shipping cattle from local ranges to railroad sidings many miles away) and Pony Express cross-country mail-carrying jobs. The sport is divided into two categories. A Competitive Ride requires contestants to cover a stipulated distance within a certain time, with penalty points given for arriving too early or too late. An Endurance Ride is a race in which the rider who crosses the finishing line first is declared the winner.

HORSE CARE
AND
STABLE MANAGEMENT

From the moment of deciding to buy a horse or pony,
a bewildering number of problems arise. In this section of
THE HORSE AND PONY MANUAL
the prospective owner can discover where and how to buy a suitable mount,
and which vital points and conformation to take into account.
The new owner must accept complete responsibility for the well-being of his animal,
often an alarming prospect.
Adequate shelter, feeding and watering, blanketing, bandaging,
fitting and upkeep of tack for riding and driving, shoeing and elementary first aid:
sensible and practical advice on all these topics is given,
illustrated with helpful annotated diagrams and photographs.
For the rider, there are hints on correct dress
for the showring and hunting field, and information on insurance and travel.
At the back of this section can be found information on riding for the disabled,
a bibliography and addresses of riding organizations
all over the world.

CONFORMATION

Buying a horse is an absorbing, challenging, time-consuming and often hazardous business. The inexperienced can be easily taken in by wily sellers; even the experienced may occasionally misjudge a horse's quality. Few can make a successful purchase without an 'eye for a horse'—an ability to judge a horse's potential, to notice its weaknesses and good points. Those who are not thus gifted, or whose eye for a horse is not yet sufficiently developed, are wise to ask for the help of someone more knowledgeable in this field. It is important to find out as much as possible about the following points: conformation and movement; soundness; suitability for proposed purpose; suitability for prospective rider; personal preferences of prospective owner; the future home; age; and value.

Conformation

The first impression is important because it covers the overall proportions and appearance of the horse. All parts of the body should together form a harmonious whole. A head that looks too heavy for the neck to carry, for example, is not only ugly but weak and is likely to cause difficulty in establishing a good head carriage.

The head

The horse's character can be reasonably judged by studying the head. An eye that is bold, round and has a kind, generous expression is a generally reliable indication of good temperament. Any experienced buyer is suspicious of a horse that flashes its eyes nervously and looks backward frequently.

The position of the eyes is also important. Those placed wide apart usually belong to a horse or pony with a generous character. A fine, elegant head is usually a sign of a well-bred horse. More common features, however, usually indicate a more sensible temperament.

The neck

By its shape and length, the neck gives an indication of the natural head carriage, and only skilled riders can improve any defects. The neck should be in proportion. If it is too short, it makes a rider feel insecure, and the horse can balance itself only by holding it rather high; if too long, it is more difficult for the horse to support.

The most elegant and strongest shape for a neck is arched (convex top line). A straight top line can normally be improved by corrective training, but a ewe neck (concave top line) is usually a permanent weakness.

The angle at which the neck joins the head is also important, as this affects respiration. If the depth from the poll to the jowl is particularly long then it will be difficult for the horse to flex without creasing the windpipe and restricting the flow of air along it.

The shoulder

The horse's movement and pulling strength can be judged by the shape of the shoulder. Thus a long, sloping shoulder, allowing more freedom of movement, is best for a riding horse. Long, sweeping strides rather than restricted ones can be taken. On the other hand, a straight shoulder provides more pulling power, and is favoured for carriage horses.

This is a very hollow back

The back

This is the weight-bearing area, and indicates the strength and power of the horse. A short back makes a horse more stable and powerful, and gives it a greater weight-carrying capacity. An unduly short back, however, is not so supple, and can restrict the speed and action of the horse. Although a long back does make the horse more supple, it needs to be broad, muscular and supported by powerful loins to offset the weakness due to its length.

The shape of the back should be slightly concave, though not too much, as a hollow back is weak (but bear in mind that a horse's back becomes hollower as it grows older). Shapes to be avoided are a sway-back (lower part of back wrenched) and a roach-back

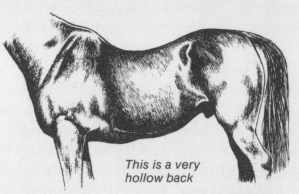

This back is too straight

(convex top line), as both normally indicate a hors that is too weak to carry heavy loads.

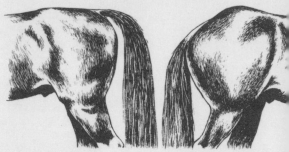

The croup is too straight and tail too high.

These hindquarter slope too steeply

The quarters

The horse's propulsive power, the spring to jum and the ability to gallop, is given by the quarters; th upper line should be rounded, not falling away or fla Large, wide quarters indicate well-developed muscle although, if they are too wide, the horse may tend t have a rolling action of the hind legs.

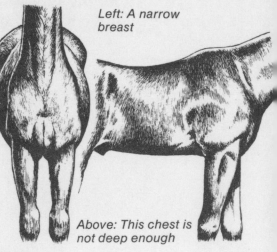

Left: A narrow breast

Above: This chest is not deep enough

The breast

This should be relatively wide, so that the foreleg can operate freely and there is plenty of room in th chest for the lungs to expand fully.

The chest

If the chest is rounded and deep, it has 'heart room and the capacity for heavy breathing; this is a goo indication of the stamina of the horse. Depth, take to be the distance from withers to belly, just behin the elbow, is considered one of the most reliabl signs of a good horse.

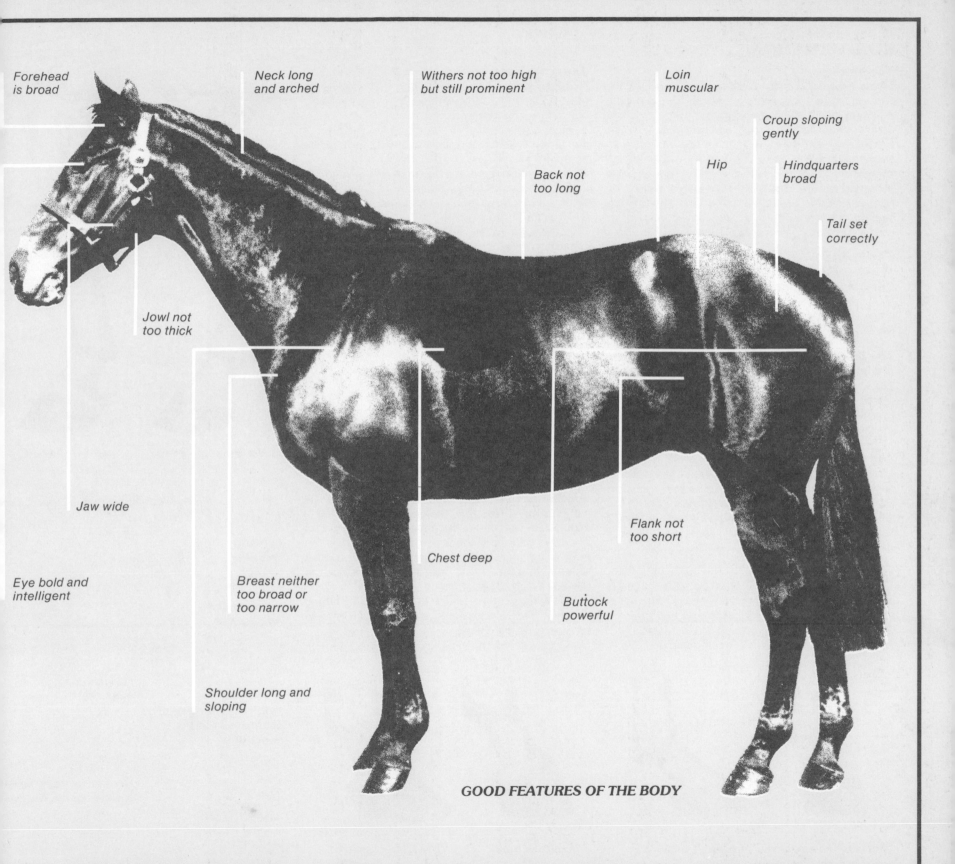

Forehead
is broad

Neck long
and arched

Withers not too high
but still prominent

Loin
muscular

Croup sloping
gently

Hip

Hindquarters
broad

Back not
too long

Tail set
correctly

Jowl not
too thick

Jaw wide

Eye bold and
intelligent

Breast neither
too broad or
too narrow

Chest deep

Flank not
too short

Buttock
powerful

Shoulder long and
sloping

GOOD FEATURES OF THE BODY

The forelegs

These have to take the strain of the horse's weight, and absorb the concussion that results from galloping and jumping. Consequently they are the commonest seat of lameness in the horse, and prospective buyers should be very wary of buying any animal with weaknesses in this area. The legs should be almost straight as far as the pastern, which should slope obliquely toward the foot. The knees should be neither 'in' nor bowed and the feet should face straight forwards. If they are turned inward or outward, such a twist is a weakness.

The knee

This should be clean, flat and well-defined. A horse that is 'over at the knee' (convex outline) puts much less strain on its tendons than one that is 'back at the knee' (concave outline). The former rarely suffers from strained tendons.

The bone

The larger the circumference (assessed by measuring the leg below the knee), the greater the weight-carrying capacity of the horse. Also the flatter and more dense the bone, the greater the horse's chance of staying sound.

The fetlock

These joints should be broad enough to provide a good area of articulation, and round joints must be treated with suspicion; puffiness in the area of the fetlock joint is a sign of strain, and a warning that it cannot stand too much work. With a young horse, it suggests he has been brought on too quickly.

The pasterns

These should be neither too short and upright, as this produces a bumpy ride; nor too long and sloping, as such pasterns are weak and place a greater strain on the tendons.

The tendons

Horses in demanding work (racing and eventing) are most liable to tendon trouble. The most reliable indications of weak tendons are:

1. Heat and soft swelling (puffiness) in the area of the tendon, which is usually evidence of a recent injury.

2. Hard swelling, in the form of either nodular lumps or overall filling, but without heat; this is evidence of a longstanding condition.

3. Heat and hard swelling.

In the case of the first, the horse may recover within a few days or it might be serious. It is better not to consider the immediate purchase of a horse in such a state but to ask to return when the heat and swelling have died down.

In the second instance, as long as the swelling is hard and cool, it is likely that the tissues have repaired. It is wise to find out, however, if the horse has been sound since the injury, and to get professional advice.

The third instance is the most serious, for it is likely to give continuous trouble.

The foot

As this is the base support for the horse it must be able to absorb jar, so a round and open-shaped hoof is best, providing a stronger and greater area to act as a shock absorber than one that is narrow, small or too upright. A large, flat foot, however, would be cumbersome. The feet should be symmetrical—matched in shape—so that the jar is shared evenly. The most important shock absorber, however, is the frog, which should be well-formed and in contact with the ground. A good blacksmith can do much to remedy defects of the frog.

Finally the material of the hoof should be strong and free from cracks, rings and any other signs of brittleness or crumbling.

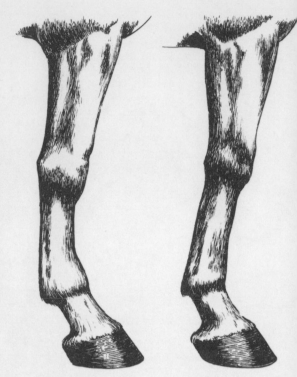

Behind at the knee   *Over at the knee*

Forearm muscular

Knee flat and well defined

Cannon bone quite short

Fetlock joints defined but not rounded or upright

Hooves in proportion to and round, not too boxy

Pastern neither too sloping nor too upright

Short, upright pastern   *Sloping pasterns*   *A narrow foot*   *A flat foot*

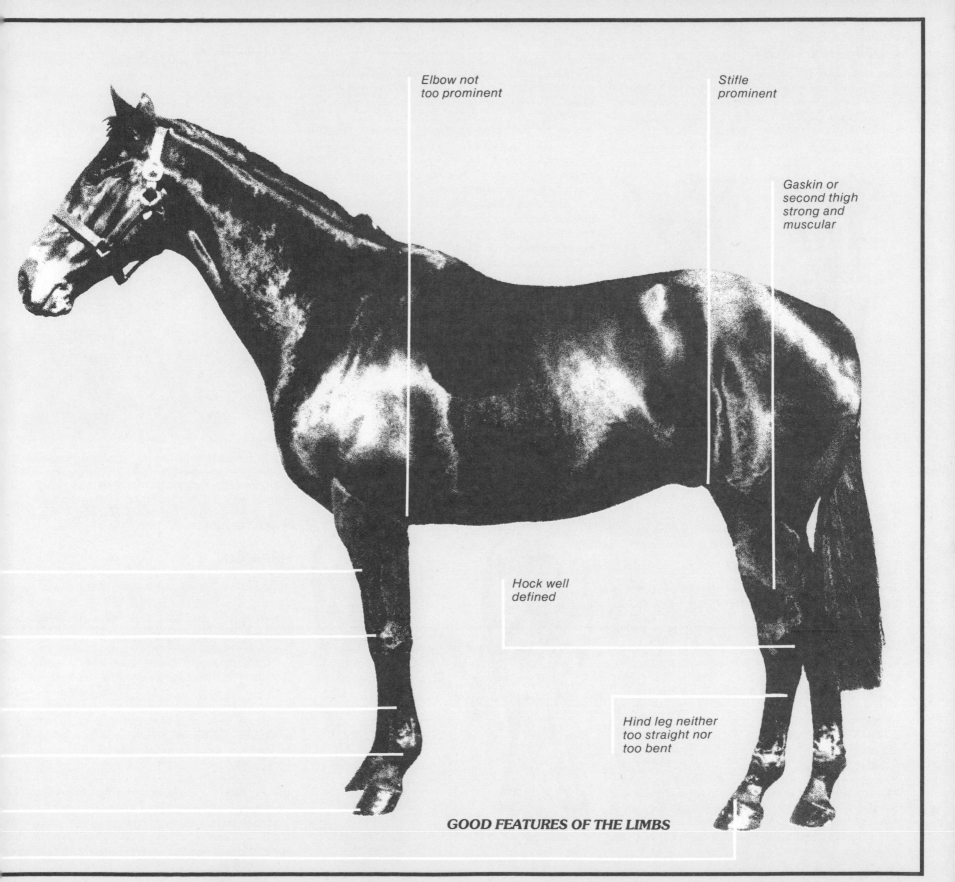

Elbow not
too prominent

Stifle
prominent

Gaskin or
second thigh
strong and
muscular

Hock well
defined

Hind leg neither
too straight nor
too bent

GOOD FEATURES OF THE LIMBS

CONFORMATION

The hind leg
This is a source of power and propulsion, most of which comes from the second thigh and the hock. Other points (joints, pasterns, etc) should be inspected for the same faults and good points as the front legs, paying good attention to the feet.

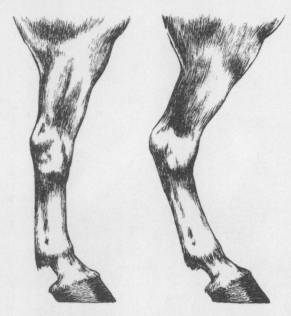

A very straight hind leg   *A very bent hind leg*

The second thigh
A broad, strong, muscular and relatively long second thigh is by far the most powerful.

The hock
This hardest-worked joint in the body is the source of much lameness, and weaknesses shown in it should, therefore, never be ignored. The shape should be wide from the front to the back; the quality should be high, with the bones neatly formed and well defined. Roundness and puffiness are warnings of possible trouble.

The most common defects of the hock are:

Cow hocks, when the points of the hocks are turned in. As long as there are no other weaknesses of the hind legs, these are not a serious problem, although a horse with cow hocks does tend to take short, rolling steps.

2. Bowed hocks, which are the reverse of cow hocks. They usually result in the legs being set well apart and the toes turning inward. Bowed hocks usually lead to the hock twisting outward each time the leg is put to the ground, which places greater strain on this vital joint than can be easily borne.

3. Sickle hocks, in which the angle of the hocks is very acute and the hind legs are in the shape of a sickle. The more severe the angle, the greater the weakness.

4. Straight hocks, which are the opposite of sickle hocks, as the hock is structured so that there is a very large angle. Straight hocks result in rather stiff short strides and a lack of flexibility in the joints, which tends to put strain on the hind legs.

5. Curby hocks have a bony formation below the point of the hock, which can be seen when looked at from the side. Though an indication of weak hocks, this is not serious if there is no heat; and especially not if there are curbs on both hocks.

When considering the effect of any weakness of the limbs on the movement of the horse it is best to examine the shoes. Abnormal wear on the front or the side signifies that the movement is affected.

In the search for a horse it will be rare to find one without quite a number of the above defects, as the horse with perfect conformation does not exist. The main point to consider is how any defects will affect the work required of the horse. Few risks can be taken in the purchase of an eventer, but the buyer who wants a horse only for hacking need not worry too much about minor weaknesses. Remember that if a weakness does exist, but is supported by particularly sound and strong surrounding parts, there is much less cause for anxiety.

Cow hocks   *Bowed hocks*

MOVEMENT

The horse should be looked at coming straight towards the examiner so that any crooked movement becomes obvious. The grey is not moving straight but twisting his foreleg which puts great strain on his joints. The bay is moving straight and well.

Movement
The horse should move with relatively straight strides. Swings and twists in action often place undue strain on one part of a limb. If the legs move close to one another, brushing can occur, although the effects of this can be prevented to some extent by the use of boots and bandages.

The forelegs should not swing inward and only a little outward (too much and the horse is said to 'dish'). The hind legs, too, should take relatively straight steps and (most important) should come well under the belly to provide driving power. The joints (especially the hocks) should articulate freely. They must not appear to restrict the action, producing stiffness.

The paces should be true — ie the walk four-time, the trot two-time and the canter three-time (*see* The gaits of the horse).

Horses used for different purposes need different styles of action. For those that pull carriages, a high knee action is acceptable; but if they are to gallop or

to perform dressage, a freely moving shoulder and sweeping action are better. Generally, good jumpers do not have too long a stride and take athletic, springy steps, especially at the trot. For the racehorse the walk is the more important indication of his value, because over-stepping by the hind foot of the fore foot on the opposite side and sweeping the ground is a good indication of the ability to gallop.

Soundness

A magnificent animal to whom the proud new owner becomes nurse and payer of veterinary bills, rather than a rider, is of little use. Although the experienced purchaser can spot many signs of unsoundness, only a vet can make a reliable diagnosis. It is best, therefore, to arrange for a veterinary examination before paying for a horse. If the horse is expensive, it is worthwhile having X-rays taken of the feet, as these will expose such serious problems as navicular (see Chapter 10).

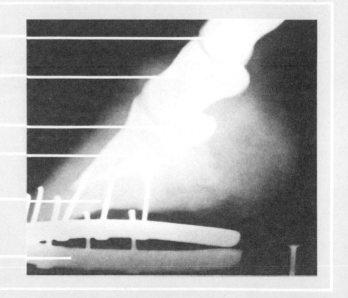

First pastern bone

Second pastern bone

Navicular bone

Pedal bone

Nails penetrating through the wall of the foot

Shoe

SUITABILITY

Suitability for proposed home
Buying a horse entails taking on an enormous responsibility. The amount of care and attention the animal needs, however, does vary from type to type. For example, if a purchaser has no stables and can only keep his animal at grass, then a hardy native breed (ie, Highland, Welsh Cob or Shetland) would be most suitable.

If the purchaser has a stable but is unable to provide constant supervision and daily exercise, then he can use the combined system of care when the horse is stabled by night in winter, and by day in summer, and turned out to grass for the other part of the 24 hours (in winter with a New Zealand rug). In this situation he can think of buying a half-bred horse, which is more refined and usually has more performance ability than the native breed, but still has the toughness and good temperament to survive without constant attention.

If the purchaser wants an animal to carry him for long days of hunting or to do well in competitions, then he will need a horse with more class (closer to, if not wholly, Thoroughbred), and he must keep him fit. Such a horse needs constant attention in the stable and exercise every day; no purchaser should contem-

plate buying a high-grade refined animal unless he has the facilities and the time to cope with the enormous amount of work involved. There is, however, an option open to the ambitious rider with too little time to look after his horse, and that is to keep him at livery. As long as a reputable yard is chosen, then the professionals can look after the animal and ride him when the owner is unable to do so.

Suitability for purpose
It is important to decide how much and what type of work will be demanded of the horse. Then the physical and temperamental assets needed to perform this work can be kept clearly in mind when examining possible animals.

Suitability for rider
It is vital that the horse is able to carry the weight of his owner, as an underhorsed rider not only looks unattractive but also puts great strain on the animal. The weight-carrying capacity of a horse is dependent on his height, depth, bone and chunkiness of body, although high class animals—Thoroughbreds and Arabs—have denser bone and are able to carry comparatively more weight than a similarly shaped native breed.

It is important to make a fair assessment of the rider's ability, for it is no use buying a sensitive, athletic, class horse if the owner is not capable of controlling such a delicate creature. A novice rider needs a horse with a good temperament much more than one with ability. He must look for a co-operative partner, one that is not upset by confused aids and clumsy riding. There is little pleasure for the novice in riding a horse that can jump brilliantly but is highly excitable. There are exceptions, but inexperienced riders should not consider either horses with great ability (most have difficult temperaments) or Thoroughbreds (as riding these demands the greatest amount of horsemanship).

The character of the rider should be considered in relation to the type of horse to buy. The young, adventurous rider might enjoy and understand an excitable, forward-going horse. A more nervous, cautious rider will prefer a horse that needs urging on. This is one of the most important aspects of horse buying—choosing one that suits the buyer, and on whom he will produce good results. This is not necessarily the most brilliant horse.

A handsome but unsuitable horse for this young rider. The boy will find it very difficult to control so large an animal as his legs are not long enough and he is too young to be strong.

TRYING THE HORSE

Owning a horse is a pleasure, not a necessity, and the buyer who has personal preferences should, therefore, indulge them. 'If you like him, buy him' is, within reason, a good maxim.

Age
It is important to determine the age of the horse, and the prospective buyer's estimate can be confirmed by the vet during his examination. The main advantages of buying a younger horse are: he is less likely to have been spoiled or frightened; his potential has not been fully realized, and he can be trained in the buyer's own way. A young horse's training, however, must be taken carefully, to avoid straining his immature limbs, although the pony, being smaller and tougher, can be brought on at a younger age than the horse. As he will have to be taught everything, he needs a patient, able rider. For the buyer who wants quick results, or who is not very capable, an older animal is advisable. This is especially the case with ponies. Wily horse-dealers break in ponies at two or three years, giving them

WHERE TO BUY

Horse-dealers
Buying a horse from a dealer has certain advantages. He probably has a large stock of horses, giving the customer a wider selection. If none is liked, he usually has enough contacts in the horse-bartering world to know where a suitable animal may be found. Furthermore, he may be willing to take back a horse that proves unsuitable and find another.

The dealer, however, does not sell bargains. He has his own profit to make, and the price of the horse will reflect this. Some dealers, too, become over-anxious to make a sale and are possibly not above deceiving or at least over-persuading the naive customer. Finally, the dealer is a master of the art of making a horse look good, jump well, etc, so try to look beyond the surface appearance.

Private sales
As private sellers are rarely professionals, they tend to be more straightforward and less adept at covering up faults. To discover where a horse is being offered for sale privately, study newspapers and equestrian journals, which carry 'Horses for Sale' columns. For inexpensive horses, local papers are a good source. For competition horses, the specialist equestrian magazines should be scrutinized. Word-of-mouth and notices at tack shops and riding schools are other fertile sources of information.

little feed and much work. Prospective buyers are easily hoodwinked into believing the pony is older and has a good temperament. All too often, when the pony is taken to a new home and given more food and less work, his lack of training and youthful exuberance shine through, revealing him as a most unsuitable mount for a child.

Value

The price of a horse, unlike that of a car, is not necessarily an indication of quality; and certainly not of the horse's suitability for the rider. It is reasonable to ask: 'What is this horse worth to me?' It should be borne in mind, too, that upkeep is expensive. It is better for a buyer to pay a little more, if necessary, to acquire the horse he really wants; the costs of maintenance will then seem less of a burden.

Trying the horse

Start by inspecting the conformation of the animal, looking at him in and out of the stable and making note of his good points and weaknesses. Then feel for weaknesses by running the hands up the tendon, the cannon bone and over the joints, looking for splints (usually only on forelegs), heat, puffiness. Lift up the feet, to ensure they are healthy and that the frog can touch the ground. Follow this close examination by asking to see the horse led away at the walk and then trotted back. Look out for weaknesses (particularly if the animal moves straight) and consider if the movement is suitable for the purpose intended.

Finally ask for the animal to be tacked up and watch the horse's reactions (fear, anger, etc), as this gives an insight into his character and past handling. Ask the owner or groom to ride the horse and show him on the flat and over fences. (If he is too young to be ridden, ask to see him lunged, or running loose.

If you are still interested, ask for a ride. It is a good idea to take the animal to a different place — such as an open field (to ensure that he is controllable), past the stables (to ensure he is not nappy, and unwilling to obey) and, if appropriate, into traffic. Taking into account his age and training, ask him to do as much as possible before making any decisions.

If the animal is to be a hunter, then most sellers will allow prospective purchasers to try him for a few hours with the local pack. This is an opportunity that will expose most major weaknesses.

The purchase

If the horse is suitable, then call in the vet to make his professional examination. He can advise whether in his opinion the animal is sound, and also whether the conformation is apt for his proposed use.

Some sellers will issue a warranty (a guarantee that they will take back the horse within a certain period if the animal fails to meet any of the specifications of the warranty, such as soundness, safeness in traffic, good manners out hunting, etc). If the buyer can obtain one of these it is to his advantage.

The other arrangement of benefit to purchasers is a trial. The horse is allowed to go to the prospective owner's home for a specified period to ensure that he is suitable. Although most sellers of ponies will allow a trial period, sellers of horses are less inclined to do so.

Agencies

These are firms of specialists who, for a percentage of the final price, will relieve would-be buyers and sellers of the problems of searching for and finding out about a horse or locating a buyer.

Prospective buyers give details of the type of horse wanted and the maximum price to be paid, and then leave the matter in the hands of the agent.

Auctions

Auctions have long been the major market for Thoroughbreds, but have been less extensively used for the purchase and sale of other types of horse. With the growing interest in riding, however, many more horses for private use are changing hands by means of auction sales than in the past.

At an auction sale there is usually a good number of horses to consider. The auctioneer carries out much of the routine work, which is convenient, and the price paid is the market value. The horse cannot be given more than an on-the-spot examination, however, which makes it difficult to form a fair picture of ability and temperament. As the buyer's inspection is so limited, weaknesses are more easily disguised and auctions have often been used as places to 'unload' bad horses. Also, bidding in itself needs experience. It is easy to be carried away by the atmosphere of the sale and to bid too highly and enthusiastically for the animal on offer in the ring.

When buying at an auction it is important to read the conditions of sale in the catalogue, particularly those covering the auctioneer's definition of a particular warranty, details of use of veterinary certificates and circumstances in which a horse is returnable. It is advisable to acquire the sale catalogue before the auction takes place so that it can be scrutinized in detail. It may be possible to inspect potential purchases at the sellers' homes.

On the day of the auction, carry out as extensive an examination as possible in the stable, have the horse led up and ask questions about it of all possible sources. If a horse is sold with a warranty, check *within the duration of the warranty* that the claims are true. If they are not, inform the auctioneers and arrange for the return of the horse. If a horse is bought with the right of re-examination by a vet, arrange such examination at an early date. Remember that a veterinary certificate is only an expression of the opinion of a qualified practitioner; it is not a warranty.

A countryside auction held in a field. The horse for sale is ridden round the ring under the eye of the auctioneer while prospective buyers look on. The local paper is the best source of information on forthcoming sales.

THE GAITS OF THE HORSE

The walk
A four beat gait.
The horse moves one leg after another so that four hoof beats can be heard.

Sequence
1. Left foreleg.
2. Right hind leg.
3. Right foreleg.
4. Left hind leg.

Two or three legs are always on the ground, so there is no moment of suspension. This makes it a comfortable pace for the rider.

Faults
1. Hoof beats not rhythmical.
2. The four hoof beats not distinct: two-time walk is possible and is a bad fault which needs correcting.
3. Hooves (usually the hinds) dragged.
4. Horse does not 'track up'; ie, hind legs do not overlap the fores. In a good walk, the hind should be placed further forward than the lateral foreleg just raised.

The trot
A two-beat gait known as the jog by Western-style riders.
The horse moves the diagonal hind and forelegs together.

Sequence
1. Left foreleg and right hind leg leave ground.
2. Right foreleg and left hind leg leave ground *before* left fore and right hind touch the ground; therefore, there is a brief moment of suspension.

At the moment when all four legs are suspended in the air, the rider finds it difficult to sit in the saddle. This has led to the development of posting (rising trot), in which the rider puts weight in the stirrups and rises out of the saddle, to sit again when the horse's legs are on the ground.

Faults
1. If trot becomes hurried and forelegs reach the ground before the hinds, four instead of two hoof-beats are heard.
2. Hind legs may be dragged so they reach the ground before forelegs. (Again, this means a four-time pace).
3. One hind leg moves further under the body than another.

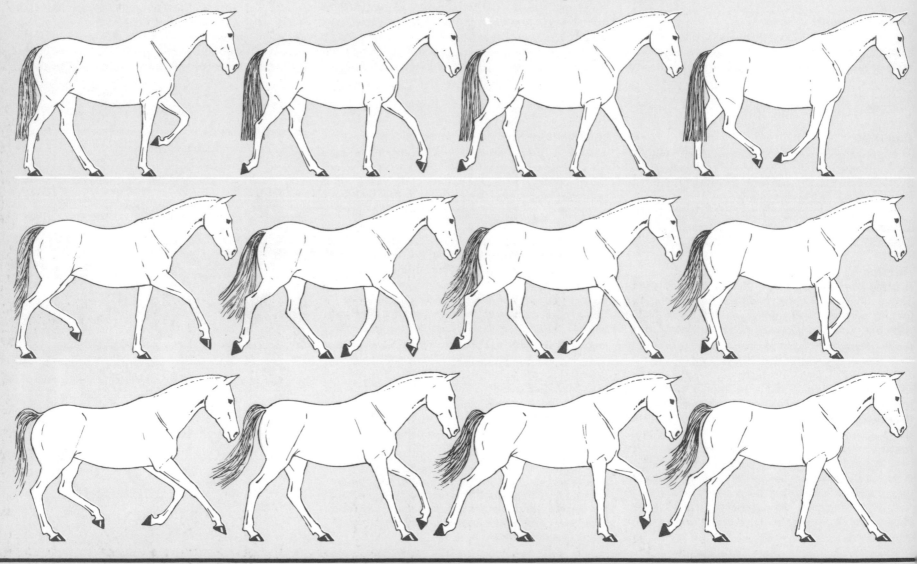

The canter

A three-beat gait known as the lope by Western-style riders.

The horse moves in bounds with either the right foreleg or the left foreleg leading.

Sequence of canter to the right

1. Left hind leg on the ground.
2. Right hind leg and left foreleg placed on ground at the same time.
3. Right foreleg placed on ground after left hind leg has risen.
4. All four legs in the air.

Faults

1. Four hoof beats are heard. This occurs when hind leg is put to the ground before corresponding foreleg (2. above), it usually happens when the horse loses impulsion (forward-driving force).
2. A disunited canter. Left leg leads in front, right leg behind, or vice versa.

The gallop

A four-beat gait.
The gallop is an unrestrained canter. The strides are longer and the moment of suspension (stage 4 in sequence) is much longer.

The pace

A two-beat gait.

Sequence

1. Left hind and left foreleg strike ground together.
2. Right hind leg and right foreleg strike the ground. This is not a comfortable pace for the rider. In America, where the saddle-horse uses five gaits, adaptations of the pace are taught.

N.B. Although these additional gaits come naturally to this breed of horse, training is needed to produce them correctly.

The stepping pace or slow gait

A four-beat gait sequence as for the pace, except that the left foreleg strikes the ground just before the left hind; similarly, right fore before right hind.

The rack

A four-beat gait.
Sequence the same as for the stepping pace but there is a longer interval between the foreleg striking the ground and the hind leg on the same side striking the ground.

The walk, *a four-beat gait*

The trot, *a two-beat diagonal gait*

The canter, *a three-beat gait. The gallop is when the canter speeds up to become a four-beat gait, and the off foreleg and near hind leg of the illustration no longer move as a pair.*

Right: **The rein-back,** *in which a foreleg and hind leg move in diagonal pairs. Sometimes they do not move quite simultaneously and it is not a fault to hear four hoof-beats.*

An event horse. *He has good depth implying he has stamina. The bone is sufficient to carry his body. His limbs are strong, and his feet good, which make it more likely for him to stand up to the rigours of eventing. He has plenty of 'class' about him (not too coarse or common) which should give him the ability to gallop.*

A child's pony. *This is a pure bred Welsh—a breed which has enormous ability but sometimes their characters are a little wilful to be ideal for children. The conformation of this one is good—stocky, compact and with a strong front. The outlook too looks genuine and kind which is the most vital factor in a child's pony.*

A western horse. *Although not very big he appears tough and stocky enabling him to turn quickly, accelerate and carry a heavy weight. He is similar to the polo pony but stockier in order to be able to carry his riders for long hours on the ranch. The pinto marking was thought good for camouflage in times of fighting, and is today rather fashionable.*

A hunter. *He has good bone enabling him to carry a good deal of weight for the long hours of hunting. He has an intelligent, bold outlook implying he will take care of his rider across country. He has strong hindquarters to give him the power to jump and a good sloping shoulder to help him in his galloping.*

A dressage horse. *Like the show jumper powerful hindquarters are needed, but not necessarily to the extent of a 'jumping bump'. These well-rounded quarters are good enough and the front is very high class—a good sloping shoulder and a long well crested neck. With such a shoulder the movement is likely to be good. The outlook certainly is, for the eye is generous and the ears broad which implies that the horse has that asset important in dressage—a good temperament.*

A driving horse. *This horse is out of an Irish Draught mare. There is plenty of bone, and good feet to stand the hammering on the roads. The shoulder is much straighter than that of the dressage horse which restricts the movement but gives more pulling power. The height of about 15.1hh is good as this gives enough strength yet more manoeuvrability than with a bigger horse.*

A showjumper. *The most important part is the hindquarters as these generate the power to spring. This horse has a distinct 'jumping bump' that is, the croup is well pointed. He has also a good hind leg and in particular a well developed second thigh. Although the forehand is not so important this horse's strong deep sloping shoulder will help in the thrust off the ground.*

A polo pony. *Although only 15hh he is wiry and tough enough to carry a big man at a gallop. He gives the appearance of being very athletic, able to turn quickly, accelerate rapidly into a gallop and stop within a few strides. He also has to be brave enough to allow his rider to 'ride off' push opponents' ponies out of the way at a gallop.*

AGEING

Nature has provided the horse with a tangible calendar—its teeth. Up to the age of eight, the teeth undergo recognizable changes each year, and it is perfectly possible, if you know the signs, to make an accurate assessment of the animal's age. From nine to 18 or so, age is less easy to pinpoint but, allowing for approximately one year's error on either side, it can still be done. Over 20, other indications of age must be sought; and the margin of error is considerable. Because of the difficulty in making a really accurate judgment, horses over the age of eight are often described as 'aged'.

Methods of ageing
The guidelines to age are the six incisors—the tearing teeth—in each jaw at the front of the mouth. In both the lower and the upper jaw they are divided into two centrals, two laterals on either side of the centrals, and two corners on either side of these. The molars—the grinding teeth—at the back may be ignored.

The sets of teeth
The horse has two sets of teeth, deciduous (milk) and permanent. By examining the types of teeth in the mouth, the age of horses up to four and a half years (the age at which the last permanent teeth erupt) can be ascertained. The teeth erupt in order; first the centrals, then the laterals, and finally the corners.

Wear of teeth
The other aid to ageing is the wear of the teeth. Horses' teeth are not enclosed in enamel, and therefore wear down. By examining the wearing surface, known as the table, age can be judged.

The table changes in shape as the tooth—which tapers toward its roots—is worn down. On a new tooth the shape of the table is oval, but with wear it becomes circular and eventually triangular.

The nature of the surface of the table changes too, as continuing wear exposes parts of the tooth closer and closer to its roots. The new tooth has a cavity in its centre called the infundibulum. As the tooth wears, this cavity is flattened and becomes dark as it is filled up with food. A tooth that has a flat table and a dark ring in the centre is said to be 'in wear'. Eventually the tooth is worn down so much that the infundibulum disappears altogether and its dark ring can no longer be seen on the table. Before this occurs, a brown line in front of the infundibulum appears, on the table of the central incisors at first, then on the table of the laterals and corners. It is called the dental star and is part of the substance of the tooth (dentine) that comes to the surface as the tooth wears down.

The profile
When the set of teeth is viewed from the side, in the case of a young horse, the profile is vertical, but as the teeth wear more behind than in front, their profile becomes increasingly horizontal with age.

Stages in the ageing process
At birth, a foal may already possess the two central incisors at top and bottom, or they may appear at any time within the first four weeks. The teeth on either side of the central incisors (the laterals) erupt within two months, and are followed during the next six months by the outside (corner) incisors. Milk teeth are white, fairly small and shell-shaped—that is, they narrow toward the base. Wear is quite noticeable on these teeth by the time the horse is two years old.

Two and a half to six years
At the age of two and a half years, the central incisors drop out and the first permanent teeth appear. These are larger than the milk teeth, have straighter sides and are brownish-yellow in colour. At three and a half to four years the teeth on either side of the central incisors (the laterals) are replaced by second teeth. At about the same time tushes, or canine teeth, will appear in stallions and geldings, although they are usually absent in mares. Between four and a half and five years the last of the milk teeth are lost and new corner incisors grow.

At first the permanent teeth are quite small, with cavities, but they gradually come into wear, and about 18 months after eruption the tables become flattened so that the dark ring of the infundibulum becomes obvious. By the time the horse is six years old, the tables of all the incisors will meet evenly, and show signs of wear. At this stage a horse is said to have a full mouth.

Seven to 15 years
At seven years old, the upper corner incisors sometimes develop a hook, called the 'seven year hook'. It disappears by the time the horse is eight years old. At seven years the dental star, a brownish line, appears on the tables of the teeth, between the infundibulum and the outer edge. It will first be seen on the central incisors, and by the time the horse is nine will be present on the corners.

The next noticeable change in the teeth occurs at about ten years. A slight depression will become apparent near the gum on the outer surface of the upper corner incisors. This feature is known as Galvayne's groove. Over the next few years, it will gradually extend down the tooth, reaching a third of the way down when the horse is 13.

During these years the blackish mark, or infundibulum, becomes lighter. It disappears from the

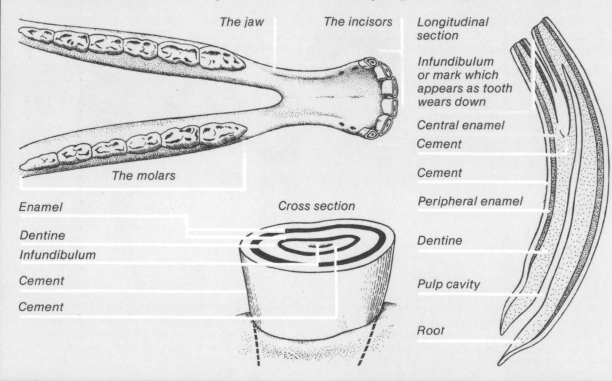

The jaw

The molars

Enamel
Dentine
Infundibulum
Cement
Cement

Cross section

The incisors

Longitudinal section

Infundibulum or mark which appears as tooth wears down

Central enamel

Cement

Cement

Peripheral enamel

Dentine

Pulp cavity

Root

central incisors at 12 and from all teeth by 15; the dental star will now be in the centre of each tooth. At the same time the wearing away of the teeth gives them a more triangular shape.

Fifteen to 30 years
From 15 onwards, age assessment is very uncertain. It is based mainly on the length of Galvayne's groove, which should be halfway down the tooth by the time the horse is 15. As Galvayne's groove lengthens, so, too, do the teeth. A 20-year-old horse will have rather long, sloping teeth and quite a pronounced Galvayne's groove. From 25 onwards Galvayne's groove starts to disappear, and by 30 it has gone completely.

A horse's life span can be anything from 20 to 40 years, and an aged appearance is not necessarily an indication of the animal's real age. In fact, as with humans, a full and interesting life may well delay the onset of old age. Provided he receives proper care, a horse can continue to lead a useful working existence well into the late 20s or 30s.

Care of teeth
Proper care includes regular attention to the teeth. Filing will be necessary from time to time, especially as the horse grows older. An old horse with overlong teeth will have difficulty in eating, and so will be unable to take in sufficient food to cope with the work he has to do. Sharp edges on the teeth can make it painful for a horse to accept the bit when ridden, so check the teeth if any mouthing problems arise.

Signs of old age
An extremely old horse will suffer from a general slowing down of his metabolism. Hollows appear above the eyes, joints may become swollen and rheumatic, and the coat will lose the shine of youth. Dark-coloured horses will show an ever-increasing number of white hairs, particularly in the winter coat and on the face and head.

It is tempting to keep an old favourite until he dies from natural causes, and modern veterinary treatment is so efficient that many an old horse can survive conditions that would have killed him in the past. But, though a long and peaceful retirement may seem a fair reward for years of loyal service, old horses may suffer acutely from boredom and loneliness even if they are not in pain. Generally speaking, it is better to have a horse humanely put down rather than allow him to pine away through lack of work and attention and a feeling of uselessness.

AGEING

Age	Teeth	Table		Profile	Diagram	
Birth—2 years 1-4 weeks 4-8 weeks 6-9 months 2 years	central incisors erupt lateral incisors erupt corner incisors erupt full mouth of deciduous teeth of uniform size	gradually teeth lose cavity and come into wear, assuming uniform size and appearance		vertical profile	At 2 years teeth uniform and almost all in wear	
2-6 years 2½ years 3½ years 4 years 4½ years 5 years 6 years	central incisors erupt lateral incisors erupt corner incisors erupt	central incisors in wear lateral incisors in wear corner incisors in wear	oval	vertical profile	At 4 years temporary teeth lost cavity-in wear permanents (still have cavity) not in wear permanents-in wear	
7-15 years 7 years 8 years 9 years 10 years 12 years 13 years 14 years 15 years	7-year hook in upper corner incisor Galvayne's groove appears Galvayne's groove half way down	dental star in centrals dental star in laterals dental star in corners infundibulum goes from centrals infundibulum goes from laterals infundibulum goes from corners infundibulum all gone	becoming more circular becoming more triangular	profile starts to change from vertical to horizontal Galvayne's groove half way down	At 10 years infundibulum present in all teeth corners still oval dental stars in all teeth centrals becoming more triangular	
15-30 years 20 years 25 years 30 years	Galvayne's groove complete Galvayne's groove half way out Galvayne's groove gone completely	infundibulum all gone and only dental stars (brown line) visible	completely triangular	increasingly horizontal	At 15 years all infundibulum gone dental stars visible	

CHOOSING A STUD

Horse-breeding is one of the most rewarding occupations in the equestrian world. It provides the challenge of gathering information about prospective parents' pedigrees, performance, records and conformation and using it to try to achieve the most complementary matings. Also it gives the great pleasure of seeing foals play, grow up and, with luck, do well in the activity for which they were bred.

Responsibilities of the breeder

Though common sense is the quality most essential to the aspiring horse-breeder, a responsible approach is also important. Mares and foals need attention; only horses used to the wild can be left to fend for themselves. Breeding is, moreover, a costly business; adequate shelter and food must be provided and veterinary assistance may sometimes be required.

Principles of selection

In view of the financial investment and the long period before results are achieved, considerable time and thought should be spent in preparation, particularly the careful selection of parents. Selection is one of the most intriguing aspects of breeding; in racing, where it reaches its most developed state, the question of basis of selection has attracted some of the best brains in the equestrian world.

Establishment of clear aims is the first stage. Two of the most important aims are to breed a sound animal and to establish the type of horse required.

To increase the chances of breeding a sound animal, parents with hereditary defects must be avoided. Defects include sickle and cow hocks, feet that turn in or out too much, very upright or sloping pasterns, a ewe neck, sway-back, parrot mouth, wind that is not clear (roarers or whistlers), eyes showing cataracts, legs with sidebones or spavins. The aim should be to use parents with good conformation, as a well-proportioned horse is not only more pleasant to look at, but also more likely to stay sound. Horses that show weaknesses in conformation, however, need not be disregarded (as must those with hereditary defects) for breeding purposes; they can simply be mated with one whose shape offsets the problem. A mare with a short neck, for instance, can be put to a stallion with a long neck.

It is advisable to decide what work the offspring will be required to carry out (showing, jumping, farming, gymkhanas, etc), so that the breeder can build up a clear picture of the assets needed (ie, size, shape, temperament, specific ability).

After the objectives have been decided, selection can begin, and this is based on four sources of information which are carefully studied.

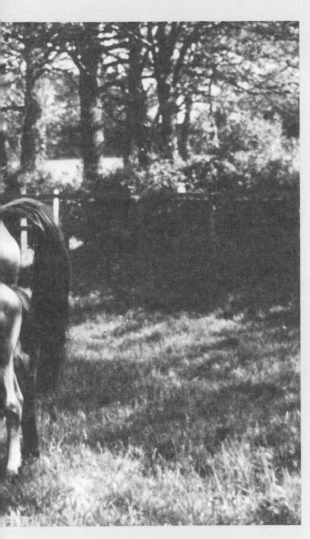

Appearance

Breeders can examine the appearance, movement and behaviour of prospective parents knowing that many of their features are likely to be passed on to their progeny. The mare, in addition, should have deep and broad hindquarters with wide hips, so that there is room for the foal to grow and be born; her genital organs and mammary glands should also be examined to make sure that they are normal.

Performance records

The performance records of mares and stallions in the show-ring, on the racecourse and across country can be studied, as the progeny of successful parents is more likely to have ability than one from unsuccessful parents.

Pedigree

Appearance and performance records, though valuable, give an inadequate picture of genetic make-up; for instance, small mares can produce large stock. Examination of the conformation and performance of the grandparents and great-grandparents, for example, helps to provide a more reliable basis of selection.

Produce

Studying the existing progeny of both mare and stallion is another valuable source of information on which to base selection. A stallion who 'stamps his stock' by transmitting definite characteristics is known as prepotent. Unfortunately, it takes time to prove a stallion's prepotency and the procedure for a mare is even slower. Most breeders have to rely on the previous three sources of information for their selection.

Choosing a stud

The other major consideration is to ensure that the mare will be well cared for if she is to be sent to a stud. Management of some studs is based on economy; feeding may be poor and mares with foals, in particular, suffer from such treatment. Also, poor facilities are usually associated with low fertility in stallions. It is wise, therefore, to make a personal visit to the proposed stud, to find out as much as possible about it from other sources and, if the mare goes there, to make regular checks on her condition.

Above: Mares and foals on a stud farm.

Far left: The long-backed stallion would be a bad partner for the mare on the right, but suitable for the shorter mare in the centre.

The stallion

Stallions (also known as studs or entires) vary in value from hundreds to millions of pounds or dollars, and the stud farms at which they stand range from ramshackle farm buildings to those where every possible equine luxury is provided.

A license

In most countries, a license must be obtained before a registered stallion can serve mares. The license is issued after a veterinary examination has confirmed that the stallion will not pass on any hereditary disease, physical abnormality or infection.

Service fees

Fees are charged for mares visiting a stallion, and there are a number of ways this can be paid. For the services of the most valuable Thoroughbred stallions it is normal either to buy a share in the stallion (up to 40 may be issued), or to buy a nomination that entitles the purchaser to send his mare for a service in that year. Nominations are usually bought at special auctions.

In general, however, a specified charge is made, either a straight fee demanded upon service or a fee payable only if a foal is born or the mare is certified in foal in the autumn. In the first case, the terms usually allow for a free return if the mare proves to be barren or the foal is born dead.

The stallions in the UK and USA are mainly privately owned, although some of those in England receive government subsidies. The UK scheme is operated through the Hunter Improvement Society, which receives a grant from the government to give selected stallions a premium. Consequently stallion owners can charge lower fees, and the services of the better horses are brought within the reach of most owners of mares.

The major contribution by governments toward breeding, however, is through their national studs. In the UK this is confined to Thoroughbred horses, but over most of Europe the national studs house stallions ranging from ponies to riding horses to work horses.

The success of a stallion

This is measured by both his ability to breed good progeny and his fertility rate.

His chances of breeding good produce are increased if good mares are sent to him. In the early years when he is unproven these are best attracted by having good stud facilities where owners of mares know their property will be well treated, by advertising, and by the stallion possessing assets required in progeny (conformation, temperament, performance record, good pedigree).

Although a high fertility rate is inherent it can be improved by ensuring that the stallion is kept fit and contented.

Care of the stallion
In the past, stallions have often been treated as dangerous animals; it is now established, however, that the more normal their handling, the more reasonably they behave.

Stabling
The stallion can be stabled near other horses, because he enjoys their company, but it is inadvisable to have mares in season too close.

Handling
This requires a combination of firmness and sympathy. The stallion must grow to trust and respect his handler, who should never show fear. In the case of ponies, Arabs and similar types, confident handling is not too difficult; but with larger and more excitable entires (eg Thoroughbreds), skill, courage and great understanding are required.

Fitness
Some stallions serve more than 100 mares in a season, which is very strenuous work, so fitness is essential if high fertility is to be maintained.

The many tougher, less valuable stallions that live out and run with the mares require no special work to get fit. Most valuable stallions, however, are kept in. Some do have a small paddock or sand pit, with high, tough fencing, in which to run free; but they still need more work.

In the past, stallions were led out on regular walks lasting an hour or 90 minutes. This method of exercising is expensive and time-consuming, however, so lungeing or riding is more often used today. Both need skilful assistants; riding, in particular, calls for high-class horsemanship to ensure that these eruptive creatures remain under control.

In winter, when the stallion's work is over, he can have a quiet period before being gradually built up to peak fitness, which must be attained by Thoroughbreds in February, and by other stallions in March or early April. It is, of course, inadvisable to allow a stallion to become completely unfit.

Feeding
During the stallion's rest time energy foods must be reduced, but as the working period approaches again they should be increased, together with

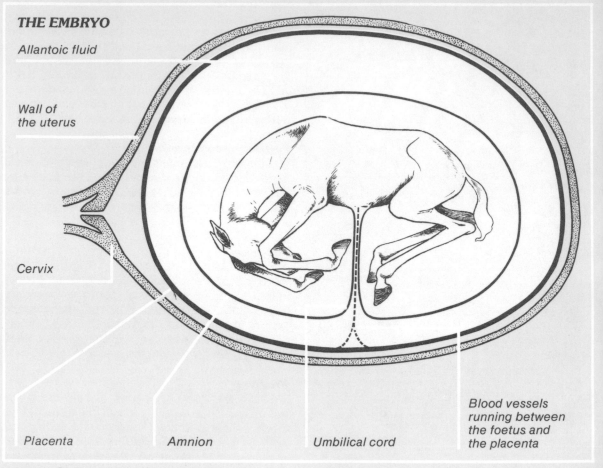

THE EMBRYO

Allantoic fluid

Wall of the uterus

Cervix

Placenta

Amnion

Umbilical cord

Blood vessels running between the foetus and the placenta

proteins. Care must be taken not to give so much energy-producing food that the result is an unmanageable stallion. Skilful feeding is vital to health, well-being and fertility.

Worming, tooth filing and foot trimming
All these should be carried out at regular intervals. Any pain or indigestion will make a stallion reluctant to serve mares.

The Mare
The heat, also called oestrum or season, lasts between five and seven days and normally occurs every three weeks, from spring to early autumn. Mares with foals come into season for two to four days beginning seven to ten days after foaling. It is only when the mare is in season that insemination can take place.

Puberty
This usually occurs at 15-24 months, though it sometimes does not take place until four years of age. It is thought inadvisable to serve mares before three years (except for well-grown two-year-olds).

Covering
In most cases mares are covered in April and May, so that the foal can benefit from the spring grass a year later. The fourth time a mare comes into season is more likely to produce successful results. Thoroughbreds intended for racing need to be covered earlier, however, so that their progeny is as mature as possible for the two- and three-year-old races. In the UK, February 15th is the official start of the Thoroughbred stud season.

A mare to be covered should be neither too fat nor too fit, but she will accept the stallion only when she is in season. She indicates that she is in season by seeking the company of other mares, raising her tail, passing urine frequently, with 'vulval winking' and protruding clitoris (a rod-like organ at the lip of the vulva), discharging mucus, and showing willingness to accept the stallion in the process known as 'teasing' or 'trying'.

Aids to getting a mare in season

The presence of a stallion, frequent teasing, the presence of other mares in season, and veterinary assistance such as hormone injection will all help get a mare in season.

Teasing or trying means taking the mare to the stallion and observing her reactions. If she is not in season, she may attack the stallion with teeth and hooves, so precautions are necessary. Such precautions include having a padded partition between the two horses, using a less valuable stallion called a teaser (if ready to be covered, the mare adopts a mating position, holding her tail to one side) and putting the mare in service hobbles and/or boots.

The service

This is usually carried out twice during the period a mare is in season. The fourth day is generally considered the best. It is advisable to have the mare swabbed before the service, which can be done only when she is in season, to ensure that she is clean.

A mare that has 'held' (is in foal) will refuse to accept a stallion when tried at her next scheduled heat periods (three weeks and six weeks). The cycle of sexual potency in a horse is, however, very irregular; up to eight weeks may pass between heats. Another danger is that pregnant mares can have 'false heats'; if served during these, they may 'slip' (give premature birth to) their foals. Consequently, the mare must be examined regularly to ensure that she does not come back into season.

Pregnancy

The mare's failure to come back into season and rejecting the stallion is a sign of pregnancy; an experienced vet can examine the rectum. To confirm, use a blood test 50 days after mating and/or a urine test after 110 days.

Duration of pregnancy

Average duration is 11 months (336 days). A variation of ten days either way is normal, however; and with maiden mares the variation might be as much as two weeks.

A stallion being led by the stud groom to his mare. He is on a long lead line for the service. The stick is carried as stallions tend to bite, and is used to give him something to nibble and to stop him biting his handler. The halter (head-collar) is left on in case the bridle should break, and secondly because it is easier when the stallion is excited to put the bridle over it. He has no shoes behind to reduce risk of damage.

The foetus

This develops within an outer membrane (bag of waters, or allantois) and an inner envelope (foal kell, or amnion), both of which contain fluid that insulates the foetus against blows or shocks. Nourishment of the foetus is achieved by a flow of blood between mare and foetus. The umbilical (navel) vein, enclosed in the navel cord, is the other connection between dam and foetus.

Abortion (slipping the foal)

Kicks, blows, colic, chills, dusty poor food, over-exertion or infection can all cause abortion, and every precaution must be taken to prevent the mare from being subjected to these risks.

Work during pregnancy

The mare needs exercise right up to the time of foaling, but work should be graded; for the first five months, anything but exceptionally strenuous work is permissible. After this, the work should be gradually reduced; the mare should not be taken across rough terrain or over-exerted. During the last three and a half months, except for the very tough breeds, running free is the only advisable exercise.

Feeding

This will depend on the breed or type of mare. Ponies need only a few oats to supplement the grass in the winter time; Thoroughbreds will need much more supplementary food.

Points to remember

The foetus grows fastest in the second half of pregnancy, so the mare will need more food then. Too rich or dusty food can be harmful. Too little food will result in the mare's drawing on her own reserves, but too much bulk food will put pressure on the stomach.

During the last three weeks of pregnancy, reduce bulk food by half because there is less room in the mare's stomach.

Give her plenty of grass, and a bran mash once or twice a week, as there is a tendency for her to become constipated. Give supplements, available from most food manufacturers, and boiled linseed.

This foal was born a few hours before in the field without assistance.

The foaling stall or box
This is needed for all but the tough breeds that foal outside, and should be at least 3.65m (12ft) square. It should be cleaned, disinfected and bedded down deeply; straw must be banked up the sides of the walls and door to help prevent draughts. The temperature should be kept at about 15°C (59°F). If possible, there should be a means of observing the mare without disturbing her.

The vet
Especially in the case of Thoroughbred mares and/or if there are only inexperienced attendants available, a vet may well be needed during the foaling. Consequently a vet should be found who has stated willingness to attend and the telephone number must be placed in a prominent place.

Equipment
It is important that this should be readily available. Equipment includes two buckets that can be filled with warm water at the onset of labour; an old bucket for the afterbirth; cotton wool or gauze (gamgee); antiseptic powder or lotion for foal's navel stump; liquid paraffin, towels and soap.

Care of mare before foaling
Cut down the amount of hay, and correct, with a bran mash, any tendency for the droppings to harden. Gently handle the udder (mammary glands) to familiarize the mare (especially a maiden mare) with the sensation.

Indication of foaling
The udder starts to enlarge and is seen to be square when viewed from behind; this is known as 'bagging up' and can occur up to two weeks before foaling.

'Waxing up' takes place (drops of honey-like secretion form at the end of the teats), and although this usually happens in the last 24 hours before foaling it has been known to occur weeks before. 'Softening of the bones' occurs two weeks to a few hours before foaling, causing grooves to appear on either side of the root of the tail. The grooves are caused by the relaxation of muscles attached to the pelvis, to ease the passage for the foal. But it is possible for the mare to show none of these signs before foaling.

Signs of imminent foaling
The mare becomes restless, swishes her tail and starts to sweat as the time for foaling approaches. She may stale (pass urine) and get down and up again. The normal time for foaling to start is in the early hours of the morning.

Foaling down
The more natural the conditions and the less fussing done, the happier the mare will be, so stay out of the box as much as possible. Although most foalings are uneventful, it is advisable to have an experienced assistant available.

The early contractions may not be seen. They start by being feeble and infrequent (one every five or ten minutes); but they should gradually become stronger and more frequent (one every half minute). Normally, within an hour from the start of contractions, the greyish water bag (the outer membrane of the foetus) appears between the lips of the vulva, then breaks to reveal the foal's forelegs wrapped in the yellowish membrane of the amnion.

When to seek veterinary advice
As long as the mare appears to be making reasonable progress, she is best left alone. However, if she is continually lying down and rising again without progress being made, and if the contractions become less frequent and/or more than an hour has passed since they started, then veterinary assistance should be sought.

Checking position of foal
When the foal appears under the tail, the position should be checked; the legs should be examined to see that knees, not hocks, are presenting. If the hocks are visible, then it is a breech presentation and a vet or experienced helper is needed.

An experienced assistant can examine the mare to feel if the foal is in the correct 'diving' position (ie, both forefeet first and head straight and slightly behind). Before checking the position, the assistant should clean his hands and wrists with disinfectant and lubricate them with liquid paraffin. After this a skilled person can slide a hand into the birth passage and, if any problems are felt, make gentle manipulative adjustment. In the case of the slightest doubt, the vet should be called.

A breech presentation is when the hind legs appear first. As the pelvis of the foal is broader than the skull, this angle of presentation makes foaling more difficult. The danger is that the umbilical cord is easily broken; if broken too soon, it can suffocate the foal. An experienced assistant may be able to pull the foal gently downward and out (*never* straight) from the mare; but professional help is normally advisable.

Appearance of the foal
In a normal foaling, the chest and shoulders will follow after the forelegs appear, and the foal will then slide out, leaving only the last part of the hindquarters in the mare.

If the amnion does not burst after this process, the foal will suffocate; if necessary, the amnion should be broken by applying pressure between the foal's feet, while protecting its eyes from the straw.

At all times, care must be taken to disturb the mare as little as possible and not to try to hurry the process.

The umbilical cord should remain intact, because it supplies the foal with blood. Only when the foal starts to kick, freeing the hind legs, should the cord break. If this does not happen within a few minutes, the cord can be cut through with sterilized scissors at least four inches from the foal's belly. The stump should then be dressed with antiseptic powder or lotion. The cord should *not* be tied.

The amnion can be stripped from the foal and the mare encouraged to lick her offspring. This is the best means of stimulating the circulation and getting the foal dry. If the mare will not do it, the foal should be rubbed with a towel for about a quarter of an hour.

The afterbirth can then be tied up with twine so that it hangs at about the level of the hocks.

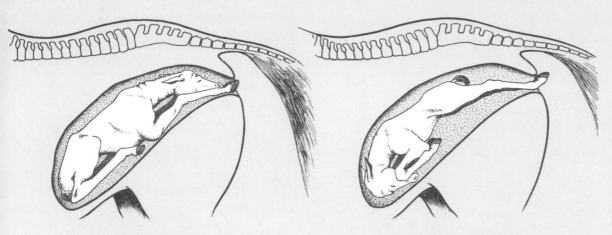

A normal presentation

A breech presentation

Care of the mare and foal

Healthy foals rise to their feet from 15 to 90 minutes after birth and start suckling milk. If the foal is weak, he may need assistance in standing up and finding his mother's udder. If the mare is a maiden or ticklish she may need to be held while the foal learns to suck. It is best to leave the mare alone until she has licked the foal; then she can be given a bran mash mixed with some linseed.

A stoppage (no bowel movement)

This in the foal can be dangerous. Normally the foal should pass a small, hard piece of wax to free the anus within four to five hours of birth. If he does not and is standing with his tail up, then a mild enema, 1-2l (1¾-3½ pt) of lukewarm soapy water, should be given. If there is no success after 18 hours, a vet should be called.

If the mare does not cleanse (expel the afterbirth)

If this has not occurred four hours after foaling, a vet should be called.

Aftercare of mare and foal

For the first few days, the mare and foal (except for hardy breeds) are best kept indoors. Then they can be let out to graze, and, depending on the weather and the type of horse, can soon be left out all the time or brought in only at night.

Feeding

In the first few days after foaling the food is intended to have a laxative effect. Bran mashes are best. Supplementary food is needed throughout the summer, according to the type of mare and the degree of nourishment to be gained from grass. Thoroughbreds need 5-7kg (12-15lb) oats, boiled linseed and 7-9kg (15-20lb) hay. Most ponies need about 450g (1lb) oats and no hay as long as the grass is good. The important point, however, is to use common sense and if the mare and/or foal start going back, to give them more hard and bulk feed. Foals will soon to eat oats and Thoroughbreds can be given up to 450g (1lb) for each month of their life.

Inadequate milk production

This may occasionally be a problem. If the mare is not producing enough milk the foal will be seen repeatedly trying to suck. In this case the mare should be given more protein (clover, lucerne, bran and linseed) and if this does not improve the milk supply, the vet must be consulted.

Worming

This is extremely important; the mare should be wormed three weeks to a month before foaling, and then not again until after she has been covered. The foal can be first wormed at eight weeks and then every month. The vet will prescribe a special dosage.

The feet

The foal's feet must be taken care of. They need regular trimming and picking out. If there are any deformities, corrections can often be made by the blacksmith; success is more likely when the bone is still relatively soft.

Weaning

The mare should not be separated from her progeny until the fourth month at the earliest. Thoroughbreds (except those that are weak and poorly formed) are usually weaned at five months, and other breeds at six months. If the mare is not in foal, weaning can be left until about eight months, as long as the mare is keeping in good condition.

Preparation for weaning

The mare's concentrates should be cut down in order to reduce her milk production. Mares out at grass are brought in seven to ten days before weaning, and the foals encouraged to learn to eat grain and hay. These should be given to them in containers separate from the mother's.

A stable or stall should be thickly bedded and any projections likely to injure the foal removed. For the last few days, the stable need not be mucked out; the mare's smell will remain in the box. The mare is led out quickly and taken far enough away to ensure that neither mare nor foal will hear the other's whinnies.

The foal is happier if left with other youngsters and he can be turned out to grass with them after two or three days. The mare's milk dries off better if the udder is left alone. Milk her only if she is very full, as milking encourages further milk production.

Care of weaners

Supplementary feeding is necessary in the autumn after weaning because the grass is not so rich. A balance must be struck between over-feeding, which causes limb troubles, and under-feeding, which restricts growth. Good hay should be basic, plus up to 2.3kg (5lb) crushed oats (depending on breed), 450g (1lb) bran, mineral supplements, and small doses of cod liver oil and linseed.

Shelter

This is necessary during the winter. If stabled at night, however, the youngsters should be allowed to run free for exercise during the day.

Worming

After weaning this is essential, preferably following a veterinary prescription.

Growth

This is at its fastest during the first year, when 80 percent of the growth in height occurs. In the second year, the bone strengthens and the body deepens. A lack of care at these stages cannot be compensated for later.

Colts and fillies

These must be separated not later than 18 months.

AT GRASS

Wild horses, roaming across acre upon acre of the grassland that is their natural home, can look after themselves. But domesticated breeds cannot, especially when they are confined to small fields. Every owner of a horse, therefore, has a responsibility to care for his animal as soon as he is turned out to grass, for statistics show that horses are even more likely to have accidents in the freedom of the field than when stabled. So looking after a horse at grass, although not as time-consuming as caring for a stabled animal, does call for a responsible, planned and thoughtful approach.

Supervision of horses at grass
Horses at grass have to be supervised. Otherwise they may damage themselves by kicking at one another or getting caught up in fences and gates. They can also very quickly lose condition through illness or bad weather. Daily checks are essential to ensure their well-being.

It is also important to handle livestock. Horses that are approached every day and patted, even when not being ridden, are unlikely to develop the infuriating habit of refusing to be caught.

The teeth of horses must be checked regularly. Rough edges on teeth make eating difficult and animals with this problem tend to lose condition. Feet, too, need constant attention. If the animal is not working, it is best to take the hind shoes off to reduce the risk of kicks damaging a field mate. Front shoes may be left on, but they must be removed regularly and hooves pared back. If the front shoes are taken off, the hooves must be trimmed at regular intervals and the feet examined for signs of cracking or crumbling. Many people recommend toe-clips as a good means of avoiding this.

The management of grassland
It is usually considered that about two to three acres per horse is sufficient. But it will only be adequate if the fields are looked after so that there is a good covering of grass. They should not be allowed to become weed-ridden, bare or poached so badly that there are potholes, ruts and mud. This means that looking after horses at grass also entails an elementary knowledge of grass management.

Horses are not good grazers. Unless it is a very large area, a field continuously grazed by them will become 'horse sick'. This means that the horses have cropped down the succulent grass and left the coarse and unpalatable remainder, so that the height of the grass is very uneven. In addition, their droppings further this unevenness by restricting growth where they fall and promoting tufts of weed around them.

Droppings are also a cause of red worm infestation of the field (see Chapter 10). It is important, therefore, to give the field a rest from horses (rotation) and to treat the grass.

Rotation
The best way of organizing rotation is to divide the land into small paddocks (if necessary, as small as half an acre) rather than have one large area. One area can then be grazed while the others are rested. A field should not be left full of horses until it is completely bare, for this makes it difficult for the grass to grow again. Ideally, when the horses are taken off they should be replaced by cattle, who are complementary grazers to them. Cattle like the long tufts, so they will level up the grass, and, as red worm do not survive when taken into their bodies, they also reduce worm infestation. If there are no cattle to graze the land, the long tufts of grass should be cut down by hand or topped with a machine.

Harrowing and rolling
The second aspect of grass management is intelligent treatment of the grass. This entails chain harrowing and, if possible, rolling. Chain harrowing both aerates the soil by pulling out moss and matted growth and scatters harmful droppings. Many new horse owners will no doubt be horrified to read of the need to harrow horse-bound fields, envisaging expensive investments in a tractor and harrow. But frequently there is a friendly farmer nearby who will help by lending his machines, or harrows can be bought cheaply secondhand, and then towed by a truck, a Land Rover, or even a small car where the land is dry. Or, as happens in an increasing number of stables, a horse can be driven as well as ridden, and harrowing provides a very practical exercise for him. Finally, if all this fails, the fork and rake can be taken out for a few hours of good healthy work. If you find the effort tiring, remember that at most major studs the droppings are collected daily by hand.

The rolling of pastures is advisable, even if it is not as essential as harrowing. The treatment compacts the soil around the roots of the herbage after they have been pulled at and loosened by grazing horses. Heavy rains and frost disturb and loosen the topsoil, and compression by rolling will aid plant growth.

Above: A good paddock with a stout post and rail fence and sensible water trough.

Left to right: A round feed tin, a haynet tied up, an enamel feed bowl, a wooden feed box and a hay rack placed high up on a wall.

Fertilizing

Rotation, harrowing and rolling prevent pastures becoming horse sick and promote a good growth of grass. Growth can also be stimulated by fertilizing and the extra cost can be set against the fact that the additional grass will provide more feed. It is advisable to get a soil analysis made by an agricultural body, who can then suggest which materials are needed to counteract deficiencies. The most common recommendations are lime, basic slag (phosphatic fertilizer), potash salts (especially for sandy soils), nitrogen and simply manure, although the last should be applied only in the autumn and on fields destined for a hay crop in the spring, not for grazing.

Drainage

The final important improvement that can be made to keep grassland in good order is drainage. This is not so necessary for sandy and chalk land, which usually drains adequately by itself, but in the case of clay it is often essential. Without drainage a clay soil is usually so boggy in winter that if the horses are turned out on it they will damage the grass by poaching it and probably get mud fever; in addition, there is unlikely to be much aeration in the subsoil, and this restricts plant growth. The digging of ditches around the field, and constant attention to keep them clear, helps drainage, but in the long run it is usually worth the expense of pipe drainage.

Feeding

Proper management of the grass will bring enormous gains in the feed value to grazing stock. However, no amount of care and attention will turn winter grass into nourishing foodstuff. It is only from May to August that the grass is really rich, and by October it has lost nearly every beneficial quality except its value as bulk. This means that the majority of horses at grass will need supplementary feeding. No hard and fast rules can be made about this; the supervisor of the livestock must keep continual watch on their condition. As soon as an animal starts to lose weight, food must be provided—initially hay, and then, as condition deteriorates further, grain.

Native or wild breeds will need little, if any, supplementary feeding, except in very bad weather. The more refined the breed, however, the greater the need to supplement the animal's natural diet. It should be added that even with supplementary feeding some horses, especially Thoroughbreds, suffer dreadfully from wintering out; so if stabling a horse is impossible, it is more sensible to buy a hardy type that can withstand the rigours of winter.

There are times when the eating of grass must be

restricted. In spring, when the grass is very rich, greedy horses often fill themselves to bursting point. This makes them too fat for their limbs, and can lead to the painful disease of laminitis. Consequently a horse that has such gluttonous habits should either be put on bare pasture, or be left free to eat the grass for only a few hours each day.

The other occasion when the eating of grass must be restricted is when the horse is being worked off grass. An animal will damage his limbs and his wind if asked to work hard when he is too fat. He will also need energy food, as grass only provides him with bulk.

The amount to feed at grass depends largely on common sense, but the following points should be taken into account: the condition of the horse; the type of horse; the state of the grass; the season of the year; whether or not any work is being demanded of the grass-kept animal.

Utensils for feeding

Laying the hay out on the ground is very wasteful, as much of it will be trodden over and never eaten. It is better to use haynets, or even to buy one of the large hay racks built specifically for this purpose.

To feed grain, heavy round feeding bins are best, as light feeding bins get turned over easily.

Water

A constant supply of fresh, clean water is essential. A horse drinks about 35l (8gal) a day. An unpolluted stream is a suitable source of water, but stagnant ponds or pools must be fenced off. A large drinking trough is the easiest container; this can be in the form of an old enamel bath tub (see section on Feeding and watering).

Shelter

The ideal field has some natural shelter, such as a stand of trees or a high hedge, which should provide the shade necessary in summer and the required protection from the wind and rain in winter. But such a natural shelter offers inadequate protection in snow and heavy rain, and actually attracts the flies that are such a menace to horses in the summertime. An artificial shelter can protect livestock against these hazards and, although horses will rarely use it except in extreme conditions, it is still worthwhile, especially as it can also provide a useful place for feeding.

An artificial field shelter need not be an elaborate structure provided it is sound enough to withstand winds. It should be at least the size of a loose box and be completely open on one side, but not into the sun; a narrow door might lead to quarrelling between animals, with the possibility of one horse being either permanently excluded or trapped inside by the horses that are outside the shelter.

The safety of a field

A field is safe for horses only when there is a strong fence around its perimeter and when there are no objects in it that could cause damage, such as broken glass or pieces of wood etc.

The fence

It is worth spending money and time on a top-quality fence to avoid the inconvenience and danger of animals straying into the countryside and along the roads; poor fencing is one of the most common causes of horses being cut and damaged. Any fence must be high enough to stop horses jumping out—a minimum of about 1.13m (3ft9in)—and strong enough to withstand being rubbed against, and it must have no pointed edges.

Of all forms of enclosure, stout post-and-rail (also called 'Man O' War') fencing, preferably three- or four-barred, is the best, both for appearance and for durability. A well-kept cut-and-laid hedge runs a close second. Hedges, unfortunately, are apt to develop weak spots and an inner rail may be necessary to prevent animals from pushing their way through. Stone walls are attractive and strong, but should be checked to see that they have not cracked and that the mortar is still intact. If they are drystone, make sure that none of the stones has shifted. Most people today, however, settle for wire, which is an excellent form of fencing if it has been properly erected. Plain, heavy-gauge, galvanized wire tightly strung between wooden creosoted posts is relatively cheap, and relatively safe provided that the lowest strand is no more than 30cm (1ft) from the ground and the wire does not sag. Electrified wire is becoming quite popular in the USA, and appears to be surprisingly safe as the shock and jolt upon contact discourages the horse without injuring him.

There are types of fencing that can damage horses: these include barbed wire (especially if it is sagging), chicken mesh, spiked iron railings and sharp-pointed chestnut palings.

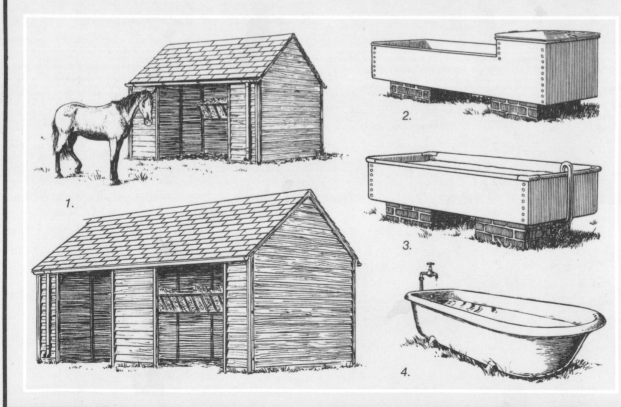

1. Shelters with hay racks inside

2. A self filling water tank

3. A tank which has to be filled by turning on a tap, but the latter has been placed underneath so the horse cannot be hurt by it.

4. The bath holds a lot of water, but a horse could be injured by the tap or overhanging lip.

Post and rail fence. This is the safest type of fencing but usually very expensive.

A very dangerous fence. Barbed wire even when tight can cut horses but when broken is even more dangerous.

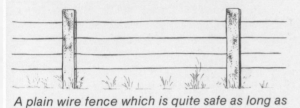

A plain wire fence which is quite safe as long as the wire is drawn tight.

A stone wall which is effective and safe as long as it is kept in good order.

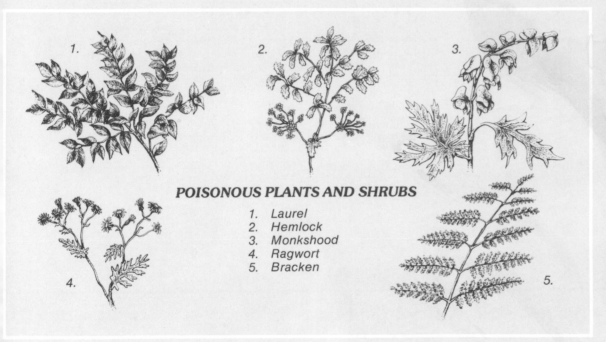

POISONOUS PLANTS AND SHRUBS

1. Laurel
2. Hemlock
3. Monkshood
4. Ragwort
5. Bracken

The gate

The gate needs to be easy for humans to open and close, but impossible for horses (it is surprising how ingenious a determined animal can be). Well-fitted five-bar gates are ideal; other means of closing and opening include slip rails secured by pins, or frame gates covered by galvanized steel mesh.

Poisonous plants and dangerous objects

The field should be checked for glass bottles, cans, pieces of metal and plastic bags are often thrown over the fence by passers-by, especially when a public footpath borders the field. Bottles and cans can lame a horse for life and it is not unknown for an animal to die after eating a plastic bag.

Any rabbit stops should be blocked up, as a horse can easily put its foot down one and this is especially dangerous to galloping animals.

Poisonous plants must be found and removed. Yew is particularly poisonous and dead clippings from this tree are fatal, as dead ragwort can be. Deadly nightshade is also toxic. Growing buttercups are poisonous, but the bitter taste of this plant makes most horses leave it alone. (In fact, once buttercups are cut and dried in hay, they completely lose their toxicity and are highly nutritious.) When ingested over a period of time, bracken may prove poisonous, although horses living in areas where bracken is common usually develop an immunity to it. Acorns, if eaten in large quantities, can have serious effects. Remember to check outside the fence as well as within, as horses will almost certainly stretch over to eat anything tempting that is within reach.

Although horses instinctively avoid poisonous foodstuffs, those that have just been turned out after a period in the stable are more at risk because they tend to be too greedy to be discerning. The same applies to animals that are being kept on particularly barren land.

Symptoms of poisoning

Purging, dryness of the mouth, distension of the stomach, colic, excessive flow of saliva, giddiness, dilated pupils, convulsions or even paralysis are all indications of possible poisoning. If these develop in a horse at grass, it is important to act quickly. Take the victim into a stable and call the vet.

Horses in work

Most horses, and all ponies, can be worked off grass. This has the advantage of avoiding the time-consuming routine of keeping them in a stable or stall. It also means that the animals need not be ridden every day, for they can exercise themselves. Care must be taken, however, to increase gradually the amount of work done off grass. Do not expect immediate fitness, and never demand fast work, or work of long duration, of grass-fed animals.

Grass provides bulk, but not energy food; so horses that are being hard ridden will need supplementary food (see Feeding section). The most common subjects for working off grass are children's horses in the school vacations, and it is a good idea to start feeding them a few weeks before the vacation begins.

There are two other important points to bear in mind when grass-kept horses are in work. The first is that in cold weather the horse relies on the grease in his coat to keep him warm. In autumn and winter, therefore, grooming should be minimal, restricted to merely getting off the mud. The second point is that horses off grass, with shaggy coats, often sweat a great deal. If colds and colic are to be avoided, the animals must not be turned out until they are completely dry.

Keeping a horse at grass is less demanding than keeping it in the stable and, as long as it is cared for in a responsible fashion, can be very successful.

IN THE STABLE

Reasons for stabling a horse

A horse may be stabled because the amount of work expected of him requires him to be in a fit condition, when he must carry no surplus flesh and his muscles must be firm, and this is impossible to achieve in a field. He has to become capable of arduous work without showing signs of distress, such as sweating or blowing, and to recover quickly from prolonged exertion. This hard condition takes time to achieve and is maintained only by giving enough of the correct type of food and the right amount of exercise. Such control is possible only in the stable.

Another reason for stabling a horse is that the animal may be too thin-skinned or constitutionally delicate to live out in all weathers. Some breeds have become so refined that they have lost the ability of native and wild breeds to bear bad weather. They cannot be left in the field throughout the winter months; if they were, they would lose condition even with special feeding.

At board or livery

A delicate breed of horse, or one needed for hard work, has therefore to be stabled; but for owners who have neither the time nor the facilities to stable their horse there is an alternative—to keep him at board or livery. This is an expensive procedure. There are two ways of cutting costs, but both entail risks. The first is to choose a riding school and allow them to use the animal for others to ride. As long as he has a tolerant temperament and is used only by good riders, the system is satisfactory; but it is likely that at some time the horse will be treated carelessly, and possibly spoilt, by inexperienced or rough riders.

The second way of reducing costs is to choose a cut-rate stable. But, unless the lower price is due to the stable being run by a hard-working family business, the chances are that the costs are cut at the expense of your horse's food, exercise and general attention. It is important to carry out extensive research into possible stables, to determine whether the stable management is good and the exercising of the horses safe and efficient. Most countries have an officially organized system, run by the National Federation, under which riding schools and stables are inspected and graded. You should examine this list, and ask the opinion of people who already have horses in the proposed stables.

If you can pay the cost of boarding or livery, it is generally worthwhile to spend a little extra money to ensure that the horse's treatment will be first class. You will also be able to enjoy better hacking, schooling, and jumping facilities when you go to ride him.

When the stables have been chosen, the best way of ensuring that the horse is properly cared for is to take a keen interest in his condition and to make a habit of discussing (without cross-examining) what work he has done in your absence. This interest will help to keep the stable managers on their toes and will also enable you to recognize quickly any deterioration in the well-being of the horse.

Attractive, well made custom-built stables. This is probably the easiest and safest type of stable to build for as long as an established firm is chosen, the dimensions and equipment will be good and tested by experience, providing both secure and comfortable accommodation for the horse.

The stable

Any stable must conform to basic standards in size, strength, safety, ventilation, insulation and drainage. If you take over an existing stable, you should check to ensure that it conforms to the standards discussed below. If it is necessary to build, whether by converting such buildings as barns, garages, or cattle sheds, or by starting from scratch, then make certain that the plans conform to these same standards.

New stables can be either custom built, or prefabricated versions erected on a concrete base. The second is probably the simpler and there are a number of manufacturers, producing stalls and stables of varying quality and size, who will provide plans and estimates. Most of these manufacturers will also erect the stables, but it may be cheaper to have it done by a local builder or even to do it yourself, if you have the necessary skill.

If you are building a new stable it will probably be necessary to get planning permission, and to adhere to local regulations about drainage and so on. These restrictions vary, usually according to how built-up the area is. It is worth taking the trouble to find out about local regulations. By keeping within them you will avoid later trouble with the authorities.

The site should preferably be close to existing electricity and water supplies, as the stable will require both these services. It is usually considered best for the stable to face south, and care should be taken that the prevailing wind will not blow straight through the doors. When designing the layout it is worth thinking about the view. Some owners prefer to give their horses something interesting to look at so that they do not become bored; others advocate a peaceful prospect for their animals so that they can rest. The preference depends largely on the work of the horse: those wanting quiet for their horses generally work them hard so that they are less likely to have the energy to get bored. Racehorses are a good example.

The stable, if built from scratch, should be laid out on 'time and motion' principles: in other words, there should be the least possible distance to cover to the vital sectors—feed room, storage facilities, tack room and manure pile.

The stables can be either straight stalls or loose boxes. In a straight stall the horse is always tied up by a rope or chain attached to his headcollar and running through a ring or hole in the manger to a light weight that rests on the bed (see diagram). This gives him freedom of movement and enables him to lie down easily. The advantages of these stalls are that they can be relatively small, cleaning

Horses in straight stalls tied up with ball and rope.

A horse in a well-equipped stall (stable) with the window protected by a grill and a fitted manger in the corner, safer than a bucket which might be kicked over.

A cast horse who cannot get his off foreleg and hind leg on the ground to give him the impetus to roll back. Sit on his neck to keep his head on the ground which will stop him from struggling and hurting himself. Get an assistant to put a rope around both hind legs and a rope around both forelegs. Get off the neck. Pull on the ropes to roll him back over so that he can get to his feet.

them out is much simpler because all the droppings are in one place, they are cheaper and easier to construct, and the horse is under better control. On the other hand, there is not much freedom for the occupants, and they tend to get bored staring at a wall all the time. In the UK and the USA, where most owners are unusually sympathetic towards their horses' feelings, these stalls are rarely seen; but all over Europe, where labour for stablework is hard to come by, they are very common.

A box stall or loose box does enable the horse to move around, and must be more comfortable for the animal. But make sure that it is large enough to minimize the risk of a horse getting hurt or cast. This is when a horse rolls over, and his legs are stopped in mid-air by the wall. Lying on his back, he is unable to roll to the original position, and so is trapped until humans can hold his legs and pull him over (see diagram).

The size will depend on the height of its occupant but the following table gives an idea of the size to choose for a box stall or loose box. Anyone choosing a small size for a small pony should remember that smaller ponies are often succeeded by bigger ones.

The doorway must be wide enough to allow the horse to pass through without bumping against the frame. It should therefore be at least 1.5m (4½ft) wide, preferably more, and not less than 2.25m (7½ft) high. Most stables have Dutch doors (in two halves), although internal boxes in a barn may have only the lower half, or a grille instead of a solid top portion. Both halves should open up a full 180°, so that they can be fastened back against the stable wall. Bolts should be carefully fitted to prevent the horse from opening the door. The lower half should be fitted with a foot-operated kick-bolt at the bottom, or a conventional bolt, as well as a bolt at the top.

Special bolts can be bought that the horse cannot open, for many mischievous horses find out how to nuzzle open a bolt, and owners may find them either trotting around on investigatory tours or getting through dangerously large quantities of foodstuff in the feed room.

Ventilation should allow plenty of fresh air, but no draughts, as these at best make a horse uncomfortable, and at worst start chills and make the animal stiff. The wall should therefore be free of cracks and holes. Windows that open should be hinged at the base so that the wind blows in at the top. Whether or not to keep the top doors shut is a debatable point. It depends partly on whether the stable faces into the wind and partly on the work of the occupant. If a horse has to face cold winds and rain when being worked (hunting, for instance), then it is probably better not to coddle him too much in the stable, and to leave the top door open. If the animal leads a protected existence, however, and if a shiny coat would be of advantage, then he can be kept much warmer in the stable, although the atmosphere should never be allowed to become stuffy.

Insulation of stables is not essential, but is certainly of benefit. An extra layer on the wall will help to keep it cooler when the weather is hot, and warmer when the weather is cold. The second layer also makes it safer for a horse or pony that tends to kick in the stable.

Roofs should be chosen for their insulation properties. Corrugated iron, although cheap, should not be used, because it is hot in summer and cold in winter. Wood or shingle covering is better.

Fittings are best kept to a minimum, to reduce the risk of a horse damaging himself on projections.

Windows provide the benefits of light and air, but can be dangerous if not protected. Horses can break them, and broken glass in the manger or on the floor may have serious consequences. It is therefore important to erect a grille on the inside of

STABLE CHART

Size of animal	Width	length	height
under 10hh	2¾m (9ft)	2¾m (9ft)	2½m (8½ft)
10-12hh	3m (10ft)	3m (10ft)	2¾m (9ft)
13-14.2hh	3¼m (11ft)	3¼m (11ft)	2¾m (9ft)
14.3-16.2hh	3½m (12ft)	3½m (12ft)	3m (10ft)
16.3-17hh	4m (13ft)	4m (13ft)	3m (10ft)
sick box foaling box	3½m (12ft)	4¾m (16ft)	3½-4¼m (12-14ft)

the window. If this is not possible, some wire mesh is usually sufficient protection.

Some horse-keepers do not have a manger fitted. Instead they give the feed in a container on the floor, which can be removed as soon as it has been cleared. This is satisfactory only if the feed tin is too heavy to be kicked or nuzzled over. For this reason plastic versions (except those specially designed not to be upset) should never be used. Iron feed tins or wooden feed boxes are thought to be the best.

The majority of stables, however, use fitted mangers, and these should be breast high. When choosing a type, ensure that it can be cleaned easily, and that it is broad enough to prevent the horse biting it and deep enough to stop the animal brushing the food out with his muzzle. Bars at the corners will also prevent food being brushed out.

Some stables use fitted hay racks, but there are disadvantages with these. The dust tends to fall into the eyes of the horse when he pulls out the hay, and also all over the person who fills it. It is better to use a haynet, which can be attached to a ring. The ring must be fitted firmly and at eye level. It is usual to fit a second similar ring to which the horse can be tied up.

It does save a great deal of time if automatically filling water bowls are fitted, but these should be sited away from the haynet and manger so that they do not become clogged with food. If using a bucket for water, a bucket container can be fitted breast high, but it is quite satisfactory to leave the bucket on the floor if it is heavy enough not to get upset.

All electric fittings must be out of the horse's reach. Switches should be of the outdoor variety and sited outside the stall or stable.

The floor of the stall or stable should be hardwearing, non-porous and non-slip, and should slope slightly towards a drain or gully at one end. Concrete is the most popular form of flooring, but it must be dense and well compacted, and finished with a slip-proof treatment. A restless, stamping horse can quickly break up poor-quality concrete, so it is worth paying extra for the best. If a drain is fitted inside the box, it must be protected by a grille. Alternatively, a channel can carry urine through the wall to an outside drain.

The bedding, if abundant, reduces the risk of a horse injuring himself and encourages him to lie down. The bed should therefore be clean, dry, thickly laid and banked up around the walls. To keep it in good shape you will need a barrow, a shovel, one pitchfork with two prongs and one with four, a broom, a skep for droppings (this can be a plastic laundry basket) and a sheet of sackcloth or similar tough material for carrying straw.

Mucking out usually takes place first thing in the morning, when the manure and soiled bedding are separated from the clean bedding with the pitchfork, and taken away to the manure heap in the barrow. The dry bedding is forked into a heap so that the floor can be cleaned and aired before the bedding is relaid as a thinner day-bed. During the day, droppings should be picked up in the skep and removed to the manure heap. At night, the day-bed is tossed up and the new bedding laid on top, with the sides of the bed banked up higher against the walls. A good deep bed is not wasteful.

It saves both bedding and time to adopt a deep litter system, when only the droppings and wet

To muck out the girl is using a four pronged pitch fork to lift the soiled bedding into the wheel barrow. The broom and spade are left outside.

patches are removed (but as frequently as possible) and small amounts of fresh bedding are added daily. The bed gradually builds up, and at some stage (every week, every month or every six months) must be removed in its entirety. The proud stable manager rarely favours this method but it does save labour.

Handling the stabled horse in the stable is important towards establishing the same respectful but trusting relationship with the horse as when riding him. The animal must learn to be obedient and well-mannered, and not frightened or spoilt into becoming a kicker, biter or spiteful animal. From the first moment the handler must be gentle in action so as not to startle him, firm in requirements so as not to confuse him, and quick to reward obedience or to reprimand the animal (with the voice or a slap on the neck) if he misbehaves. At all times he should be approached from the head so that he can see what is happening. He should be talked to before any action is taken and during any handling. He will quickly learn the difference in tone between being soothed and being scolded.

Tying up is often thought unnecessary by trustful owners who may like to leave their horses free, but this is a mistake. A horse never becomes as obedient as a dog, and most of them will seize an opportunity to escape through the door. And when a horse is free in the stable, accidents happen so easily—pitch-forks are stepped on, people kicked, and the like—so it is much fairer on the horse, and on everyone, to tie him up when mucking out, feeding, grooming and saddling up.

To tie the horse up, approach with the halter (headcollar) from the front, talk to him and pat his neck. Pass the free end of the rope around the neck. Put the noseband over the muzzle and the head-piece over the ears. A rope halter is then knotted on the near side (see picture), and a leather halter (headcollar) is buckled up. Lead him then to the ring on the wall and use a quick release knot.

Blanketing (rugging up) is necessary in all but the hottest weather for the horse kept in a stall or stable. To put it on, tie the horse up, take the blanket (rug) at the front and gently swing it over the horse to lie centrally along the back but high up on the neck. Buckle up the front and then slide back into position, but not so far that it drags on the shoulders.

If there is no surcingle attached to the blanket (rug), use a roller pad under a roller. Position this pad behind the withers and put the roller over it, ensuring that there are no twists (see diagram). Buckle up the roller so that it is firm, but not squeezing the horse. Run the fingers between the roller and the rug to ensure that there are no lumps. Check that the rug is not too small, and is not pulling on the shoulders and withers, as this can make the animal sore.

In cold weather a clipped horse may need an additional blanket for warmth. This is put on first, again well forward, and slid back so that it nearly touches the root of the tail at the back. The blanket (rug) is then added, the roller done up and the free portion of the under blanket, at the front, folded back over the rug, to make it neat and stop it slipping back.

To take the blanket (rug) off, remove the roller

TYING UP

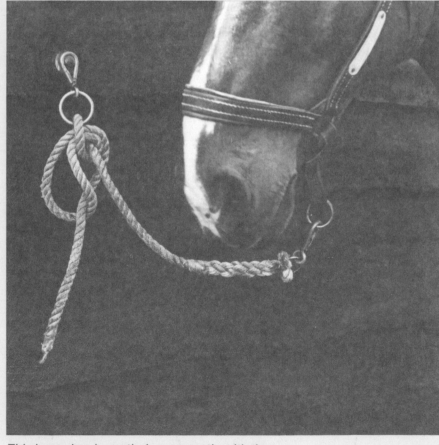

This horse has been tied up correctly with the free end through the loop so that the horse can not pull the knot out.

RUGGING UP

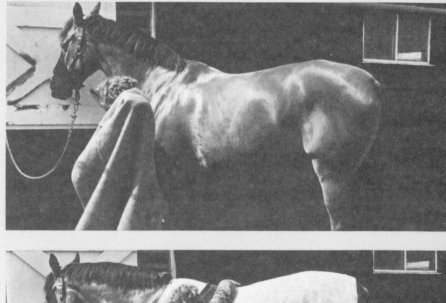

and unfasten the front buckle. With the left hand grasp the part of the rug that is over the withers, and with the right hand the part over the back. Slide it off in the direction of the hair and fold it up four-square.

Stable routine
A timetable for a normal day in the stable is given here;

7am	Tie up horse and inspect for injury. Refill water bucket unless the stall has an automatic water fountain. Refill haynet. Muck out stable. Brush over horse without completely removing blanket (rug). Pick out feet. Lay day-bed.
7.45am	Give the horse his first feed.
9.30am	Remove droppings. Remove rugs. Saddle up and exercise the horse. On return refill water bucket.
Noon	Tie up horse. Groom thoroughly. Put on blanket (day rug). Refill water bucket. Untie horse.
12.30pm	Give second feed. Refill haynet.
4.00pm	Tie up horse and pick out feet. Remove droppings and shake up bedding. Remove day rug (blanket), brush over and put on night rug (blanket). Refill water bucket. Untie horse.
5.00pm	Give third feed.
7.30pm	Remove droppings. Lay night-bed, and refill water bucket and haynet.
8.00pm	Give final feed.
Last thing at night.	Visit stable to ensure that all is well.

The combined system
From this timetable, it can be seen that caring for a stabled horse is a full-time occupation, unless the duties can be shared. If there is no one to help during the day, or it is difficult to exercise the horse regularly, it is better to turn him out into a field in the daytime, and stable him only at night. When the weather is very hot and the flies are troublesome during the day, the procedure can be reversed so that the horse is at grass during the night.

In the winter a stabled horse, especially if he is clipped, will find the fields very cold. The New Zealand rug has been specially designed to be worn by horses at grass. It is waterproof and has special straps to keep it in place even when the wearer rolls.

The blanket is thrown gently over the horse to fall on the neck, and slid back into place. The front buckle is done up, the roller is lifted on and unless well padded, a pad placed underneath. It is done up and any wrinkles smoothed out.

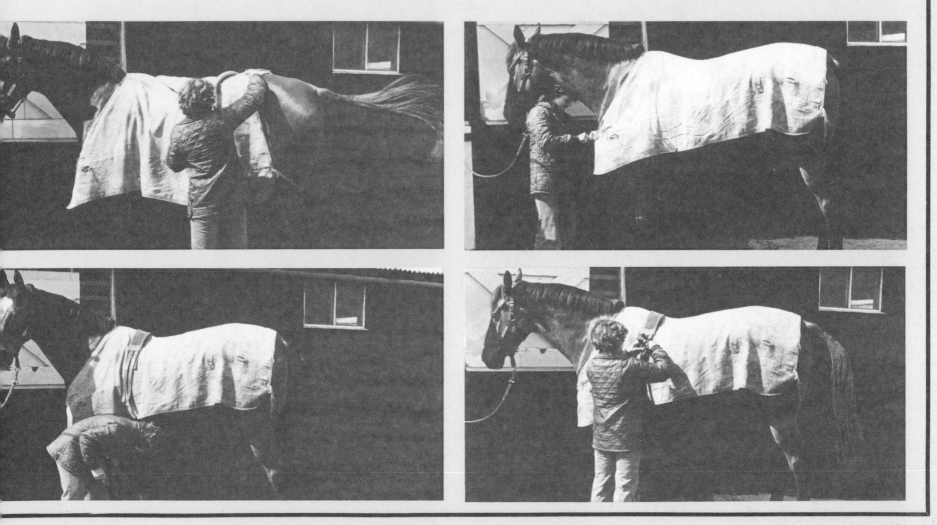

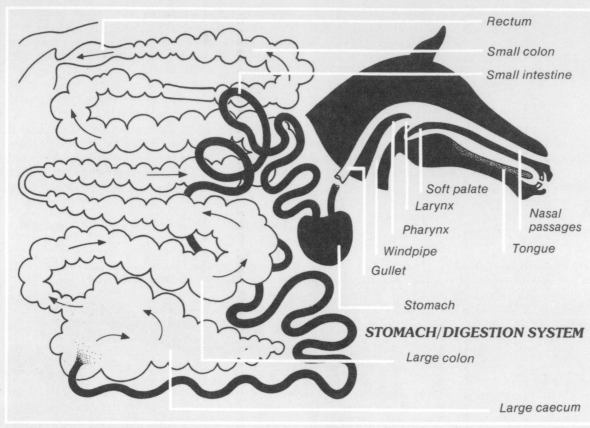

Rectum
Small colon
Small intestine
Soft palate
Larynx
Pharynx
Nasal passages
Windpipe
Tongue
Gullet
Stomach

STOMACH/DIGESTION SYSTEM

Large colon
Large caecum

Horses have a very small stomach in relation to their size, and food passes through several digestive processes before waste matter is evacuated. The intestine narrows at various points, and bottle-necks can occur when food becomes impacted at these places; this leads to a build-up of doughy matter, the formation of gases, and ultimately an attack of colic.

It is essential, therefore, that horses should be fed small amounts several times a day and that their diet should contain plenty of fibrous foods to prevent impaction and fermentation. Grass, hay (dried grass) and, to a certain degree, bran (the outer husk of wheat grain) contain plenty of fibre. They also contain other nutrients, principally carbohydrates, some proteins, and minerals such as calcium, phosphorus and magnesium, as well as a number of essential trace elements. A horse that is required to do little work beyond gentle weekend hacking, and is living out with access to adequate grazing, needs no food other than grass in the summer and hay in the winter. Indeed, most native horses, with their powerful constitutions and extreme hardiness, fare better on a year-round diet composed entirely of grass or hay without any grain supplement.

But horses doing hard work, and refined breeds require more proteins and carbohydrates than fields can provide. Proteins (nitrogenous substances) are needed to build and repair tissues (in particular, muscle tissue); and carbohydrates are needed for energy. Minerals and vitamins are also essential in small quantities; without them, health tends to decline, and such ailments as rickets develop in young stock.

Types of food
It is important to remember that concentrates rich in protein and carbohydrates are given in addition to grass and hay, never as substitutes. Bulk or roughage is essential to help the digestive process. Overfeeding of concentrates (especially protein) will upset the metabolism.

Hay
This is the staple diet of horses, however kept. The best hay for horses is seed hay, which contains a mixture of grasses especially sown for a hay crop (in other words, the hay comes from arable land where it is one of a rotation of crops). Clover hay, which is highly nutritious, should be mixed with another type of hay before feeding; on its own, it is too rich and heating for horses. Meadow hay comes from permanent grassland and may be good or bad, depending on its source. In many countries lucerne hay (alfalfa) is in common use. It is very rich in protein and a horse not used to eating it should be given only very small quantities at first.

Good-quality hay is greenish in colour, sweet smelling, free of dust, not too coarse, and between six and 18 months old. Yellow, blackish, damp or mouldy hay must be rejected, and every effort should be made to get good hay (the best if a horse is in fast work). Hay forms between one half and two thirds of the diet of a stabled horse and its quality will have a major effect on the animal's condition. During the winter months, from November to March, a horse may get through two tons of hay or more.

Bran
This is a by-product of the milling processes of wheat. Although it is bulky and rich in proteins, bran contains relatively few energy-giving carbohydrates. The best bran is broad in flake, dry and not musty. It has a tendency to absorb moisture and become sour, so unless dry storage facilities are available it should be bought in small quantities.

Bran has two opposite effects on the horse's system according to how it is fed. If fed wet, in mash form, it acts as a laxative, but if fed dry, it tends to constipate. In a normal feed it is dampened, and is usually mixed with oats, in the ratio of three units of oats to one unit of bran.

Oats
This is the most effective energizing food for horses and must be used cautiously with spirited animals or children's mounts. Oats can be used whole but it is more usual to crush, roll or bruise them, so that the kernel is exposed to the digestive juices. This helps the process of digestion. Oats should not be crushed flat, which makes them lose their floury content, nor should they be kept for more than a few weeks after crushing, as they begin to lose their food value. The best oats are dry, without must, plump and short, more or less uniform in size and pale gold, light grey, dark chocolate brown or black in colour.

Barley
This is an excellent grain for improving condition. When used for this purpose, it should be boiled before being given to a horse. Raw barley should always be crushed and introduced to the diet very gradually. It is not a good substitute for oats if the

horse is used for very demanding or fast work.

Wheat
Except in very small quantities, this is not a suitable grain for horses. It should be crushed or boiled, then fed with other concentrates.

Corn (Maize)
High in energy value but poor in proteins and minerals, it has good fattening effects but should not be fed in large quantities. It should never make up more than a quarter of the grain ration. As it is rather indigestible, it is best fed flaked.

Peas and beans
These are rich in protein and they should therefore be used sparingly, and only for a horse in hard work, one whose condition has deteriorated badly, or one that is wintering out at grass. Peas and beans should be split or crushed with a hammer before being mixed with the feed.

Sugar beet
Usually available dried and pulped, this must be soaked in water overnight before being mixed with the feed. If fed dry it would swell in the stomach, and could cause colic. It is a good conditioner.

Horse cubes
Known in the USA as pellets, these contain most of the required nutrients in well-balanced proportions. According to the market for grain, they are made up of varying quantities of oats, bran, maize, barley, locust bean, linseed cake, groundnut meal, grass meal, molasses, vitamins and minerals. They have great advantages as a foodstuff. They are convenient to store, and as they provide a balanced diet they can be used on their own, making it unnecessary to mix the feed. Because they create less energy, they are an especially beneficial substitute for oats when feeding spirited horses and children's mounts. Their only drawback is that they are relatively expensive.

Chaff
This is chopped hay or oat straw. About 450g (1lb) of chaff should be added to all feeds, as it ensures proper chewing of concentrates and acts as an abrasive on teeth. The chaff sold by feed merchants tends to be of very poor quality and is therefore of little use. The only sure way of getting good chaff is to

Filling a hay net. The girl is taking small handfuls of hay from an opened bale, shaking them and pushing them into the hay net.

use a chaff cutter; these can be bought secondhand, or perhaps a neighbour will lend one at regular intervals.

If neither of these alternatives is possible, chaff may be left out of the diet; although advisable, it is not essential. Bran and horse cubes both to some extent stop bolting of food.

Root vegetables
These help to provide variety and a different taste for horses that are stabled. Roots are of special value to poor feeders and to horses in bad condition. Carrots are probably the best, but turnips, mangels, swedes, and parsnips are thoroughly appreciated by most horses. Roots should be sliced into finger-shaped pieces and mixed with the regular food.

Molasses
This may be sprinkled on a feed, to encourage a finicky eater on to promote a shiny coat. It should never be used to disguise mouldy, dustry or poor-quality hay. Hay in bad condition will not become more nutritious as a result of being made more palatable, and it may even be harmful.

Cod liver oil
This helps to build up condition and improve the horse's coat. As it has an unpleasant taste, manufacturers make it more attractive to shy feeders by mixing it with more tasty materials. It is then sold under a brand name as either cake or liquid.

Mineral salt licks
There are a number of mineral salt licks available, which can be fixed into special containers and attached to the wall, or simply left in the manger. Some horse keepers, however, prefer to use lumps of rock salt rather than these prepared licks.

Linseed
This is rich in oil, which makes it an excellent means of improving condition and giving gloss to a coat. It must be well cooked to destroy the poisonous enzyme that is present in raw linseed. The linseed can be made into a jelly or tea, according to the amount of water used. To make jelly, soak the linseed in water for 24 hours, then add more water and bring to the boil. After being allowed to cool, the jelly is tipped out and mixed with the feed. Linseed tea is prepared in the same way as jelly but more water is added; the resulting liquid can be used to make linseed mash. Linseed can also be bought as cubes and fed directly, which relieves the feeder of this preparation process.

FEEDING AND WATERING

A bran mash

Usually fed the night before a rest day, or after great exertion, such as a day's hunting, it is an excellent laxative. To make it, pour boiling water over half a bucket of bran, stir it well, cover with a sack, and leave it to steam until it is cool enough to be eaten. The mash should be 'crumbled dry', neither stiff nor thin and watery. About a quarter of an ounce of salt may be added to half a bucket of bran.

Basics of good feeding in the stable

1. Feed little and often. Times of feed will vary according to stable routine, but an acceptable timetable would be feeds at 7am, 12 noon, 4.30pm and 7.30pm.

2. Feed plenty of bulk food (hay or grass). Using a haynet prevents hay from being wasted, but it should be tied securely and high enough to prevent the horse getting his feet tangled in it. A haynet should be given about three times a day, and total quantity divided unevenly, with the smallest amount in the morning and the largest amount in the evening.

3. The amount of the feed should be adjusted according to the work being done by the horse, and the size and temperament of the animal. A horse that becomes excitable and difficult to manage should have its oat ration decreased; cubes should be given instead.

4. Any change in types of food or times of feed should be gradual and spread over several days.

5. Avoid using musty, dusty foodstuffs and always dampen (but do not soak) the feed.

6. Do not work a horse hard immediately after feeding, or when the stomach is full of grass. Quiet work is possible after a small feed of 1-1.5kg (2-3lb), but after a full feed no strenuous work should be done for 1½ hours.

7. Water before feeding.

8. Always use clean feeding utensils. The trough or manger, bucket, pan or feeding bowl must be kept clean; any remains of the previous feed must be removed before a fresh feed is given.

Good feeding is an acquired skill; it demands experience and a close interest in the animals, as each individual will have varying requirements. Some animals look well on very little feed and become too excitable if fed any more; others need as much feed as they will take, to maintain their energy and condition. Although there can be no absolute rules about quantities to feed, the following table does provide a rough guide, but it must be used in conjunction with continual observation so that any changes in condition or performance can be noted at an early stage, and the feed adjusted accordingly.

Specimen diets

NB These are for horses with a sensible temperament. If the animal becomes unmanageable, substitute cubes for oats, or turn him out to grass for a few hours each day, or do both.

In the field

For owners of horses turned out in pastures, the usual problem is when to start feeding hay in the autumn and when to stop in the spring. But so much depends on the extent and quality of the available grazing; there can be no hard and fast rules. Weather is also a factor. During a mild winter, the grass will continue to grow and will contain some nutritive value, right up to the end of the year. The wisest plan is to start offering hay as early as October but discontinue for a while if the hay is ignored. By December, however, a daily haynet will be necessary. Once the grass starts to grow again in spring, the horse should be encouraged to eat some hay; you may have to tie the animal up and give it a haynet for two or three hours each day. Too much rich grass eaten too quickly may cause colic or laminitis (see Chapter 10). By May, it should be possible to stop giving hay.

Concentrates may be given at any time, if the horse is in work or losing condition. Ponies, however, are usually best kept on cubes. Oats often go to their heads, turning them into unruly beasts.

The feed should be taken to the field at the same time each day to avoid any impatient fretting, which can impair the digestion.

But horses doing hard work, and refined breeds, require more proteins and carbohydrates than fields can provide. Proteins (nitrogenous substances) are needed to build and repair tissues (in particular, muscle tissue); and carbohydrates are needed for energy. Minerals and vitamins are also essential in small quantities; without them, health tends to decline, and such ailments as rickets develop in young stock.

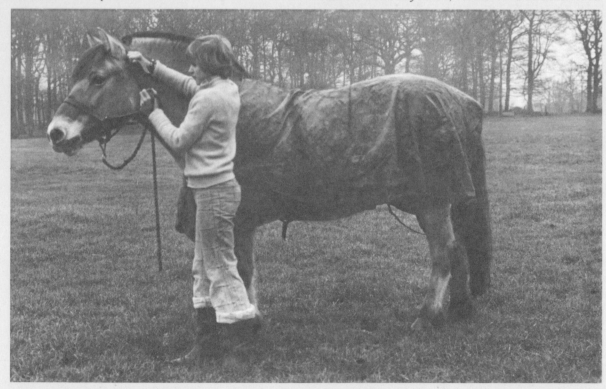

Turning a pony out to grass with a waterproof New Zealand rug to keep him warm. Straps around his hind legs stop it from slipping.

FEEDING CHART

Type of horse	7am	12 noon	4.30pm	7.30pm
Hunter, working or event horse more than 16hh	2lb oats, 1lb bran plus chaff, 2lb hay	3lb oats 1lb bran plus chaff, 5lb hay	3lb oats, 1lb bran, linseed jelly, roots, chaff	4lb oats, 1lb bran, chaff, 7lb hay
Hunter, working or event horse less than 16hh	2lb oats, 1lb bran plus chaff, 2lb hay	3lb oats, 1lb bran plus chaff, 4lb hay	2lb oats, 1lb bran, linseed jelly, roots, chaff	3lb oats, 1lb bran, chaff, 6lb hay
14.2hh pony, working, hunting or eventing (turned out for a few hours)	2lb cubes, 1lb bran, chaff, 2lb hay	turned out	2lb oats, 1lb bran, chaff	2lb oats, 1lb cubes, 1lb bran, 6lb hay
Show-jumper over 16hh	2lb oats, 1lb bran, chaff, 2lb hay	2lb oats, 1lb cubes, 1lb bran, chaff, 5lb hay	3lb oats, 1lb cubes, 1lb bran, chaff	3lb oats, 1lb cubes, 1lb bran, chaff, 7lb hay
Riding horse of about 15hh (turned out by night in summer, or for a few hours during the day)	1lb oats, 2lb cubes, 1lb bran, 2lb hay	1lb oats, 2lb cubes, 1lb flaked maize, 1lb bran, chaff, 3lb hay	2lb oats, 1lb cubes, 1lb bran, roots, 6lb hay	
Child's pony of about 13.2hh being worked daily (but turned out for a few hours)	1lb cubes, 1lb bran, 1lb hay	2lb cubes, 1lb bran, 2lb hay	1lb oats, 2lb bran, chaff, 1lb carrots, 5lb hay	

Watering

This is as important as feed to a horse. Although the animal could stay alive for about a month without food, it would die in about a week if deprived of water. As a general rule, water should be offered to horses before a meal and after exercise; watering on a full stomach, or immediately before energetic work, may cause pain and distress. Some horses, however, seem to like the opportunity of taking a light drink after a feed, and as long as they have been able to drink deeply beforehand, this should do no harm.

Watering in the stable

In the stable, water is usually contained in a bucket, which can be emptied and refilled four or five times a day. It should be placed in a corner away from the manger and haynet, so that it cannot become contaminated by loose hay or spilt feed. A bucket-holder will prevent it from being knocked over. Alternatively, an automatic drinking bowl may be fitted in the box; the bowl should be checked regularly, however, to ensure that the mechanism is working and has not become clogged. Problems are especially likely to arise in cold weather when the supply pipes can freeze.

Watering in the field

Far less control over a horse's drinking habits is possible in a field, but here the animal will most probably conform to the routine followed by horses in the wild, drinking at morning and evening but rarely in between.

A pastured (grass-kept) horse is visited less often than a stabled one, however, and it is easy to forget to check the water container at every visit. If the field possesses a running stream or an automatic water trough, fresh water will always be available. A running stream is the best watering system, provided that the ground bordering it is sound and that neither the ground nor the bed of the stream is composed of boulders or thick mud. A stagnant pond is better fenced off.

Automatic troughs draw water from pipes, with the supply being controlled by a ballcock and valve mechanism or a stopcock. The troughs should be situated in the open, away from hedges or over-hanging trees, so that several horses can drink at the same time and falling leaves will not pollute the If no other source is available, water must be supplied manually, by means of a hose or buckets. An old bath makes an adequate container, but it should be cleaned regularly and should be boxed in to prevent any sharp rim from injuring the horse. Buckets by themselves are unsatisfactory as they hold little water and are easily knocked over. A horse may drink as much as eight gallons during a day, so capacity is an important factor to consider.

In freezing weather, ice on the surface of the water must be frequently broken and removed. During a prolonged frost, water in the trough may freeze solid; in these circumstances, carrying water in buckets will be the only means of ensuring that your horse has enough to drink.

The purpose of grooming

First and foremost, grooming keeps a horse clean. It also massages, stimulates circulation of the blood and lymph, and tones up the muscles. Thus, grooming is a means of preventing disease (especially of the skin), of maintaining condition, and of improving appearance. For the horse in the stable, deprived of a natural life, daily grooming is essential to its well-being.

The grooming routine

Brief grooming, or quartering, is a five- or ten-minute grooming before a stable horse is worked. The feet are picked out and stable marks removed with a dandy brush or, if necessary, a damp sponge. The mane and tail are brushed with a body brush and put in place with a water brush. The eyes, muzzle and dock are sponged.

Grooming after exercise

When the horse returns to the stable after exercise the feet, if muddy, should be washed and then picked out. Any dry sweat marks may be removed with a dandy or body brush, but not until the coat is completely dry. If the horse is hot or wet, he may need to be sponged down before being dried off.

Thorough grooming (strapping)

Thorough grooming is the hardest part of the grooming routine; the best effects will be achieved only by 'elbow grease'.

Start with the dandy brush, to remove mud and sweat marks. This can be done only if the dirt has dried. Although it is possible to sponge marks off, it can lead to chapping and sores unless the area is dried adequately afterwards.

The field-kept horse stimulates his circulation by moving around, and the grease in his coat acts as a natural waterproofing agent. Because a horse kept in the stable has lost both these safeguards, it is best to avoid wetting the coat. Brush off dirt wherever possible.

The real hard work starts with application of the body brush. The bristles must be driven through the horse's coat, beginning at the neck on the near side, to remove all the dirt and dried sweat. Stand far enough away from the horse to get your weight behind the brush. More force can be put into the task if the brush is held in the left hand on the nearside and in the right hand on the offside. With a strong, circular motion, work the brush from the neck along the body, occasionally cleaning the brush with the curry comb. The belly, the flank and the area

Sponge

Large mane comb

Sweat scraper

Hoof pick

Small mane comb

Grooming kit bag

Curry comb

Water brush

Stable rubber

Body brush

Dandy brush

between the forelegs should be covered. When grooming the hind legs, it is best to stand as close as possible at the side (not behind), so as to feel and see more easily if the horse is about to kick or move.

The head, especially around the eyes and ears, is a very sensitive area; use the brush gently but firmly. A dandy brush must never be used on the head. The mane and tail should be groomed into place and the hairs separated with the body brush. A dampened water brush can then be applied to keep the mane lying over. The tail can be bandaged to keep it in the correct shape.

The dock, eyes and nostrils should then be cleaned with the sponge, and the finishing touch is to wipe the horse over with a damp stable rubber.

A good grooming, however, should include some wisping, which both develops and hardens the muscles and stimulates the circulation. To be effective the dampened wisp must be brought down with some force on the horse to follow the lie of the hair. Aim for a rhythmical pattern of lift, down, thump and along. This wisping should be done in the regions of the muscles, ie, the shoulders and neck; the head, loins, belly and legs should not be wisped.

Setting fair (touch-ups)

Most horses have an additional blanket or thicker rug put on them at the end of the day. This is a good opportunity to give them a quick brush-over and wisping.

To make a wisp

Twist some dampened hay into a rope of about 2m (7ft). At one end, arrange the rope into two loops, one slightly longer than the other. Twist each loop in turn under the rest of the rope, until there is none left. To finish, twist end of rope through end of each loop and tuck in (see diagram).

To pick out the feet

Stand beside the horse's shoulder or hindquarters. Run the hand down the back of the leg toward the hoof, which the average animal will then pick up. If it does not, push on the shoulder or hindquarters to make it transfer its weight to the other leg and pinch the back of the leg with the hand. When the leg is lifted, hold it firmly around the coronet and pick out the hoof with a blunt-ended hoof pick, starting from the heel and working toward the toe.

THE GROOMING KIT

Item	Purpose	Method of use
Hoof pick	Removal of dirt and stones from feet	Pick out each foot in turn. Remove stones, mud, bedding, etc., with point of pick. Work from the heel to the toe and take care not to force down on the side, or on the cleft of the frog, too hard.
Dandy brush (stiff)	Removal of caked mud and sweat	Use with firm 'to and fro' motion on a horse or pony with a thick coat, on legs and under the saddle. It is too hard for the tender regions of a horse with a fine coat. A rubber curry comb is a gentler means of removing mud and sweat marks.
Body brush (soft, with close-set hairs)	Removal of dust and scurf from coat. Also used on mane and tail.	Use short, circular strokes in the direction of the lie of the hair. As much force as possible should be put behind the brush without thumping horse or pony. Mane and tail brushed by separating and brushing a few locks at a time. Head is cleaned after removal of head collar, which is then fastened around the neck.
Curry comb	Removal of dirt from body brush. If made of rubber, comb can be used on horse, to remove hair and dirt.	Curry comb in one hand; body brush in the other. Brush is drawn through it after every four or five strokes. Curry comb is cleaned by being tapped on floor. Do not use comb when brushing mane, tail and head; a free hand is needed at these times.
Wisp	Stimulates circulation and massages	Bring down with a bang in the direction of the lie of the coat. Use on side of neck, quarters and thigh; but not on bony, tender areas.
Water brush (soft)	Dampening of mane and tail, and washing of feet	Dampen and brush over mane to required position. Wash feet, if dirty.
Sponge	Cleans eyes, lips, nostrils and dock.	Dampen sponge, clean dirt from around eyes, then muzzle. Lift tail and clean dock region. Rinse sponge between cleaning of these areas.
Stable rubber	Gives final polish after grooming	Arrange into flat bundle, dampen and wipe coat in direction of lie of hair.
Sweat scraper	Removal of water and/or sweat from coat	A horse that has been washed or has sweated profusely can have its coat scraped gently but firmly in direction of the lie of the hair.

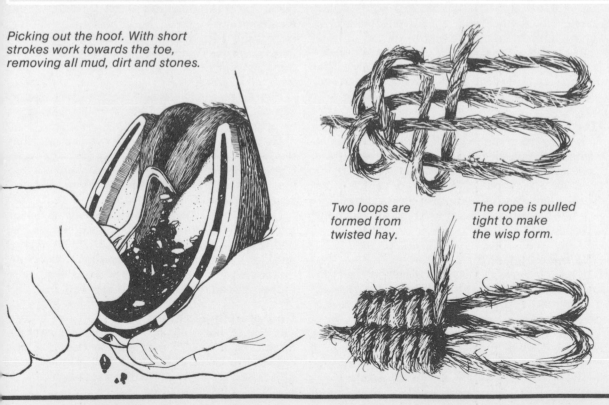

Picking out the hoof. With short strokes work towards the toe, removing all mud, dirt and stones.

Two loops are formed from twisted hay.

The rope is pulled tight to make the wisp form.

The grass-kept horse

Only limited grooming is needed for animals living outside. The grease and dandruff in the coat help to waterproof the hair and keep the animal warm; it is inadvisable, therefore, to clean a grass-kept horse too vigorously, in case his natural means of protection is removed.

Grooming should be limited to picking out his feet, removing mud with a dandy brush or rubber curry comb, brushing mane and tail with a body brush, laying the mane with a water brush, and finally sponging the muzzle, eyes and dock.

The grooming machine

Grooming machines (vacuum cleaners) are a great help in busy stables. They must, however, be operated intelligently; it is easy to frighten a horse and to damage the machine. It is inadvisable to groom with them every day—normal practice is to use them once or twice a week. On the other days, the horse can be groomed by hand, a process that usually takes much less time than a normal grooming because so much of the grease and dirt has been removed by the machine on the preceding day.

CLIPPING AND TRIMMING

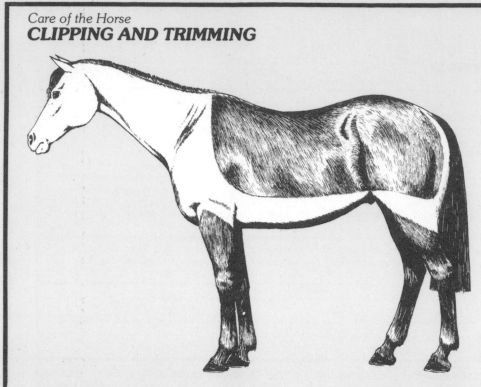

Left: A blanket clip

Right: A hunter clip

Removal of all or part of a thick coat is needed for horses in hard, regular work. Clipping both prevents excessive sweating and enables the horse to dry quickly afterwards. It also makes him look trim and neat, although this is not the main reason for clipping.

The first clip of the season is carried out as soon as the new winter coat is well established, usually about October. The first sign that the winter coat is on the way is the disappearance of the high gloss of summer. Suddenly, the coat feels more woolly beneath the fingers as the short hairs thicken, the top hairs grow longer and the fine summer hairs begin to fall out. At work the horse sweats more easily.

Electrically operated clippers are the most efficient means of removing the coat. They are quick, easy to use after some practice and, when oiled during the cut and sharpened at intervals, give a satisfactory clip. Hand-operated clippers are good, but rather tiring to use.

Types of clip
The extent of the clipping should depend on the work the horse will be expected to do, and on how much he sweats.

A full clip
This clip is one in which all the hair is removed from the head (except muzzle and ears), neck, body and legs of the horse. This is used on heavily coated animals, on whom the hair on the legs is ugly and so thick that it becomes difficult to dry.

The hunter clip
This leaves hair on the legs as far as the elbow and top of the thighs. This protects the horse against gorse, thorns and other matter encountered in cross-country riding, and reduces the risk of heels cracking. Sometimes, a patch of hair is left on the back under the saddle to help stop rubbing, but if the hair is excessively thick it is best removed to prevent excessive sweating.

The blanket clip
This leaves most of the body hair (in the shape of a blanket) and all the leg hair. The head, neck, belly, part of the thighs and a thin strip up the back of the quarters are clipped. It is used in particular for Thoroughbreds who, because of their fine coats, do not need to have so much removed to reduce the sweating.

The trace-high clip
The briefest clip of all, this removes hair only from the belly, chest, and part of the thighs and up the back of the quarters. A strip on the underside of the neck is also sometimes removed. The trace-high clip is popular for horses that are to be kept out during the winter but will be hunted during winter holidays; it prevents excessive sweating without removing any of the animal's protection against the weather.

How to clip
Clipping takes time and patience. An assistant should be available to help if required.

The horse's coat should be as dry and well-groomed as possible. The most important factor is not to upset the animal. Before the clip is started, the assistant should hold the horse, talk to it, pat it, and be reassuring. If it becomes restless when the ticklish areas (for instance, the belly) are being clipped, the assistant can lift one of its legs to prevent the horse from moving around.

Start clipping in the areas that are least ticklish and sensitive, such as the shoulders—not the head, groin or belly.

Ensure that the clippers do not overheat, and that the blades are sharp and do not pull the hairs; clippers must be run flat along the skin and not dug into the horse, and they should be guided, not pushed, against the lie of the coat.

Do not clip into the sides of the mane or the root of the tail, or inside the ears. The backs of the tendon and fetlock are usually better dealt with by scissors and comb. The comb and scissors should be moved upward against the hair, in the same way as a professional hairdresser trims human hair.

Care of a clipped horse
The clipped horse needs a blanket to compensate for the loss of his thick coat. A blanket made of jute or hemp and lined with wool is used in most cases, with or without an additional blanket underneath. A

recent innovation in the UK is a quilted rug, which is warm and light and can be used in place of the night-rug and blanket.

Mane- and tail-pulling

These tasks are forgotten by many horse owners, who perhaps worry that they may do a poor job and produce more problems than they solve. But a well-pulled mane and tail give a good appearance and, in the case of the mane, make it easier to plait for hunting or showing.

Pulling thin hair from the mane makes the ends even (scissors should never be used) and helps it to lie flat. The task is best carried out when the horse is warm and the pores of the skin are open so that hairs will come out easily and without discomfort. Always remove the hairs from the underside of the mane, and never take out more than a few hairs with each pull. It is best to do a little each day rather than keep going for a long time, which could make the animal sore.

Tail-pulling means removing (never with scissors) the short, bushy hairs from the top of the tail. It is done solely to give a neat appearance. It should not be carried out on grass-kept animals, who need the short hairs at the top of the tail to protect the region around the dock.

Mane- and tail-braiding (plaiting)

These give the final touch to the overall show-ring appearance of a horse, and show off his neck and quarters to best advantage. Braiding is also a useful means of making an unruly mane lie flat on the correct side.

Braiding a mane

The mane should be braided on the morning of the show, and the braids must be taken out at the end of the show to avoid damaging the hair by splitting or tearing.

Braids are made from withers to forelock, usually about a mane-comb's length apart. There should be an uneven number of braids up the length of the neck.

The hair is first damped with a water brush and divided into sections. Each section in turn is then braided so that the top of the braid is tight against the roots of the hair. The end is then secured, by means of a needle and thread passed through the plait and wound tightly around it, before being folded under and stitched to the braid about half way up. The resulting loop is then rolled up tightly until it forms a knob close to the poll, where it is stitched firmly in place. Sharp-pointed embroidery

scissors are needed to remove the stitches at the end of the day.

Braiding with rubber bands is a quicker method, but it is difficult to achieve such a smart result as that given by needle and thread. The hair is braided in the same manner and a rubber band is looped around the long braid several times. The end is then turned up into the desired position and the band looped around the entire braid to make it secure.

Tail braiding

Tail braiding is carried out in a similar manner, starting at the top of the tail, braiding down the centre and drawing in the side hairs on the way. When the braid is two thirds of the way down the tail bone, start leaving out the side hairs. Continue the braid, using only the centre hairs. The end of the braid should be stitched and bound securely with needle and thread, doubled under and attached to the point where the braiding of the side hairs ends.

Tail Braiding

1.

2.

3.

4.

5.

6.

7.

Step-by-step diagrams of how to braid a mane.

BEFORE AND AFTER EXERCISE

A stabled horse must be regularly exercised. Otherwise he runs the risk of swollen legs, azoturia, and colic, and is also likely to show spirited behaviour when ridden. One rest day a week is acceptable, but on the evening before this it is advisable to give a laxative bran mash.

The amount of exercise given to the horse will depend on his type (Thoroughbreds need more than ponies), the type of work being prepared for (three-day eventers need more than hacks), the amount of energy food the animal is receiving (horses being given large quantities of oats need more than those on pellets [cubes]), and his fitness (a horse that has been in work for only a week requires less than one that is ready to go hunting).

Preparation for exercise

Exercise should not take place until at least one-and-a-half hours after a large feed, or one hour after a small one. It is also advisable to take the hay away one hour before exercise, as a horse or pony stuffed full of hay will find breathing more difficult. In the case of a horse about to be put to fast work, this precaution is essential, and must be observed.

When ready to exercise the horse, he should be tied up and quartered (see Grooming above) before tacking up. If boots or bandages are worn, these should be put on first. Yorkshire boots are used if the horse brushes his hind fetlocks; they are attached firmly just above the fetlock so that they cannot slip down. Brushing boots are used on the forelegs, and are advisable on all valuable horses as they reduce the likelihood of injuries or splints being caused by blows or brushing. The brushing boots should be put on with the ends of the straps pointing towards the hind legs. The bottom strap should be done up first, to stop the boot slipping down, and the straps should be tight enough to prevent the boot passing over the fetlock joint.

Some horse owners use exercise bandages, either because they like the additional protection these provide, or because the horse has weak tendons that need support. Others argue that this regular support to the leg prevents it hardening up to withstand the strain. Bandages need to be put on very carefully, because if they are too tight they can cause damage and if too loose they will slip. They should be applied over a layer of tissue or gamgee and should be neither so high nor so low as to interfere with the action of the joints. They should be applied firmly in the manner shown (see diagram). The tapes should be knotted in a bow at the side of the leg; not at the front or at the back, where they might interfere with the bone or the tendon. Ends of tapes should be tucked in.

If the exercise includes jumping, all but small ponies should wear over-reach boots, which are worn just above the hoof. Some varieties of these boots can be buckled into position, but many have no buckles and have to be pulled on. It is best to start by turning them inside out. The foot is then picked up and rested on the attendant's knees while the over-reach boot is held by the broader rim and pulled over the hoof. When the narrower rim is over the hoof, the boot can be turned the right way out, to hang in the correct place.

After all the necessary clothing protecting the legs is in position, the saddle and martingales, and finally the bridle, can be put on (see Chapter 9).

The horse is then ready, but in stables where turnout is considered important, hoof oil is put on the feet to add a finishing touch, to his appearance.

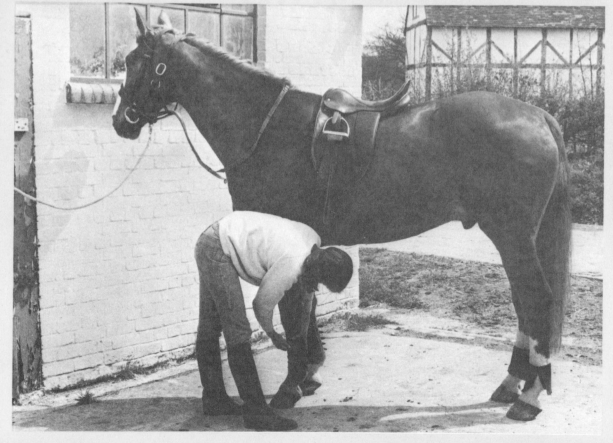

Above: After exercise, when the horse has been inspected for injury and his feet picked out, the blanket (rug) can be turned inside out and folded back. This allows more air to get to the horse and cool him off.

Left: Almost ready for exercise. The horse is tacked up, the Yorkshire boots are in place on the hind legs and the girl is just buckling up the brushing boots, with the straps pointing towards the hind legs.

Care after exercise

Ideally the horse's exercise should end with a walk so that he returns to the stable cool and relaxed. The bridle can then be taken off, and the horse can be tied up before the saddle and leg clothing are removed. The animal should then be inspected for any injuries and feet picked out to clear them of mud and to ensure that no stones or foreign bodies are lodged in them. The feet may be washed if muddy, but try not to get the heels wet; if this is unavoidable, take care to dry them out, or cracked heels may develop.

Depending on the stable routine, the exercised horse may be strapped immediately or merely have the saddle and bridle sweat marks brushed or sponged off before being rugged up. In the latter case the strapping can be done at a more convenient time. This is more usual, because the horse is so often warm after exercise, and a sticky sweaty coat cannot be groomed properly.

Occasionally the horse cannot be returned to the stable dry and relaxed—for instance, if his coat has been soaked by rain. In this case it is better to trot the animal back to the stable so that he is warm on arrival. Untack the horse as before and rub him down with straw, a stable rubber or an old towel. When he is reasonably dry put a sweat sheet on him or cover his back with a layer of straw. A blanket (night rug) can then be put on top, but it is advisable to turn it inside out so that the lining does not get damp. It is also best to fold it back over the horse's shoulders (see picture) so that the air can get to, and dry, the neck and shoulders. The vital area to keep warm is the back.

There are always occasions, such as during strenuous work, or in a summer heatwave, when the horse gets very hot. Then he will need to be sponged down, preferably with buckets of lukewarm water. Some people advocate bathing him all over, whereas others just sponge the sweaty areas, fearing that too much water will take the grease out of the horse's coat and make him susceptible to chills. These objections are valid, but there is little danger if proper precautions are taken. The horse should not be bathed every day, and should be thoroughly dried before being returned to the stall or box.

The drying process starts (in the case of both a sponge and a washdown) with the sweat scraper. This is run firmly along the coat in the direction of the lay of the hair to squeeze out the water. In order to be effective the edge of the sweat scraper should be relatively sharp, and therefore should not be used on sensitive areas such as the head.

After being scraped the horse may be rubbed down. Ideally a cooler or sweat sheet should then be put on, and the horse led around until dry. On returning to the stable it is a wise precaution to leave the cooler or sweat sheet on, and to put the blanket (night rug) over it, folded back and upside down.

A horse that has been hunted or worked in competitions will need special attention when he returns to his stable. Colic or chills may develop unless this treatment is thorough. Firstly the horse should be given a drink of warm water. Then, if he likes to roll, turn him loose in a thickly bedded stable for a few minutes. Do not leave the horse, however, if he stands still and does not roll, for he must be kept warm.

Tie the horse up and remove sweat and wet mud with a damp sponge. Rug him up with a cooler or sweat sheet or straw under a folded-back rug (blanket) and inspect him for any injuries. If there is dry mud on the legs, brush this off; any that remains can be washed off as long as the legs are dried immediately afterwards. The feet can then be picked out and if necessary washed, but the heels must be dried.

If his coat is not sticky with sweat, the horse can be unrugged for a few minutes and given a quick going-over with the body brush. Finally, he should be given a good warm bran mash and left to rest. Check later to ensure that the horse has eaten up and is warm enough, but has not started to sweat. If he has started to sweat he should be rubbed down and walked around. To find out if he is cold, feel his ears. If they are not warm at the base, remedies are needed. The ears themselves should be rubbed and more blankets should be put on the horse.

Some horse-keepers think they can keep their horse warmer and happier by using stable bandages. These are put on in the manner described in Chapter 9.

Washing down after hard exercise. The horse has been sponged down all over and the girl is using the sweat scraper to remove as much of the water and sweat as possible. It is important after a sponge down and scrape that the horse is rubbed down and led around until he is dry. As an added precaution an anti-sweat rug or cooler should be put on to avoid a possible chill.

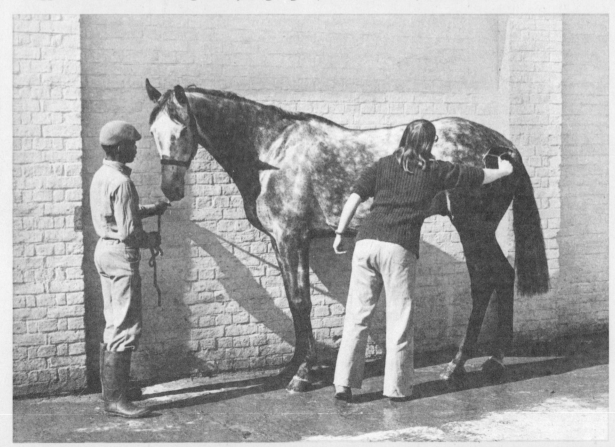

PREPARATION FOR RALLIES SHOWS AND HUNTING

In order to make the most of a rally, competition or hunt, it is vital to plan the preparations. If this is not done, everything may be ruined by arriving too late, getting into a panic or forgetting some vital piece of equipment. But these preparations are fun, for almost everyone enjoys the excitement of anticipating the sport ahead, whether that sport is to be in the hunting field, in the competition arena or with the Pony Club. It is no hardship, therefore, to put aside time on the preceding days to organize a timetable, and to prepare the equipment, the horse and the rider.

The arrangements for transportation
The method of travel should be planned well in advance. If the event is to take place up to ten miles away, it should be possible to hack, and an average fit horse should walk and trot the distance at about 6mph. An animal that is off grass, however, should be kept to the walk as much as possible, which will reduce the average speed by about 2mph.

If the distance is too far to be hacked, those without transport will have to hire a trailer or lorry and driver, hire a trailer that they can tow behind their own car, or persuade friends to collect the horse. Whichever method is decided upon, it must be arranged well ahead of the event.

Those with their own transportation may enjoy the independence, but it does entail more work. The fuel tank, tyre pressures, and condition of the vehicle all need to be checked, in addition to preparing accommodation for the horse. The travelling compartment must be clean, and a haynet hung up to keep the animal happy on the journey. If he is expected to work hard soon after arrival, though, the filled haynet should be put out of reach until the work has been done. The vehicle should then be loaded with all the equipment needed at the rally, show or meet.

Preparation of tack and clothing
Those who travel to many events find it best to list all the necessary equipment and to keep the list in the tack room, where each item can be checked off as it is loaded into the transport. This list will vary according to the type of activity, and those who are hacking to a rally or meet do not need one at all, for nothing is needed other than the tack the horse wears. The only important thing is that the tack is cleaned the day before and inspected to make sure that it is in good order.

For those going by trailer or lorry the list expands to include a fork, shovel and brush to keep the transport clean; a haynet for the journey; a feed if the horse is to be away for a long time; a blanket (day rug) or sheet and bandages, for travelling; a cooler or sweat sheet to place under the rugs to help the horse cool down if he gets hot; a spare halter or headcollar in case one gets broken; water in a container, and a bucket from which to drink it.

If going hunting, and if the journey is not too long, it is probably easiest to transport the horse or pony tacked up, with a rug over the top of the saddle and a tail bandage to prevent any rubbing. If going to a competition, as the animal is usually more valuable and the journey longer, special clothing for travelling may be used to give the best possible protection (see Transportation below). The competition horse will also need additional equipment when he arrives, and most seasoned travellers to competitions have trunks in which to keep it. A full grooming kit will be needed: studs if the going is likely to be slippery; brushing, Yorkshire and over-reach boots, and exercise bandages, as necessary. Then there is the saddlery, which can include a line and cavesson for lungeing to get some of the spirits out of over-fresh or excitable horses. A first-aid box should be part of the kit (see Chapter 10), and when the going is very hard this can include a cooling wash to be applied to the legs after work. A useful luxury is a mackintosh sheet to keep the horse dry in heavy rain.

Preparation of the rider
It is a tradition in the horse world to pay great attention to the turnout of the rider. A handsome effect, it is thought, gives horse and rider a feeling of pride that makes them perform just a little bit better. Although expensive and beautifully fitting clothes can be an advantage, the most valued factor is cleanliness. Gleaming boots, brushed jackets and hats and clean breeches make rack or 'off the peg' equipment look just as good as the custom-made or tailored items, and so, before any event, time must be set aside for polishing boots and washing and brushing clothes.

Clothes are not the only key to smartness; hair is often overlooked. Girls should experiment to find out how their hair can be arranged for the most becoming and tidy effect. The coiffure should be fastened securely, for overhanging branches and hedges can play havoc with any tresses that are precariously arranged.

Men may consider themselves exempt from this aspect of the preparations, but modern trends are changing this. The flowing locks of many young men do not look so attractive when poking out from under a cap or derby (bowler). If the rider is to impress the judges he should consider a short hair style.

The dress for children under about 16 years can be the same for all activities. It consists of:
a riding crop;
jodhpur boots (brown with a tweed jacket, or black with a black or blue jacket);
spurs—but only for lazy ponies with good riders;
jodhpurs, although children sometimes prefer breeches and top boots;
a white shirt;
a tie—if the child is a member, the Pony Club tie may be worn;
a tie pin to keep the tie from blowing around;
a waistcoat or V-necked sweater in cold weather;
a tweed jacket (although a black or blue coat may be used for smart occasions);
a riding cap (or a derby (bowler) for hunting);
gloves.

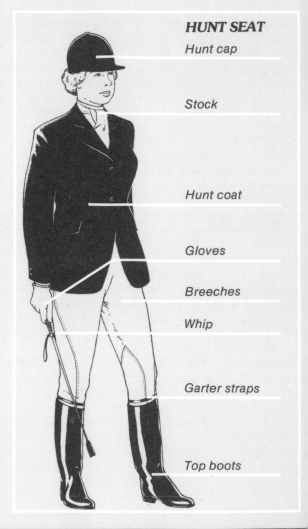

HUNT SEAT

Hunt cap

Stock

Hunt coat

Gloves

Breeches

Whip

Garter straps

Top boots

The riding attire for older riders should vary according to the activity, with well-kept clothes presenting a smart, neat turnout.

Hunting has the strongest traditions with regard to dress, but certain modernizations are becoming acceptable. For instance, although a hunting whip is correct, more and more people carry a crop in the hunting field. Top boots are more normal than jodhpur boots, but modern manufacturers make such good rubber versions (which can be polished) that there is no need to buy expensive leather ones. Spurs should be worn, but a rider with a skittish animal would probably be forgiven for leaving them off. Jodhpurs may be worn, but breeches are more acceptable and are usually cheaper. It is best to buy thick ones; skimpy nylon breeches will not be warm enough. The hunting shirt is made of wool or silk, and is thus warmer than a normal shirt; it has no collar, which makes it easier to wear the hunting tie (stock). The stock can be bought ready tied but it takes only a little study and practice to tie one's own. An ordinary shirt and tie may be worn with a tweed jacket. The coat can be tweed, but it is smarter to wear black or blue. Traditionally, only the hunt servants and farmers had the right to wear hunting caps; followers were supposed to wear a derby (bowler) or top hat: fewer and fewer hunts, however, are enforcing this rule. Gloves are essential for all but the very tough in winter time. When in doubt what to wear, ask the Master or Honorary Secretary's advice.

In competitions the dress was originally based on what was acceptable in the hunting field, but practical variations have crept in. Breeches, coats and shirts are now more lightweight, as competitors do not have to wait about for long periods in the cold and rain. The tie worn with a blue, black or red coat is rarely a stock, simply a white or blue tie. Most types of spurs and crops are accepted and the hat is normally a hunting cap.

In dressage those in the higher echelons (Prix St Georges and above) are expected to wear top hats and tail coats.

In the cross-country phase of eventing the emphasis is on protection, so crash helmets are worn. Coats are replaced by high-necked sweaters or shirts.

Riders competing in Saddle-horse classes wear saddle suits consisting of a long-skirted jacket and bell-bottomed (Kentucky) jodhpurs of the same material and colour, and occasionally a matching vest (waistcoat). Other items are a derby (bowler) or soft hat, shirt and tie, and jodhpur boots. More conservative colours are preferred for evening classes.

Western Division riders must wear a Western-style hat, a long-sleeved shirt, and cowboy boots. The choice of trousers is left to the competitor, although most people wear either slim-cut frontier pants or jeans. Unless the rules provide otherwise, chaps must be worn.

Preparation of the horse

Little can be done to prepare the horse the day before an event other than giving him an extra good grooming, and washing his mane and tail, and even this might have to be done again if they are of a light colour and get stained during the night.

If the horse is normally kept at grass, bring him in the night before if possible. This will help to keep him cleaner and save time in the morning. It is on the day of the show that so much of the work has to be done, and the vital factor is that it starts early enough to avoid panic and rush.

The initial work should consist of the normal stable routine: watering, feeding and mucking out. After this the horse can be groomed, and (if there is time) given as good a strapping as possible. For most events the mane must be braided (plaited) and the tail bandaged.

The final preparations will depend on the intended · programme. Horses for rallies, and hunters, can be saddled up. Competition horses can have their legs bandaged (see Chapter 9), and a blanket (day rug) or sheet put on for travelling.

After all this, it is to be hoped that there will be time to set things right for the return, ensuring that the mash can be prepared easily, that the horse's bed is clean and that water and hay are ready.

The preparations over, it is at last time for the start of the action.

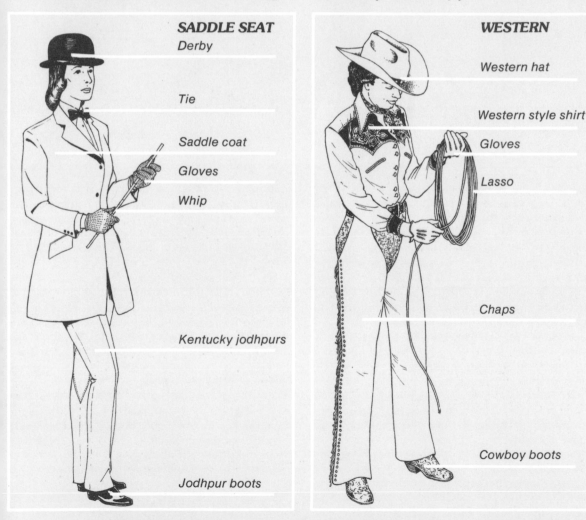

SADDLE SEAT
Derby
Tie
Saddle coat
Gloves
Whip
Kentucky jodhpurs
Jodhpur boots

WESTERN
Western hat
Western style shirt
Gloves
Lasso
Chaps
Cowboy boots

TRANSPORTATION

Barely 150 years ago, the only means of travelling any distance by land was on horseback. Now, ironically, except on long-distance rides, mounted expeditions or pony treks, the last method to be considered for getting a horse from A to B is on his own legs. Today, horses travel by trailer, horse-box, plane, or even occasionally by ship. A few years ago trains could have been added to the list, but in most countries it is becoming less and less popular as a means of transporting horses, and in the UK the rolling stock of British Rail no longer includes a horse-wagon.

The journey
Fortunately, most horses travel well, and appear to suffer no ill effects from a long journey. The interior of a trailer or horse-box is well padded and designed to give the animal support against jolting and swaying when the vehicle is under way. A haynet should be all that is necessary to keep the horse occupied while on the move but, if desired, a light feed may be given in a nosebag.

If the journey is to take several hours, arrangements should be made for occasional stops so that the horse can be watered. He can also be unloaded and walked around to ease any stiffness. The horse will appreciate the chance to graze quietly for 20 minutes or so. If the journey is to last more than about four hours, the diet should be fairly light during the 24 hours before departure, with the oat ration reduced by half.

Clothing
Valuable animals should be equipped with protective clothing. Flannel or wool travelling bandages should always be worn, as should a tail guard or tail bandage to stop the top of the tail being rubbed. On long journeys or for bad travellers, knee caps and hock boots are advisable to protect these highly susceptible joints. On an air journey, when the horse may have to pass under a low beam or doorway, a poll pad is desirable to guard against injury to the top of the head. If no poll pad is available, cotton wool or foam rubber, wrapped round the headpiece of the halter or head-collar and held in place by a stable bandage, will serve instead.

All horses should wear a well-fitting halter. Blankets or rugs are necessary only if the horse is accustomed to wearing one in the stable. On a hot day, a cooler (anti-sweat rug) or a summer sheet is advisable.

Loading
Loading should present no problems as long as the

horse has been carefully loaded and driven in the past. But it is very easy to frighten an animal by not being patient and thoughtful when first getting him accustomed to being loaded, and by driving too fast, especially before he has learned to balance himself with the strange movement. Horses must be driven smoothly and steadily, so that they are not swung off their feet when the vehicle goes around corners, or jolted backwards and forwards by heavy braking and acceleration.

If there is any possibility of a horse being a 'shy loader', or if he is travelling for the first time, the timetable should allow for delays.

The person leading a horse into the transport should walk confidently ahead, and should not look behind and pull. Staring at the horse tends to put him off going forward. Any helpers should be behind the horse.

Apart from thoughtless driving and handling, one of the main reasons for reluctance to load is fear of the ramp, which reverberates when struck by the horse's hoof. Straw may be liberally spread on it to deaden the sound, and a non-slip mat is an

advantage. A reluctant traveller will sometimes enter the trailer or horse-box quiet readily if he can follow a stable companion, or a feed bucket containing a few oats may tempt a greedy one. If all else fails, you may have to resort to ropes attached to the rails of the ramp and crossed behind the horse just above his hocks. Two assistants are needed to hold the loose ends of the ropes, and to tighten them as the horse and his handler approach the ramp. If ropes are not available, the linked arms of the two assistants can be used to push against the horse's rump.

Forms of road transport
Those who do not transport their horses very often may prefer to hire the services of professional transporters. Although this is relatively expensive, there are enormous benefits. The drivers are experienced in loading and driving, and the horse owner avoids the expense and worry of maintaining personal transport.

But as journeys become more frequent, it becomes inconvenient to have to rely on others. Most horse

owners start by buying a trailer. These come in various sizes and can be towed behind any powerful car or jeep, which means that no special lorry license is needed. In the USA these trailers have been developed into a very sophisticated method of horse transportation, but the versions in the UK are more primitive and have disadvantages. They must be driven slowly or the trailer starts to sway, and even the largest is not suitable to carry more than two medium-sized horses.

So, particularly in the UK, horse-boxes are more popular than trailers with people who have to travel their horses for long distances. In them the horses enjoy a smoother ride, but the driver does need to be experienced to manage such a large vehicle. Today most governments require drivers to take special heavy goods vehicle tests before a license is granted to drive vehicles over a specified weight.

Air travel

Though more expensive than sea travel, air travel is becoming a much more usual means of taking horses abroad. Racehorses going abroad to race are carried in freight planes. These are especially chartered by blood-stock agencies, who normally make all arrangements, including the supply of trained grooms to attend the horses on their journey. It is also possible to make private arrangements with air-ferry companies.

Legal formalities when travelling abroad

All over the world there are strict controls regarding the import and export of horses, and this includes temporary visits to a foreign country for races or competitions. Anyone contemplating taking a horse abroad should contact the appropriate government department, and an agent who specializes in the transport of horses, for advice about documents required (ie, import/export license and veterinary certificates).

The major purpose of these restrictions is to prevent the spread of contagious diseases. South Africa is one country that has these precautions. Europeans, fearful that African horse-sickness could be introduced into their territory, have banned the import of horses from South Africa.

Insurance when travelling

Special insurance policies are available to cover animals against transportation risks, either during a specific journey or for a period of time, for instance during the show season. Most professional transporters, however, are covered against the risk of damaging horses that are travelling in their vehicles.

Above left: A horse dressed for travelling, wearing a halter (headcollar), day rug, roller with felt pad attached, knee caps, travelling bandages, hock boots and a tail bandage. If he was travelling by air he would also wear a poll pad to guard against injury to the top of the head.

Above: A horse loading willingly. The assistant is walking confidently by his side, and is not pulling or looking back at him.

Right: A horse unloading. The most important point is to ensure that he comes out steadily and not in a rush when he might stumble or slip.

SHOEING

The blacksmith is a very important person in a horse's life, for a good smith can correct certain faults of conformation, improve the condition of the feet and prevent weaknesses from developing. A bad one can ruin a horse for life.

The choice of blacksmith must, therefore, be made with care. Few places these days have a forge, and more often the blacksmith has to come to the horse, rather than wait for his clients to visit him. Conversely, the necessity of going outside the immediate locality in search of a smith may offer a choice of two or three of them. The best method of selection is to find out which blacksmith visits neighbouring horses and arrange for your own horse to be shod at the same time.

Hot and cold shoeing

The lack of forges has led to an increase in cold shoeing. This is the system whereby a smith measures a horse's feet, and makes a set of shoes at his forge, then fits them cold. At this stage, he cannot make any further adjustment to the shoes; so they are unlikely to be as good a fit as with hot shoeing. In hot shoeing, the shoe is heated on the spot. It is then hammered into shape and placed on the foot for a few seconds to char a brown rim on the hoof. The shoe can then be altered if necessary, and so can the hoof; for an incomplete brown rim indicates that there is some space between the shoe and the hoof. The bearing surface of the hoof should be made level by rasping it before attaching the shoe.

The shoe

The horseshoe has changed little in style since the first iron shoe was nailed by a Celtic horseman to his horse's hoof nearly 2,000 years ago, but it has undergone certain refinements. Most shoes are now fullered (that is, they have a groove on the underside to improve grip with the ground). Most, too, are concave, so that they are narrower on the ground surface than above. This makes the shoe lighter and less likely to be pulled off in sticky ground.

Clips help to keep the shoe in place. These are small triangular extensions of the outer edge of the shoe that fit into the wall of the hoof. It is usual to have one clip on each fore shoe, and two clips on each hind shoe (one on each side). Central clips are rare on hind shoes, for without them there is less risk of the metal causing an over-reach.

Grip is an important requirement of a shoe. A fullered surface helps, and there are other possible modifications. Calks or calkins can be forged on the heels of hind shoes by turning the ends of the shoe downward to provide a small projection. Even more

grip can be obtained with the small mordax studs that the blacksmith can attach to the hind shoes. They are especially beneficial for horses that do a lot of roadwork (for instance, hunters and driving horses). The greatest grip of all is provided, however, by studs larger than the mordax versions. They are too large to leave in permanently, as they would make walking on hard surfaces very awkward. Consequently, the smith prepares screw holes on the outer edge of the hind shoes, and sometimes on the fore shoes too. Studs can then be screwed into the holes as required for such activities as show-jumping.

A horseshoe should be held securely by nails that are hammered through the horny part of the foot until they emerge higher up, when their points are twisted off and the ends, known as clenches, are hammered down. A properly fitting shoe should not interfere in any way with the functions of the various parts of the foot.

The foot

It is important for keepers of horses to have an elementary understanding of the structure of the foot so that they can recognize if the work of the blacksmith is good or bad.

The inner core of the foot consists of three major bones: the lower section of the coronet bone (short pastern); the coffin, or pedal, bone; and, situated between the wings of the pedal bone, the navicular bone. These bones are surrounded by very sensitive fleshy parts that, if pricked or damaged, will make a horse lame. These sensitive parts produce corresponding horny and insensitive structures that form the protective outer casing of the foot.

A blacksmith trying a shoe against the hoof to check that it is the right size.

The wall

This is the horny insensitive structure seen when the foot is on the ground. It is comparable to our finger nails and, like them, is always growing. This growth is downward, originating from the area of the coronary band. Some water is present in the horn, adding flexibility to this casing of the foot, and its evaporation is reduced by a thin layer of hard 'varnish' to the outside.

The wall is divided into three areas: the toe, which is at the front and is the highest section; the quarters, which are at the sides; and the heels, which are at the back where the wall curves inward to form the bars.

The horn of the wall is continuously growing. When the foot is unshod, the horn will wear down with friction, but when shoes are attached, it will start to spread after a few weeks and can eventually overlap the shoe, break away from the nail holes and possibly make the horse lame. The shoes must therefore be removed at regular intervals and the hoof pared into shape.

The sole

This protects the foot from injury from below. Although horny and insensitive, its outer layer grows from the sensitive area of the sole, which covers the under part of the pedal bone. The outer layer is thin; it can very easily be pierced or damaged and the sensitive area made vulnerable.

The healthy sole is slightly concave to the ground. Dividing it and the wall is a white line, visible from below, which is a layer of soft horn. Its position is important, for it indicates to the smith the thickness of the wall and consequently how much room there is for the nails, which must never penetrate the sole.

The frog

It is visible from below as a triangular area of horn at a lower level than the sole. The sensitive or fleshy

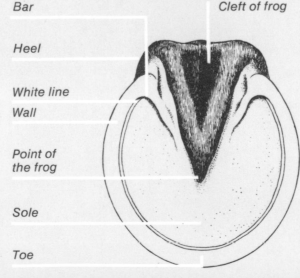

Bar

Heel

White line

Wall

Point of the frog

Sole

Toe

Cleft of frog

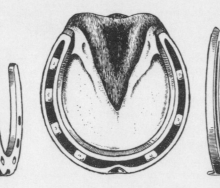

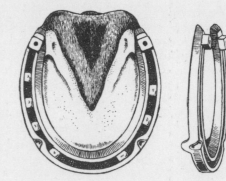

A half shoe of a fore foot.   *A fullered fore shoe with toe clip*   *A fore shoe with a feathered edge*   *A hind shoe with studs.*

frog is above it, inside the hoof, and like the sensitive sole, produces the horn of its insensitive area. The sections of the frog are made of relatively elastic material, providing the foot with both a shock absorber and a non-slip device. The heel meets the ground before the toe, so that it is this area that bears the brunt of the shock. For the frog to carry out this vital function it must be in contact with the ground. The smith, therefore, must never pare it back, but only remove any ragged ends. It is important, though, that the frog, like the sole, does not get any sharp objects lodged in it. It should therefore be picked out regularly with a hoof pick.

Reasons for shoeing
People sometimes wonder whether shoeing is strictly necessary, because a horse in the wild wears no shoes at all. As with additional feeding, the answer to this depends on the sort of work the animal has to do.

Plenty of work, part of it on solid surfaces such as roads, will wear the hoof down faster than it grows and lead to friction, soreness and finally lameness, as the softer parts of the foot have to take the weight. Another factor is climate; in the temperate zones of the Northern Hemisphere, the hard part of the foot tends to be comparatively soft. In Mediterranean countries, the Arab has traditionally gone unshod for centuries; but atmosphere is drier there and hooves harder, so that the hoof wears more slowly and evenly.

Shoeing is not necessary on hardy animals doing light work on grass or in sandy areas, provided their feet are in good shape and regularly inspected and trimmed by the smith. If their hooves are brittle, however, with a tendency to crack or split, shoeing is essential and may be the only means of preventing lameness. For example, a horse with severe sandcrack (in which a crack in the hoof extends upward into the coronary and downward towards the bottom of the hoof) may be helped by the trimming of the foot and the use of a special corrective shoe to prevent pressure on the wall.

Checks to be made on a newly shod foot
1. The type of shoe should be suitable for the work required of the horse, and the weight of iron proportional to the size of the animal. Normally a horse's set weighs in the region of 2kg (4-5lb), whereas a pony of about 12hh needs a set weighing just over 1kg (2½lb).

2. The shoe should be made to fit the foot, not the foot made to fit the shoe (so not too much rasping and severe paring back of the hoof).

3. The length of the foot should have been reduced evenly at toe and heel.

4. The frog should be in contact with the ground.

5. An adequate number of nails should have been used, but not too many. The usual number is three on the inside and four on the outside.

6. The clenches should be neat, in line and the right distance up the wall.

7. There should be no space between shoe and foot.

8. The heels of the shoe should be neither too long nor too short.

9. The clip should fit well on each shoe.

Special types of shoe
Horses with conformation faults (such as a tendency to brush and injure the opposite leg) can be fitted with feather-edged shoes. The inner side of such a shoe is very much thinner than that of a normal shoe, so that it fits close in under the inside wall. Nails are used only around the toe and outer arm of the shoe.

Hunters out at pasture during the summer usually have their shoes removed and replaced by toe-clips. These small, half-size shoes, fitted only to the toe, prevent the hoof from cracking and encourage the frog to come into full contact with the ground.

Racehorses use two types of shoes: a light fullered concave shoe of mild steel for training, and a fullered, concave 'plate', usually of aluminium, for racing. A set of racehorse plates weighs only 250-500g (½-1lb) a set.

Great improvements have been made in recent years to the materials used for hoof pads. Various forms and shapes of plastics have been developed which, when placed between the shoe and the hoof, help to reduce jar. They are being used more and more for horses with foot or tendon problems and for horses that are required to jump on hard ground or to do much road work.

Indications that re-shoeing is necessary
1. Loose shoe

2. 'Cast' shoe (one that has been lost)

3. Shoe wearing thin

4. Clenches rising and standing out from the wall

5. Long foot and/or one that has lost its shape.

Depending on the amount of work a horse does, re-shoeing is usually necessary about once a month; either new shoes or 'removes' can be fitted. Removes are old shoes that, if not worn too thin, can be replaced after the foot has been trimmed.

THE HORSE IN LAW AND INSURANCE

Basic law
The law relating to horses is basically simple, although it can be complicated by such factors as the duty of care and contributory negligence. There is a saying that every dog is allowed one bite, which means that, the first time a dog bites anyone, its owner can plead ignorance of the vice. The same applies to horses; the first kick does not constitute breach of the duty to take care on the part of the person in charge of the horse. The second kick does, provided it can be proved that the owner was aware of the previous incident or of the horse's general temperament.

Previous knowledge
There are subtle interpretations to be put on incidents in which previous knowledge is claimed by the injured party. Every horseman knows that a red ribbon tied to a horse's tail indicates that the horse is a kicker—that is to say, a kicker of horses—and injury to any horse it kicked would be the responsibility of its owner. But if, while wearing the red ribbon, it kicked a person or a car, which it had never done before, legal liability would not rest with the owner, although the onus of proving ignorance would fall on him.

Similarly, liability in damages lies with the owner only where a vice, such as kicking or biting, is concerned. Playfulness, at least in law, is not deemed a vice and the owner is not necessarily liable if his horse knocks someone over in play. This is important in relation to a public footpath passing through a field in which horses are kept.

Reason and the law
The law seeks at all times to be reasonable. It would not be reasonable for someone to claim damages if he was bitten by a horse while feeding it with tit-bits over a fence, even if the owner was aware of its tendency to bite. If, however, the land close to the outside of the fence was a public footpath and people passing along the footpath were within reach of the biter, it would be the responsibility of the owner either to see that the horse could not reach the passers-by, or to erect a warning sign that is clearly visible from the footpath.

Straying animals
In the UK the Animals Act of 1971 laid down for the first time that damage caused by straying livestock is the responsibility of the person having possession of the stock. There are a few exceptions, such as straying from a highway that the animal is using lawfully, or from unfenced common land; but, generally speaking, it is up to the owner to see that

fences enclosing his horses are adequate for their purpose.

In the USA the law is similar and the touchstone in torts (the lawyer's word for civil liability) is 'reasonable standard of care'. That is to say, liability occurs when someone's behaviour falls below what a reasonable and prudent person would or should have done under similar circumstances. Consequently, an owner who leaves a paddock gate unlocked, enabling a horse to break out and cause damage, is liable.

Nevertheless, accidents do happen. Gates are left open or unlatched, and animals have an annoying habit of finding weak spots in hedges before the owner does. This seems invariably to happen at dusk; often the first the owner knows about it is a telephone call or visit from a neighbour. Almost always the horse can be retrieved and the gap closed at a cost of nothing more than a few wasted hours. Perhaps once in 100 such incidents, however, horse and owner find themselves in trouble: there may be damage to a person or car, or a loved horse may be killed or injured; and later, litigation may add further worry to a distressing occurrence.

Contributory negligence
If an incident results in an action being brought, there may be grounds for the defendant to claim contributory negligence on the part of the plaintiff. Patting a confirmed biter when asked not to do so might constitute contributory negligence, as would taunting a horse until it became savage. Sounding a car horn right beside a known kicker of cars could also be held in law to have contributed to the resulting damage.

The acceptance of risk
Knowledge and acceptance of the risks involved could absolve the owner from any liability. Injuries from a fall, in circumstances where falls are possible, would not form the basis of a claim—for example, on a racecourse, or hunting, or in a cross-country event. Similarly, a groom who is kicked and injured, after willingly entering the stable of a horse that is known to kick, cannot claim damages from his employer.

Riding schools and public stables
Anyone who runs a riding school or public stable is deemed to owe a higher standard of care (because of the profit motive) than a person who merely lends a horse without compensation. Although posted notices may disclaim liability for accidents, an establishment cannot contract away gross negligence, such as renting a horse known to be difficult to an obviously inexperienced rider, or failing to inform about dangerous conditions along trails where

accidents have previously happened. As a practical matter, insurance will cover most liability, but no school or stable wants to be known as a place where accidents are a frequent occurrence.

A sales contract
In the USA it is becoming more common to use a written sales contract when purchasing a horse. A written agreement is better than a handshake to hold both buyer and seller to all terms and conditions. The method of payment should be spelled out; for

Premiums vary according to the horse's activities, but those that go steeplechasing and eventing have to pay the highest insurance premiums.

These pictures, showing some spectacular falls, make this understandable.

property, an entry on the expenditure side of his balance sheet as necessary as the price of a ton of hay.

A decision is difficult to reach if the horse concerned has a comparatively low market value. Though a family horse's sentimental worth may be high, the premium for insuring it may represent the cost of several weeks of winter forage, a new bridle or a visit to the farrier. For this reason, many animals live out their lives without ever appearing on an insurance company's books.

The size of the premium depends on:
1. The age of the horse (those over 12 years are more expensive to insure).

2. The use of the horse. A low rate is quoted for hacking, gymkhanas, driving and dressage; a slightly higher rate for show-jumping; still more for eventing, point-to-pointing and hunting; and the highest rate of all for steeplechasing.

The type of cover
1. Death from accident.

2. Death from accident, illness or disease.

3. Death from accident, illness or disease, or loss of use of the horse.

A combination policy
It is possible, however, to take out a combination policy, which covers a number of risks connected with horses and riding. These include: death or humane slaughter resulting from accidental injury or illness (foaling [except in the case of mares over 12 years old having their first foal], fire, lightning and travelling are covered); permanent loss of use; veterinary fees and expenses incurred in foaling and protective inoculations; loss by theft or straying. Riders are insured against death or injury, and the personal liability of the policy-holder is covered. Saddles, bridles and other tack are covered against any accidental loss, damage or theft, provided that they are kept in a private house or in locked premises.

The average premium in the UK for such a policy is about six percent of the sum insured—minimum £150—for horses kept for private hacking, showing, gymkhana events, driving, Pony Club events, show-jumping, polo, hunting, hunter trials and one-day events, or five percent if the last five are excluded. Cover is further limited when horses reach 15 years of age, and are more likely to become unsound.

example, one half now, and the balance as soon as a ...et of the buyer's choice has certified that the horse is ...ound and in good health. It is advisable to include ...ny claims made by the seller, as well as the duration ...f any trial period during which the purchaser may ...ssess the suitability of the horse.

nsurance against liability for damages
...he only essential insurance for any horse owner is ...ersonal liability coverage. This protects the policy-...older, or anyone riding or driving the animal with the policy-holder's permission, against legal liability for personal injury to, or damage to the property of, third parties, caused by the insured horse.

The insurance of a horse
The problem of what insurance to take out may be difficult to settle. The owner of a valuable animal does not hesitate: his horse is insured as a matter of course to protect his investment. However much the owner may wince at the premiums, they constitute part of the expected annual cost of maintaining his

THE SADDLE

Good-quality, well-cared-for tack is an essential part of any efficiently run stable. For the sake of safety, appearance, durability and comfort, it is advisable to buy the best leather and metalwork, and to look after it.

The saddle
The framework is known as the 'tree', and was traditionally made of beech wood, but laminated wood or metal is more usual today. A 'spring tree' is used in most modern saddles. This has two pieces of tempered steel running lengthwise along the tree from the front arch to the cantle. This makes the seat more resilient and so more comfortable for the rider, who can feel and follow the horse's movements more closely.

The seat
Built on to the tree, this is usually made of pigskin.

The flaps
These are attached to the seat.

The panels
These are stuffed with wool or shaped felt, and act as a cushion between the tree and the horse. There is a channel (gullet) running through the centre, which ensures that weight is not placed on the horse's spine. The panels may be full (reaching almost to the bottom of the saddle flap) or half (reaching only halfway down).

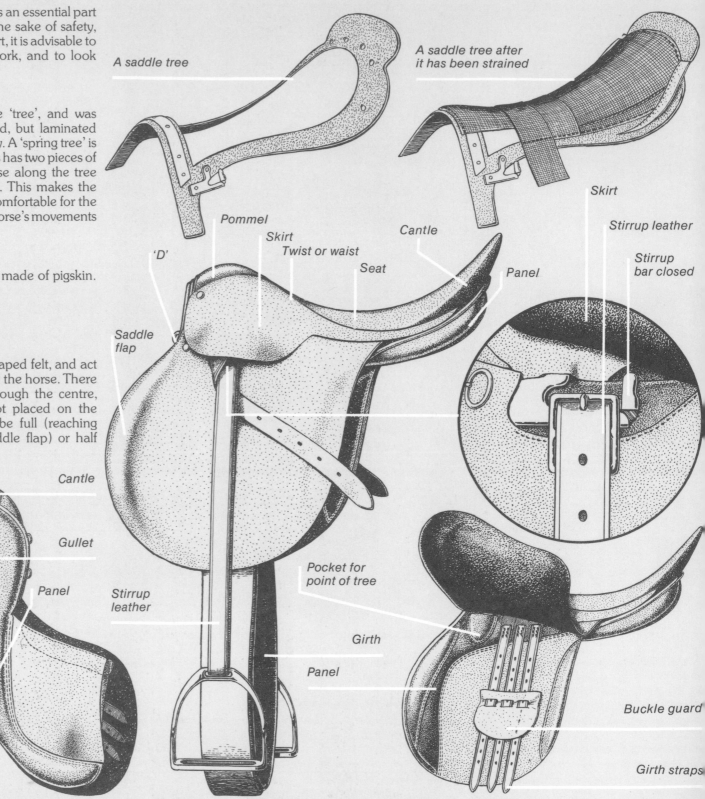

A saddle tree

A saddle tree after it has been strained

Pommel

Skirt

Twist or waist

'D'

Seat

Cantle

Panel

Skirt

Stirrup leather

Stirrup bar closed

Saddle flap

Cantle

Gullet

Lining

Panel

Saddle flap

Stirrup leather

Pocket for point of tree

Girth

Panel

Buckle guard

Girth straps

The types of saddle
Variation in the design of the tree, panels, etc, are made because the best place for the rider's weight is as near as possible to the centre of gravity of the horse. This varies with changes in the posture and speed of the horse: for example, in racing, the horse is extended and the rider's weight needs to be well forward. In dressage, the horse is collected and the weight needs to be further back.

The jumping saddle
This has to bring the rider's weight well forward. To do this the bars for the stirrup irons are placed forward, the panel is extended and forward cut with rolls to support knee and thigh, and the tree is deep (ie, concave).

The all-purpose saddle
This saddle is a modification of the above, with panel and flap less forward cut, thus making it possible to ride with longer stirrups.

The dressage saddle
As the rider has to use very long stirrups and to have a deep seat, the dressage saddle is straighter cut, the roll for lower thigh is on the forward edge of the panel, and the dip in the tree is deep, positioning the rider well back.

The show or saddle seat saddle
This is designed to show the front of the horse to its best advantage. It is therefore excessively straight cut and it fits as closely as possible to the horse's back with normally a half panel used, having little padding and no knee rolls.

The racing saddle
The seat is unimportant because the rider rarely sits. Its outstanding feature is that it is very light, weighing about 0.5-1kg (1-2lb). Light materials are used, such as kangaroo-skin and aluminium, the panels are cut to a minimum and the stirrup bars are usually omitted, leathers passing over side bars of the tree.

The stock saddle
This is used for the Western style of riding and has a high pommel with horn in front for securing a lasso when roping. The cantle is also high. Fenders (like long narrow saddle flaps) on each side protect the rider's legs from sweat. There are leather thongs along the back on which to tie lassos, saddlebags and other gear, and the cinch (girth) is secured by two thongs in cloverleaf knots. The stirrups are wide and made of solid wood.

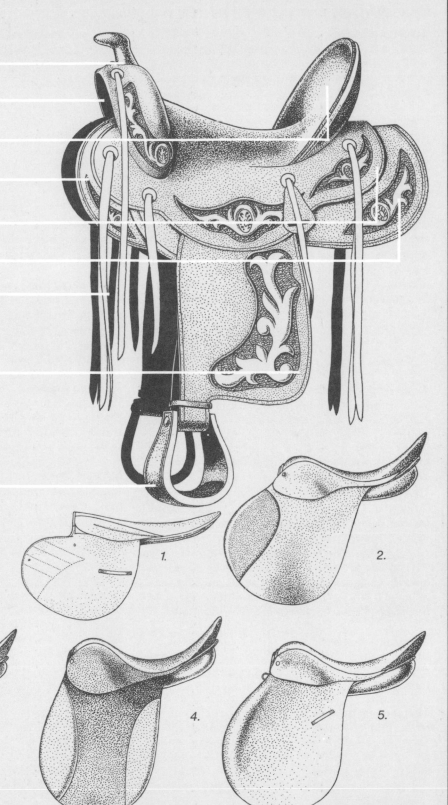

Horn

Gullet

Cantle

Front skirt

Rear housing

Rear skirts

Saddle strings

Fender

Stirrup

1. Racing saddle
2. Jumping saddle
3. Showing saddle
4. Dressage saddle
5. All purpose saddle

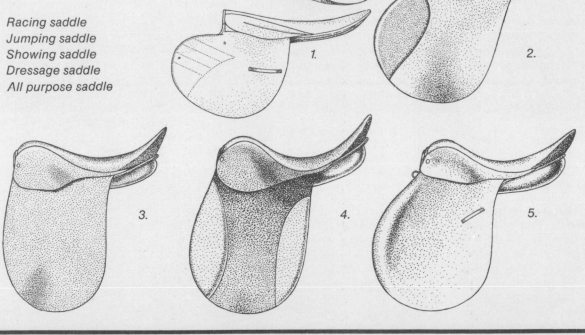

THE SADDLE AND THE BRIDLE

To fit a saddle

An ill-fitting saddle can make both horse and rider sore, and make it difficult for the rider to get into the correct position. It is important to check the saddle carefully, bearing the following points in mind.

The weight must not be concentrated on a particular point but distributed evenly over the back muscles. None must fall on the loin muscles or on the spine. The withers must not be restricted: the front arch of the saddle should be high and wide enough to prevent them from being pinched or pressed upon. The horse's shoulder blades must be able to move freely. Panels must be stuffed so that the rider sits in the correct position. Too much or too little stuffing, or wrong tilting, can result in the rider's seat not being in contact with the horse and/or sliding backwards. It is possible for a tree to break in a fall, or if the saddle itself is dropped. The saddle with a broken tree must not be used, because it would hurt the horse.

To ensure that the saddle fits correctly, it is advisable for the saddler to carry out an annual check-up.

Care of the saddle

When placing the saddle on the ground, rest it on the front arch (not flat), taking care that the leather is not scratched. When carrying, place the front arch in the crook of the elbow. Clean regularly in accordance with general instructions (see below).

Cleaning the lining

Take care to use the appropriate materials. A leather lining should be sponged off, ensuring that water does not run under the lining to dampen the stuffing. Dry with chamois leather, and finally soap. If it is made of linen, sponge or scrub it first, and dry away from direct heat with the saddle standing on its arch. A serge or wool lining should be dried and brushed. Do not scrub it unless it is very dirty.

Washing leather

Make sure that the small black spots of grease found under the flap are removed: a small pad of horse-hair is the best means of doing this.

The pad or numnah

Worn underneath the saddle, the numnah helps to protect the horse's back. It is made in many types of material, the most common being leather, felt, sponge rubber, synthetic fibres and sheepskin.

It is usually held in place by straps attached to the girth straps. Correctly fitted, it should be large enough to project about 2cm(1in) all round the

saddle. Before the girths are tightened, the forward part of the numnah should be pulled up in order not to put pressure on the withers or spine.

Cleaning a numnah depends on the material from which it is made. Leather should be washed with pure soap; felt and sheepskin should be dried and brushed (scrub only when necessary). A synthetic fibre pad may be washed in a machine.

The girth

The girth secures the saddle and there are a number of types.

Web girths

These wear out more quickly than other types and can snap. Always use two.

Leather girths

Excellent as long as they are kept supple and used with caution on soft, unfit horses, when the leather can cause girth galls. They may be shaped, straight, cross-over or three-fold. The last-mentioned should have an oiled flannel inside the fold to keep it soft.

Balding girths

These are narrow in the centre and reduce the chance of rubbing. They allow air to circulate. They are easy to clean with a brush, although an occasional wash is advisable.

Stirrup irons

The best are made of hand-forged stainless steel. Rubber treads are a useful addition as they help to prevent the rider's foot from slipping. Safety irons are used by many children and these have a rubber band on one side of the stirrup, allowing the foot to come free in a fall. (The rubber is worn on the outside.) This iron does have disadvantages, as it does not hang straight and the rubber often breaks.

A well-fitting stirrup iron should leave the rider's foot with 13mm (½in) on either side, between it and the iron. Less space means the foot might be wedged in a fall, and more can cause the entire foot to slip through.

The bridle

The major purpose of the bridle is to hold the bit in the mouth. The snaffle bridle provides attachments for one bit and the double bridle for two bits.

The snaffle bridle

This, the simpler of the two bridles, consists of the following:
the headpiece and throat latch (lash) are in one

1.

2.

3.

1. A bosal bridle

2. A western bridle with a roping bit

3. A cutting horse bit attached to a split ear bridle

4. A double bridle

5. A Hackamore bridle

6. A snaffle bridle with a drop noseband

7. A snaffle bridle

7.

Head piece

Brow band

Cheek piece

Cavesson noseband

Throat latch (lash)

Snaffle bit

Curb bit

Bridoon

Curb chain

Lipstrap

4.

5.

6.

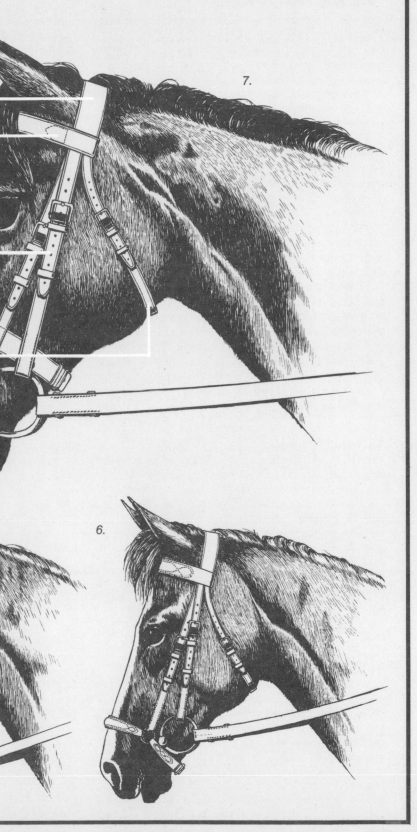

THE BRIDLE AND BIT

piece, with the throat lash preventing the bridle from slipping forwards;

the brow band prevents the bridle from slipping backwards;

the two cheek pieces are attached at one end to the headpiece and at the other to the bit. The noseband is on its own headpiece. There are three basic types of noseband.

The cavesson fastens below the projecting cheek bone and normally serves no purpose other than providing an attachment for the standing martingale. A dropped noseband is fastened under the bit and prevents the horse from evading the bit by opening his mouth. The crossed, or grackle noseband has two crossed straps fastening above and below the bit. The pressure preventing the mouth from opening and the jaws from crossing is higher with the grackle than with the dropped noseband.

The bit is attached to the cheek pieces and the rein by either stitches (neater), studs (convenient for bit changes) or buckles (convenient, but clumsy in appearance).

The reins have a central buckle. They can be plain, plaited or laced leather (the last two are less likely to slip), covered in a rubber grip (which is the best means of preventing slipping), or plaited or plain linen or nylon.

The double bridle
The double bridle has the same constituents as the snaffle bridle, plus the following:

the bridoon headpiece and one cheek piece;

two bits, comprising a bridoon (thin snaffle) and a curb bit (usually called 'the bit');

an additional pair of reins of which both are of plain leather, but one (the bridoon rein) is wider than the curb bit rein;

the curb chain, which is attached to hooks on either side of the curb bit;

and the lip strap, which is attached to the small 'D's on the curb bit and runs through the fly link of the curb chain.

To fit the bridle
The throat lash should be loose enough to allow an adult's fist to be placed between it and the jawbone (if too tight, it restricts the breathing and flexion; if too loose, it will not serve its purpose of preventing the bridle from coming over the horse's head, which could lead to a serious accident.

The brow band prevents the bridle from slipping back to for, but must not be so tight that it touches the ears or pulls on the headpice. The fit of the

noseband varies a great deal according to the type.

A cavesson should lie halfway between the projecting cheek bone and the corners of the mouth. Normally, it should be loose enough to allow two fingers between it and the horse's nose but if done up tightly it can help to prevent the mouth from opening.

A dropped noseband is the normal way of preventing the mouth from opening, but it can be used only with a snaffle bridle and it must be very carefully fitted if it is not to pinch or restrict breathing. The front piece must be well above the nostrils and the back strap should lie in the chin groove, firmly but not tightly fastened.

The bit must be of the right width and attached so that it hangs in the correct position. If it is too narrow or too high, it will wrinkle or pinch the horse's lips. Too wide or low, it will fall on the teeth. In a double bridle, the bridoon should be higher than the curb bit.

The curb chain is attached to the hook on the offside of the bit, twisted until flat and then attached to the nearside. The length should be such that it comes into play when the bit is drawn back to an angle of 45°.

The lip strap is attached to one side of the curb bit, passed through the fly link of the curb chain and buckled to the other side of the curb bit.

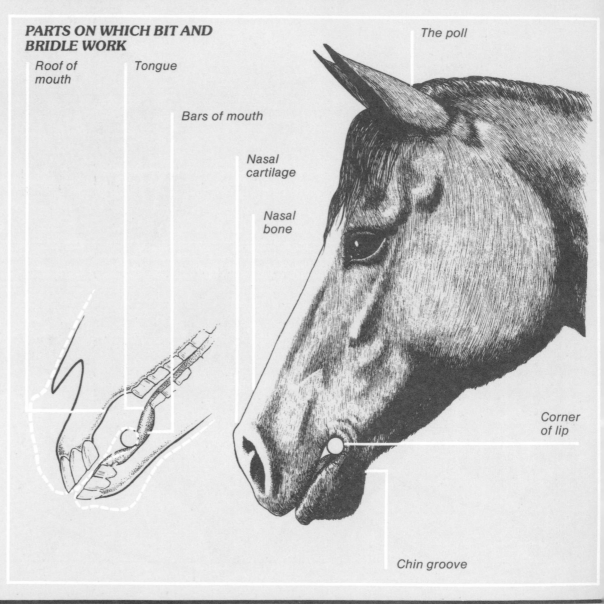

PARTS ON WHICH BIT AND BRIDLE WORK

Roof of mouth

Tongue

Bars of mouth

Nasal cartilage

Nasal bone

The poll

Corner of lip

Chin groove

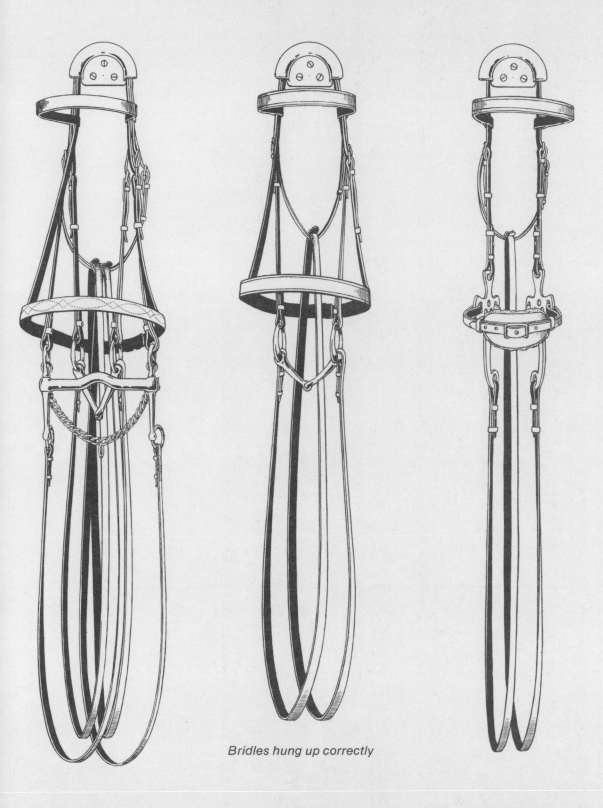

A double bridle   A snaffle bridle   A Hackamore

Bridles hung up correctly

The bit

Bits can be made of various materials. Nickel has a yellow appearance. It is relatively cheap but tends to wear badly, resulting in rough edges, and it may bend or break. Plated steel is stronger than nickel but tends to chip. Hand-forged steel is the strongest but also the most expensive material. Mouthpieces of rubber, rubber-coated metal or vulcanite are comparatively soft, producing a very mild bit.

The purpose of the bit

The bit is used in conjunction with the rider's seat and legs to control the horse. The pressure of the bit on the mouth conveys a message to the horse. With good training, the horse will react by relaxing his jaw and will not resist. He will obey not out of fear or pain but because he has learned to understand and trust his rider. Consequently the key to any horse's mouth does not lie among the numerous types of bits that apply varying degrees of pressure to different parts of the mouth and chin, but in good training, and reliance on a rider with a firm seat and good hands. Mechanical contrivances should be resorted to only if the horse has already been spoilt.

The snaffle

This has a single mouthpiece, which acts upwards against the corners of the lips, particularly when the horse's head is low, on the bars of the lower jaw, particularly when the horse's head is high, and on the tongue. There are many different types and shapes of snaffle.

The half-moon (slightly curved) or straight bar snaffle is a very mild bit, especially if made of rubber, and can be used on young, sensitive horses or those with injured mouths.

The single-jointed snaffle has a joint in the centre of the mouthpiece. This creates a 'nutcracker' action causing more pressure to be applied than with the half-moon. It is the most common type of snaffle and has a number of variations.

The thickness of the mouthpiece alters the severity of the bit. The thinner the mouthpiece, the more severe the bit becomes, because the pressure is more concentrated. The thin version is known as a racing snaffle, and the thick one as a German snaffle. The latter is a gentle bit and most riders use it on their young horses.

The rings can be large, small, fixed to the mouthpiece or loose (traversing rings). The two most common types are the egg-butt snaffle (in which the rings are fixed to the mouthpiece and are straight where attached, so that they are less likely to pinch the lips) and the Fulmer snaffle (which has

TYPES OF BIT

metal cheek pieces to prevent the bit from rubbing the mouth and to ensure the bit is not pulled through from one side to the other). The rings are the loose (traversing) type.

The texture of the mouthpiece also varies. A rough texture helps to prevent the horse or pony from leaning on the bit. The most common variation is the twisted snaffle, in which the mouthpiece is twisted, sharpening the pressure on the horse's mouth. It is a severe bit and should be used only on hard-mouthed horses. Other variations are ridged or square mouthpieces and those with chains and rollers. These are all hard on a mouth and should be used only with caution.

The method of attaching the bit to the leather cheek piece can affect the severity of the bit. The cheek pieces are normally looped on to the rings of the bit, but in the gag-bit they are rounded and pass through holes at the top and bottom of the ring so that the rein is attached directly to the cheek piece. A pull on the rein results in the bit rising against the corners of the horse's mouth. It has a very severe action and the gag-bit should be used only in the last resort.

A double-jointed snaffle has two joints, thus reducing the 'nutcracker' action. Furthermore, the bit will not rest so low and gives the horse more freedom to move its tongue. Sensitive horses and those that put their tongue over the bit are often more relaxed in this snaffle.

The bits of the double bridle

These give a more precise control, and a double bridle, therefore, should not be used until the horse accepts a snaffle bit. To use it before a horse or pony has learned to relax will tend to frighten him, and get him to stiffen against it, so he will obey only because of its severity. The result of this is that he develops resistances in order to try to avoid the action of the bits. The double bridle has two bits.

The bridoon is a snaffle that is usually thinner than the simple snaffle. The curb bit provides additional control and makes possible more refined aids. It acts partly on the tongue, and the pressure is greatest when the mouthpiece is straight. If there is a port in the centre of the curb bit, then there is more there is more room for the tongue to move.

Pressure is also felt on the bars of the mouth (area of gum between the incisor and molar teeth) through the action of the metal cheek piece, which may be fixed (action more direct) or movable; in either case, it has a lever effect.

The third area of pressure is on the curb groove, for as the metal cheek pieces are pulled back, they cause the curb chain to apply pressure on the curb groove. The greater the length of the cheek piece, the greater the leverage and the severity of it and the curb chain.

The fourth area of pressure is on the poll; when the metal cheeks are pulled back, the eye (the ring of the bit to which the leather cheek pieces are attached) goes forward and, as it is connected to the bridle, exerts a downward pressure on the poll.

The Pelham

This aims to combine the effect of a snaffle and a curb bit in one. Two reins are normally used. The bridoon rein is attached to rings level with the mouthpiece, and the curb rein to the bottom of the metal cheek piece, thus obtaining the lever and curb chain effect. The mouthpiece may be vulcanite and straight or half-moon, with a port or even jointed.

A 'Pelham converter' or leather roundings are curved couplings that join the bridoon and curb rings on a Pelham bit, so that only one rein need be used. Having only one rein reduces the variations in

1. *Egg-butt snaffle*
2. *Rubber snaffle*
3. *Double-jointed snaffle*
4. *Gag-bit*
5. *Pelham*
6. *Kimblewick*
7. *Bridoon and Curb bits of a double bridle*
8. *Fulmer snaffle*
9. *German snaffle*
10. *Twisted snaffle*

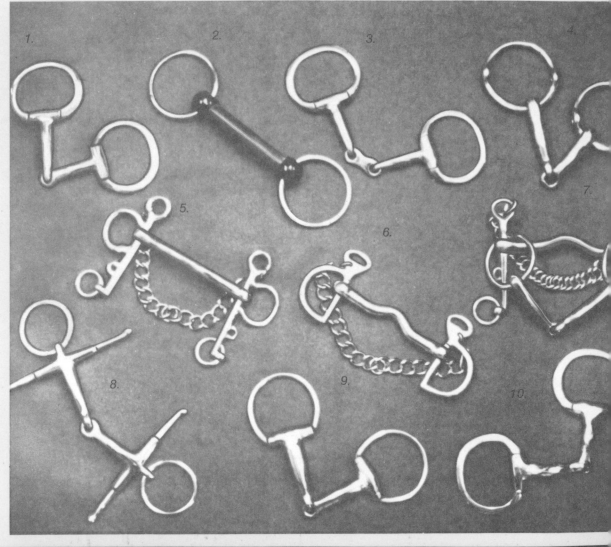

pressure that can be applied, but it is simpler for the rider to handle.

The Kimblewick
Using the same principle of roundings, it consists of a single, large metal 'D' running from the mouthpiece to the bottom of the cheek piece. It is a severe bit, and must be used with caution.

The bitless bridle
This bridle has no mouthpiece; pressure is placed on the nose and chin. The hackamore is the best-known type; it has two long metal cheeks that are curved so that their leather attachments act across the nose and behind the chin when the rider pulls on the reins. The hackamore is sometimes called a bosal.

The principles of bitting
Whenever possible, use the mildest bit. A severe bit can often worry a horse so much that he becomes more excitable and more difficult to control. If the horse resists the bit or is too strong, always consider other possible causes before selecting another bit. These could include bad riding, rough teeth, too much energy-giving food, an injured mouth, a badly fitting bit or bridle, or simply that the horse is too inexperienced to do what is asked.

If none of these applies, the next step is to analyze the form of resistance before making a selection. If the horse or pony is too strong and has the experience and temperament to accept a stronger bit then try one, but with caution and good hands. If the resistance takes the form of crossing his jaw and opening his mouth, a dropped or crossed noseband should be used. If the tongue is brought over the bit, then the bit is acting only on the bars of the mouth and not on the tongue. To prevent this from occurring make sure the bit is high in the mouth, use a dropped or crossed noseband (as the horse needs to open his mouth to get its tongue over) or try a mouthpiece that has a port or is double-jointed (as these give more freedom for the tongue to lie beneath the bit). If all else fails then a device to prevent the tongue from getting over the bit can be used.

The most common forms of resistance are going behind the bit when the head is tucked in, or going above the bit when the head is raised. In the former case a less severe bit is needed, so that the horse will not be frightened to take hold of it. The latter might be due to a lack of training or fear of a severe bit (shown by nervous jerks of the head), and only if the mouth is hard can a curb bit help.

ACCESSORIES

The halter
There are two types of halter, both used to tie up or lead a horse. One is made of hemp or cotton and usually has no throat lash or buckles. The more expensive variety is made of leather or nylon and fitted with buckles and a throat lash. In the USA the term halter still applies, but in the UK this type is known as a headcollar or headstall.

Martingales
These are used to control the position of the horse's head. There are various types.

The standing martingale
Consisting of a strap running from the girth to a cavesson noseband (never to a dropped noseband, as this can restrict breathing), it prevents a horse from throwing his head in the air.

The running martingale
This is a strap that runs from the girth, divides in two and ends in rings running along the reins. The effect of this martingale is thus felt on the bit, and a very short running martingale has a severe lever action the mouth. It should be fitted so that the rings are in line with the withers, thus discouraging the horse from raising his head above this level. The neck strap must not be too tight, as this would rub the animal. Leather or rubber stoppers should be used on the reins to prevent the rings from getting caught on the buckles of the reins.

The Irish martingale
Used to stop the reins from going over the head.

The Chambon
Is a strap which runs from the girth through the bit to rings on an attachment over the poll. It is advisable to use the Chambon only on the lunge. It is harmful if used too tightly and is useful only in the hands of an expert.

The draw rein
This runs from the girth through the rings of the bit to the rider's hands, giving him greater control over the horse's head position. It is frequently used by top show-jumpers but can do much damage in the hands of a rider with limited experience or rough hands.

The breastplate
This is a neck strap with attachments to two 'D's of the saddle and to the girth, which prevents the saddle from slipping back. To fit the breastplate ensure the neck strap is not too tight and that the attachments are not strained.

Below: Draw reins

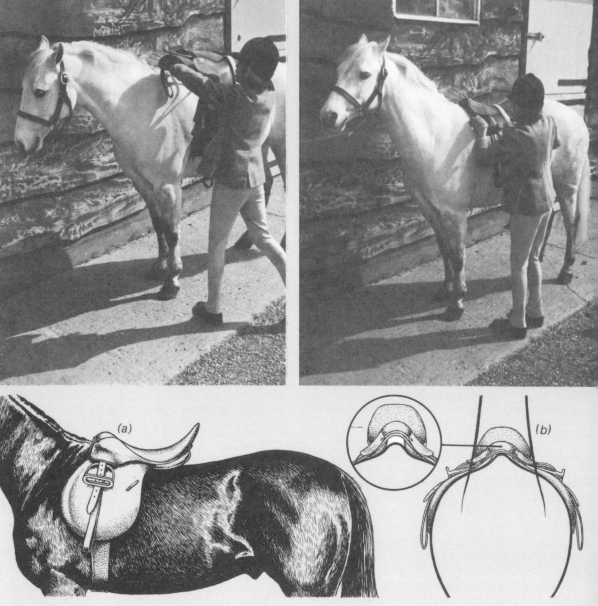

Putting on the saddle and bridle

Tie up the horse on the halter or headcollar before collecting the saddlery from the tack room. The saddle should be carried with the front arch in the crook of the elbow, with the irons run up, the girth attached on the offside lying over the seat and the pad/numnah (if being used) underneath them all. The bridle and martingale can be hung over the shoulder of the same arm (see picture).

The martingale and the saddle are put on first, so the bridle can be hung up nearby. Check that there is no mud or dirt on the horse where the saddle will lie. Put the neck strap of the martingale over the head so that the buckle is on the nearside.

Putting on the saddle

With the left hand on the front arch and the right hand on the cantle, approach the nearside and place the saddle well forward of the withers. Slide it back so that it sits in the deep part of the back. Check to see that the flaps are straight, and if a numnah is used that it too is flat, pulled well up into the arch of the saddle and protruding evenly around the entire rim of the saddle.

Go to the offside, let down the girth and check that it is straight. Return to the nearside, take the girth, put it through the martingale, if using one, and buckle up. Ensure that the girth is not pinching the skin and that there are enough holes left to be able to tighten it later. Where two webbing girths are used the two should overlap, with the underneath one attached to the forward buckles on either side. Make sure it is done up tightly before mounting.

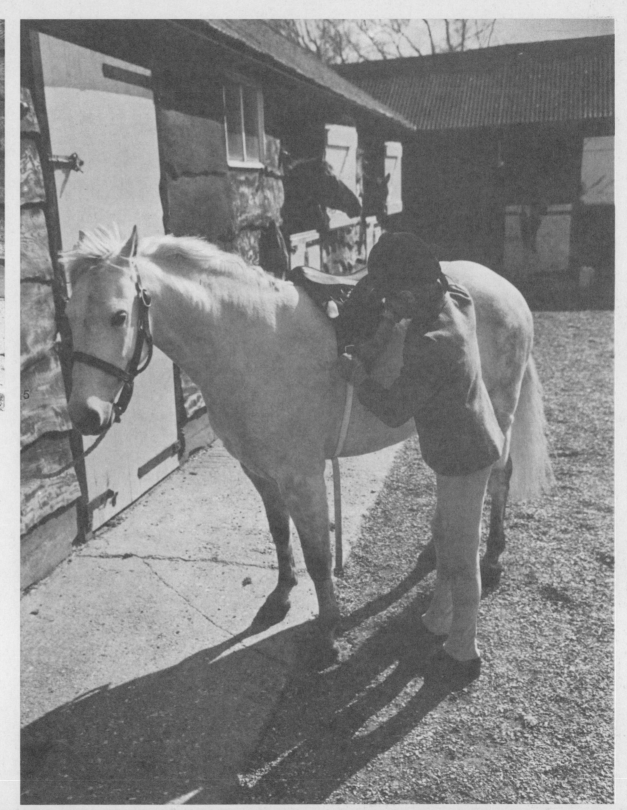

1. The boy is carrying the bridle over his left shoulder so that the arm is free to be used. The saddle is carried on the lower half of the arm and can be on this same arm, or as in the picture.

2. The saddle with the girth over the top and the stirrups run up is put on the pony's neck above the wither.

3. The saddle is then slid back to rest in the lowest part of the back. It is important not to push it forward as this will be against the lie of the hair and could lead to rubbing.

4. The girth is then slipped over and allowed to drop. After making sure it is straight (going around to the other side if necessary) it is done up on the near side.

5. The girth is done up loosely at first. The fingers are then run down between it and the pony to make sure there are no wrinkles that might rub before the girth is done up tightly.

Above left: The saddle is incorrectly placed (a) too far forward and (b) resting on the wither. The inset shows the correct position.

Saddlery
PUTTING ON THE TACK

Putting on the bridle

Untie the horse and put the reins over his head. Still holding the bridle, remove the halter and hang it up. With the right hand take the headpiece of the bridle and let the bit rest against the left hand, which is then positioned under the muzzle. Insert the thumb or first finger where there is a gap between the horse's teeth and gently prise the mouth open. The bridle can then be lifted with the right hand while the left hand guides the bit into the horse's mouth. Use both hands to ease the headpiece over the ears, ensuring that no skin or hair is pinched and that the leather is not twisted.

The buckles can then be done up, starting with the throat lash and followed by the noseband, which must lie inside the cheek pieces. All the keepers have to be checked to ensure that the flaps are held in place. With a curb bit, the curb chain must be fastened, twisting it until straight, followed by the lip strap (if there is one).

Check that the bridle is on straight and that the bit is level (ie, that the buckles on both cheek pieces are in matching holes).

With a running martingale the reins should then be undone and put through its rings. With a standing martingale, the loop should be hooked to the noseband before the latter is buckled up.

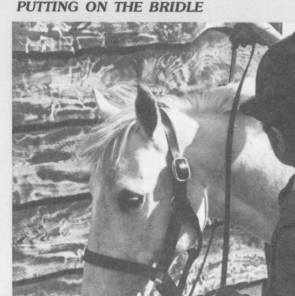

The pony is still tied up by his halter (headcollar) and the first stage is to hold the bridle in the left hand and take the reins over the head.

The halter can be undone and allowed to drop to the ground as soon as the reins are securely around the pony's neck.

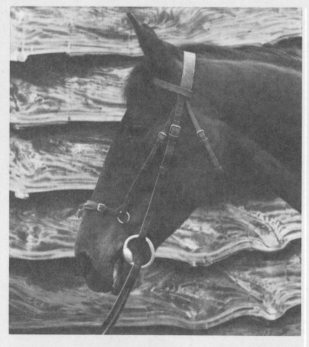

A badly fitting bridle. The bit is far too low in the mouth and the drop noseband has been fastened above the bit and is likely to pinch him.

When the bit goes into the mouth the headpiece of the bridle is lifted over the ears taking care not to pinch them.

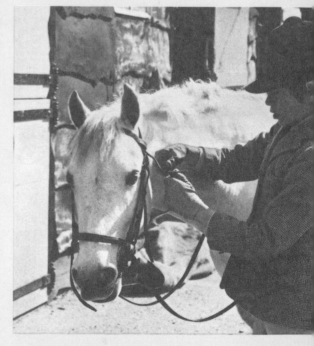

The first buckle to be done up is the throat latch (lash). It should be possible to put a fist between the latch and the pony's jowl.

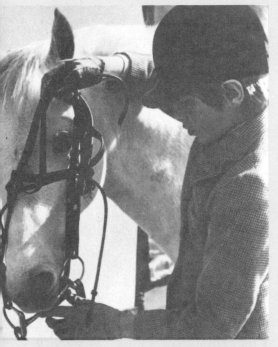

The bit is held between the thumb and first finger of the left hand and the top of the bridle in the right.

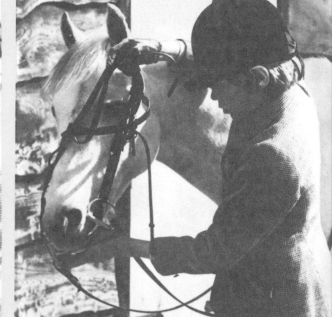

The pony's mouth is opened by pushing the thumb into the area of the mouth where there are no teeth—between the molars and the incisors.

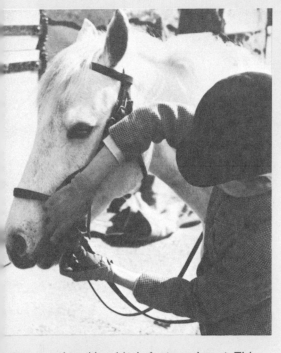

The noseband buckle is fastened next. This pony has a drop noseband which must not restrict breathing by being too low or tight.

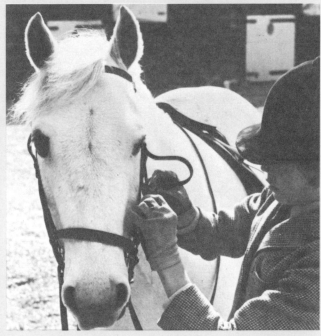

The final stage is to tuck all the straps into their keepers, and in this case the noseband has still got to be straightened.

DRIVING HARNESS

The collar
The collar is a pad that encircles the horse's neck. It can be straight or bent back and is lined with leather, wool or serge, with the outside of brown leather or black patent leather.

It is vital that the collar fits, or the rubbing will cause sores. It should be possible to put the flat of the hand between the top of the collar and the neck; the flat of the fingers at the sides; and the hand and wrist at the bottom.

The breast collar
This serves the same purpose as the collar and is a broad padded strap fitting around the chest and held up by a strap passing over the neck in front of the withers. Although simpler to fit than the collar, it is not considered so smart, nor can such heavy loads be pulled by it.

The hames
These are metal arms that fit around the collar and to which the traces are attached. The hames must fit into the groove of the collar behind the rim. At the top are driving rings, through which the reins pass.

The hame strap
This fastens the hames at the top and bears a great deal of strain so it must be regularly examined to ensure that it has not stretched or weakened.

The pad or saddle
The saddle should be used if the horse or pony has to take any of the weight of the vehicle on its back. The pad is a lighter version of the saddle. Like a riding saddle, neither should bear down upon the back and both should be held securely by the girth.

The crupper
The crupper prevents the pad or saddle from slipping forward. It is a back strap connecting the pad or saddle to a crupper dock, which goes under the tail.

The breeching
This enables the horse or pony to stop the vehicle without the assistance of brakes. It hangs horizontally just above the level of the shafts so that when the horse is pulling down hills the strap goes against the animal's quarters, enabling it to hold the vehicle back.

The traces
These connect the collar to the vehicle and bear the strain of pulling the vehicle. They are usually made of leather.

THE DRIVING HARNESS

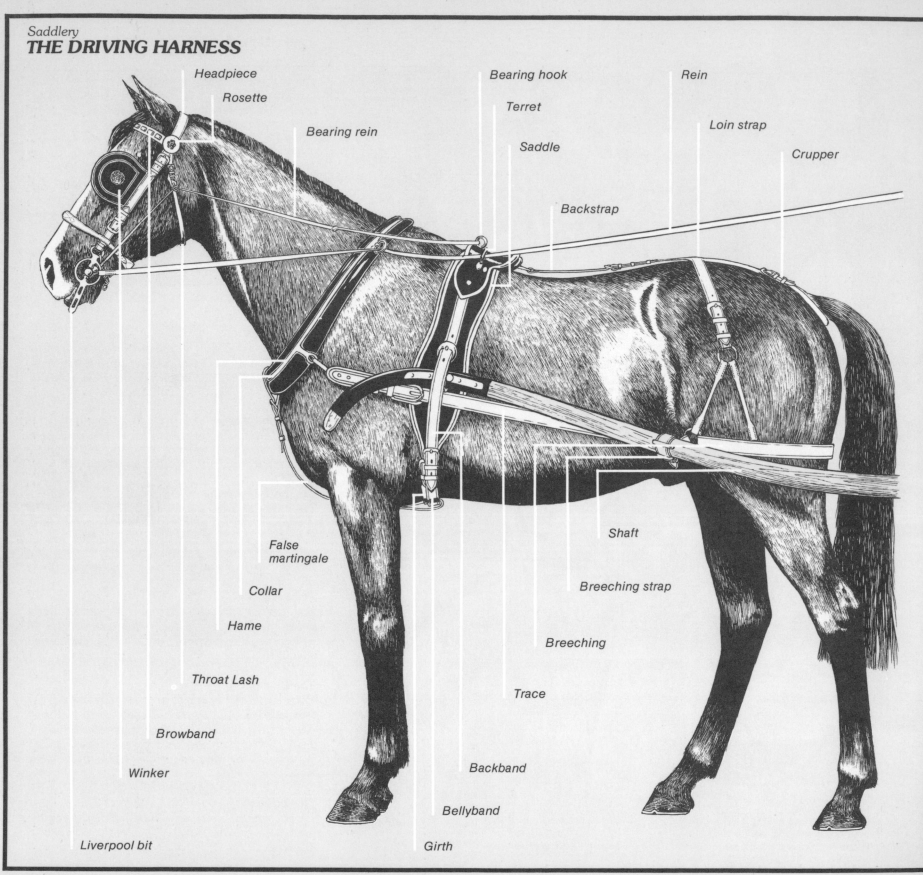

Headpiece

Rosette

Bearing rein

Bearing hook

Terret

Saddle

Rein

Loin strap

Crupper

Backstrap

False martingale

Collar

Hame

Throat Lash

Browband

Winker

Liverpool bit

Girth

Bellyband

Backband

Trace

Breeching

Breeching strap

Shaft

The bridle

There is basically no difference between this and the bridle on a riding horse, but blinkers are usually attached to the cheek pieces. The lower parts of the cheek pieces pass through loops on the inside of the noseband, around the rings of the bit and up to loops on the outside of the noseband, before being buckled.

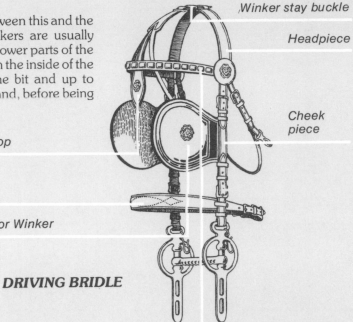

Winker stay buckle

Headpiece

Face drop

Noseband

Blinker or Winker

Browband

DRIVING BRIDLE

Headpiece

Crown loop

Browband

Browband tab

Cheek piece

Bridlehead

Noseband

ARMY BRIDLE

Backstay

Jowl piece

The bits

These are again basically the same as for riding. The snaffle, however, has two rings on either side. One is fixed on the mouthpiece and the other, which floats along the mouthpiece, is used for the attachment of the bridle's cheek pieces. For more severe action the reins are attached to the floating rings but for gentler control they are buckled to the fixed rings.

The most common curb bits are the Liverpool and the Buxton, the severity of each depending on where the reins are attached to the metal cheeks of the bit; if low down there is a strong leverage but if level with the mouthpiece there is none (see diagram).

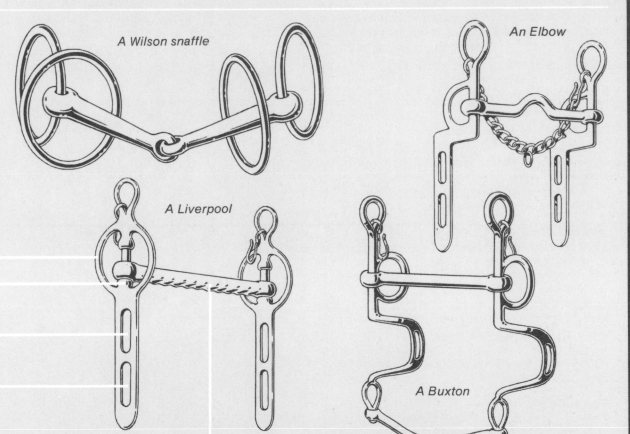

A Wilson snaffle

An Elbow

A Liverpool

Plain cheek

Rough cheek

Middle bar

Bottom bar

A Buxton

Reversible
sliding mouth

CARE OF TACK

Regular inspections are essential, because it is safer and cheaper to replace rotting stitches or repair cracked leather in the early stages of deterioration. Tack should always be hung up or stored carefully so that air can circulate around it and prevent mildew. It must be kept clean and the leather pliant.

Equipment for cleaning tack

In order to clean tack efficiently, the following equipment is needed: a towel for washing; sponge for saddle soap; chamois leather for drying; saddle soap; metal polish and several soft cloths; rubber for drying metal work; dandy brush for removing mud from girths, lining, etc; nail for cleaning out curb hooks, etc; glycerine for covering tack to be stored; a bucket; a hook on which to hang bridles; and a saddle horse.

The Do's of tack cleaning

Hang bridle and leather accessories on tack-cleaning hook, and place the saddle on a saddle horse. Undo all buckles and remove fittings (bit, stirrup leathers, irons, etc). Wash leather and metal with lukewarm water and dry with chamois leather. Apply saddle soap to leather with a sponge, using as little water as possible. If using bar soap, it is best to dampen the soap and not the sponge. Apply metal polish to metal and then thoroughly clean off. On any parts of the tack that need washing (eg, girths, pads) use pure soap, not detergent. When cleaning is finished put all the parts together again.

The Dont's of tack cleaning

Never wash leather with washing soda or hot water, or saturate it with water. Never let it dry too close to a strong heat. Never use linseed, neatsfoot oil or mineral oils; use saddle soap, glycerine, olive oil or castor oil to keep leather soft.

Storing the tack

The bridle should be hung up by placing the rein or reins through the throat lash (see p.175) and the noseband outside cheek pieces. There is no need to buckle, but the end of the strap should be put through the keepers. Put the bridle on a wide bridle rack so that the leather keeps its shape and does not crack. Do not use a nail or coat hook. If there is no special hanger, an empty round saddle soap or coffee can, nailed to the wall, makes a good substitute.

The saddle

Place the saddle on a bracket about 45cm (18in) long attached to the wall. The accessories can be hung beside the saddle.

BOOTS

Brushing boots
These can be made of many types of material (felt, leather, etc). They are worn around the cannon bone and the upper half of the fetlock joint.

Over-reach boots
These are bell-shaped and fit over the hoof to protect the heels of the forelegs.

Knee caps
Horses' knees can be protected when travelling by the use of knee caps. It is also advisable to use them when exercising on hard roads, in case of a fall.

Hock boots
Worn over the hock, they are made of heavy wool and protect the horse when travelling or, in the stable, if he is a kicker.

Yorkshire boots
These are worn to protect the hind fetlocks and/or coronet.

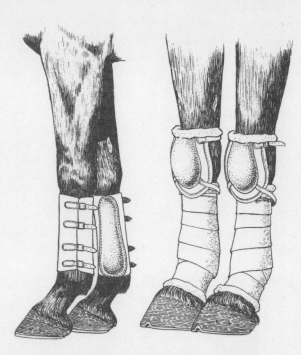

Brushing boots showing leather protection pad on inside leg.

Knee caps with travelling bandages.

Over reach boots

Yorkshire boot tied firmly above fetlock joint

Yorkshire boot fitted

Yorkshire boot

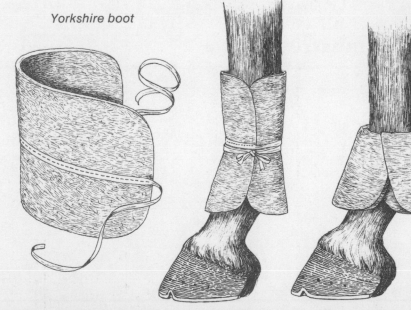

A hock boot

Saddlery
BANDAGES

Exercise bandages
Made of stockinette or crepe, 65-75mm (2½-3in) wide, they are used for support and protection. They cover the legs below the knee or hock and above the fetlock joint.

Stable or travelling bandages
These are made of flannel or wool and are about 10cm × 2.5m (4in × 7-8ft). They are used to keep the horse warm, and for protection when travelling. They should cover as much of the leg as possible, from the knee or hock down to the coronet. They should be firmly, but not too tightly, applied over gamgee or cotton wool. Start at the top and wind it around the leg until the fetlock is covered, then work upward until the starting point is reached.

Tail bandages
Made of stockinette or crepe, 65-75mm (2½-3in) wide, these are used to protect the tail when travelling and/or to improve its appearance by getting the hairs to lie flat. To apply, dampen the tail. Unroll 15cm (6in) of the bandage and hold the end under the tail. Make two turns, to secure the bandage, and then two above, to cover the highest part of the tail; then wind downward around the tail to the end of the tail-bone, where the tapes should be tied. To remove, slide off, grasping bandage at the top of the tail.

To roll up bandages
Tuck tapes in on the side where they are sewn in; then roll up with the sewn side facing inward.

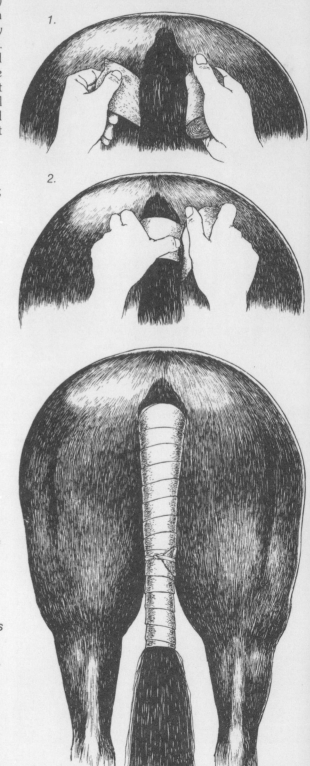

EXERCISE BANDAGE

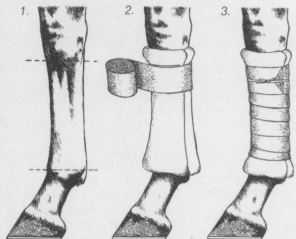

1. The bandage will cover the leg between the knee and the fetlock.
2. The bandage is begun at the top and must be firm.
3. The correct, finished exercise bandage.

Tail Bandage

Right:

1. The bandage is started from the top of the dampened tail.
2. It is important that the bandage be started correctly to ensure it stays firmly in place.
3. The correct bandage finishes at the end of the tail bone.

STABLE OR TRAVELLING BANDAGE

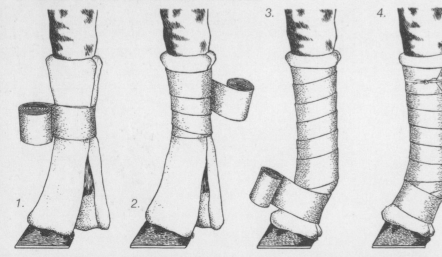

1. The bandage is started about centre of the cannon bone.
2. It is continued up to just below the knee and down again.
3. Coming down the leg the bandage covers the pastern.
4. The bandage is correctly finished off at the top.

BLANKETS AND RUGS

The stable blanket or rug
This is made of heavy jute, hemp or sail canvas and is lined with wool blanketing. It is used in the stable to keep the horse warm.

The day blanket or rug
A wool rug, often decorated with braid, it is used to keep the horse warm when travelling, and on any occasion when he needs to look smart.

The woollen blankets
Worn under rugs to give extra warmth when it is cold. It is not shaped, but oblong or square.

The roller
This is used to keep rugs in place and is made of leather, web or jute, padded on either side where it passes over the backbone so that pressure does not fall on the spine (a pad is often used in addition to give further protection against pressure on the spine). Surcingles, which have no padding, should be used with caution; they often cause sore backs.

The anti-cast roller
Two pads are joined by a metal hoop which prevents the horse from rolling over and getting cast.(for a description of this, see p.156).

The summer sheet
Made of cotton, this is used instead of a rug in hot weather. It provides some warmth and is a protection against flies and dust in the summer months.

The cooler or anti-sweat sheet
The holes in this sheet made of open cotton mesh allow ventilation; it is therefore used for cooling off horses that have sweated. If worn under a rug, it provides a layer of insulation against heat and cold and helps to prevent a horse from 'breaking out' (sweating) after heavy work or other strain.

The New Zealand rug
This is made of waterproof canvas, partly lined with wool, and has special straps to stop it from slipping. It is used to keep horses warm when turned out to grass. For a horse with a full coat, this is unnecessary, but for stabled horses, who may be turned out for a few hours during the day, New Zealand rugs are advisable, in cold weather.

1

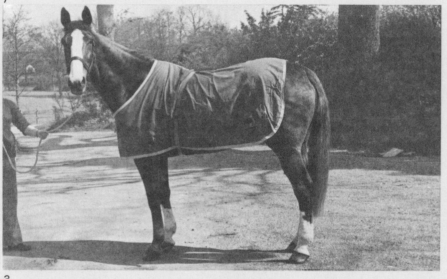

2

3

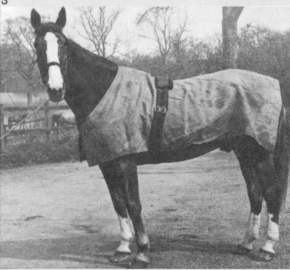

1. A summer sheet used when the weather gets too hot to wear a blanket (rug).

2. A day blanket (rug) Used when the horse needs to look smart.

3. A night blanket (rug) for general use, worn by the horse in his stall (stable).

4. A cooler (anti-sweat rug) used when a horse is likely to sweat, ie after exercise.

4

THE VETERINARY PROFESSION

Horses are remarkably tough creatures. In spite of the hazards they have to face in everyday life—poisonous plants, barbed wire, thoughtless motorists, bad weather and sometimes, regrettably, ignorant owners—the occasions on which they require the attentions of the veterinary profession are usually few and far between. Though the many ailments and injuries that horses can suffer occur only rarely, every horse owner should keep near the telephone the name and number of a reliable vet. A professional is trained to recognize symptoms that a layman can easily miss.

Training
Like a doctor, a vet has to undergo a long training; in the UK the course is within a university and takes five years. In addition to the basic sciences the subject covered are veterinary anatomy, animal management, veterinary hygiene and dietetics, pharmacology, bacteriology, pathology, parasitology, medicine and surgery. Those who succeed in their final examinations are awarded a Bachelor of Veterinary Science degree and Membership of the Royal College of Veterinary Surgeons (MRCVS). In the USA the title is Doctor of Veterinary Medicine (DVM), which university graduates can earn after three years at vet school.

During a vet's training years, there is no special course in equine medicine. Horses are studied as part of the general curriculum and any specialist study must be undertaken as post-graduate work.

Veterinary practice
The qualified vet who wishes to work with horses should choose a veterinary practice specializing in the equine field. The majority of practices in the UK, and an even greater proportion in the USA, have limited dealings with horses as they usually concentrate on either small animals or farm stock. Consequently owners of horses should bear this in mind and take care to call in a vet from a practice experienced in horses. These horse practices tend to mushroom in areas where there is a high concentration of riding schools or racecourse training stables.

Duties of a vet
A very large part of the work entails personal visits to the stables and farms in the area where the vet examines, diagnoses and prescribes treatment for horses. Consequently for a large part the travelling vets save owners the inconvenience of transporting their animals to the clinic or surgery.

This veterinary work in the field involves not only treating illness and lameness but also issuing certificates of soundness. These consist of a full description of the animal, the results of a thorough examination, and the final conclusion as to whether in the opinion of the vet the animal is sound or unsound in wind, eye, heart and limb. If requested, the vet will usually also give his opinion as to the suitability of the horse for the proposed work and its chances of remaining sound in the future. In issuing these certificates the vet plays a major part in the buying and selling of horses, and in their insurance (a company will not insure an animal without such a certificate).

Vets are also trained as surgeons, and in this field there have been great advances due to improvements in anaesthesia that allow a horse to be kept safely unconscious for longer periods. As with doctors, many vets specialize in different aspects of horse treatment. Major operations are usually performed in special operating theatres found at the top veterinary schools, research centres and leading equine practices. Minor operations, though, can still be performed at the patient's stable.

X-rays play a large part in equine diagnosis and, although there are some mobile units that can be brought to the stables, the best results—especially in difficult areas such as the back—are gained from bringing patients to a practice where there is a permanent machine.

Research
Although all too little research has been done into equine medicine—no cure, for example, has yet been discovered for that all too prevalent ailment of navicular—research work is on the increase. In the UK most of such research is carried out at the Equine Research Station at Newmarket. Owned by the Animal Health Trust (a registered charity), the Station was established in 1946, and although much of its research work is carried out on behalf of the bloodstock industry, its findings inevitably help horses everywhere.

The research covers many fields. There is a well-equipped surgical department, and a clinical department to which horses can be admitted at the request of a veterinary surgeon. There is a radiological unit with up-to-date X-ray equipment, and an Ear, Nose and Throat department. In the pathology department, the largest at the Station, are studied a number of conditions from congenital deformities of foals to simple skin diseases. Pasturage for horses and the best methods of maintenance are another vital area of research currently under way.

The Station is supported partly by a grant from the Horserace Betting Levy Board, partly by private subscription, and partly by clinical and laboratory charges on those who directly use the Station's services. It has a staff of about 80, including scientists, laboratory technicians and animal attendants.

In the USA, although some equine research is being done by the Department of Agriculture, most is carried out on a private basis. An important establishment is the University of Pennsylvania's New Bolton Veterinary Center, where many new research projects are being investigated and used to to treat horses.

Professional etiquette
Vets are governed by rules of professional conduct, and owners are most affected by the one forbidding a vet to take over a case from another vet without agreement. If a horse owner is dissatisfied with the treatment his animal is receiving, he should inform the vet that he no longer wishes him to attend the case, ask for him to bring in a 'second opinion', or if it is a serious case request a consultant specialist in the particular field. If an owner fails to follow this procedure, he may find it difficult in the future to get the co-operation of a vet.

This section should help those looking after horses to prevent ill health as far as possible, and to recognize it when it does occur. It is vital, however, to consult a vet whenever there is cause for doubt or anxiety as this is too brief a study to provide a guide to home treatment for any but the least serious problems, that occur from day to day.

Outer splint bone

Cannon bone

Sesamoid bones

Long pastern bone

Short pastern bone

Pedal bone

Sensitive wall

Horny wall

Sensitive sole

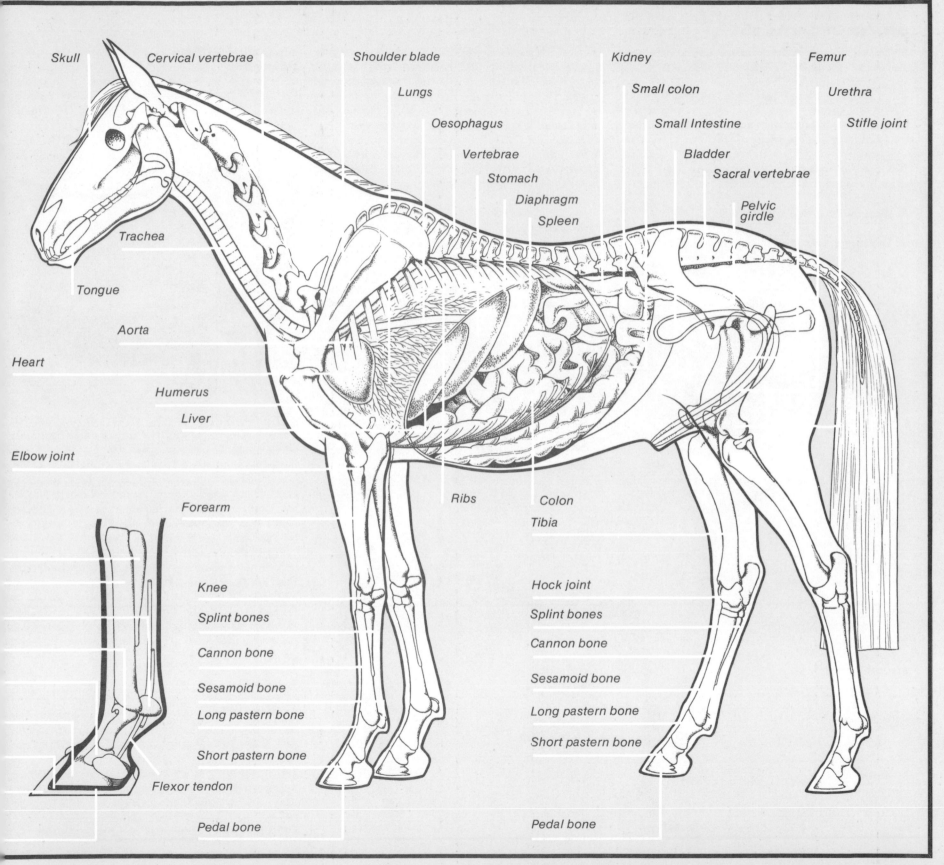

Skull

Cervical vertebrae

Shoulder blade

Kidney

Femur

Lungs

Small colon

Urethra

Oesophagus

Small Intestine

Stifle joint

Vertebrae

Bladder

Stomach

Sacral vertebrae

Diaphragm

Pelvic girdle

Spleen

Trachea

Tongue

Aorta

Heart

Humerus

Liver

Elbow joint

Forearm

Ribs

Colon

Tibia

Knee

Hock joint

Splint bones

Splint bones

Cannon bone

Cannon bone

Sesamoid bone

Sesamoid bone

Long pastern bone

Long pastern bone

Short pastern bone

Short pastern bone

Flexor tendon

Pedal bone

Pedal bone

SIGNS OF ILLNESS

1. Lacks interest in feed, loses weight, becomes 'tucked up' (hind part of abdomen gets smaller).

2. Droppings—no longer round balls that break on hitting the ground; bad smell; shape and/or consistency changes; mucus or parasites visible in them; may not be passed regularly.

3. Coat becomes dull, 'staring' and/or tight. Horse starts sweating.

4. Eyes become dull and unalert.

5. Discharge from eyes and nostrils.

6. Legs become puffy.

7. Temperature above or below the normal 37.8°C (100°-101°F). Temperature should be taken with clinical thermometer that has been lubricated with oil or soap. The tail is raised and the thermometer inserted into the rectum. Thermometer must touch one side and not stay in the middle, where it would measure only the temperature of the faeces.

8. Breathing looks restricted and respiratory rate rises (normal rate is 10-15 a minute; can be counted by watching flank rise and fall).

Any of these signs of illness should lead to a careful examination to ascertain whether a simple explanation (eg, sweats due to hot weather) can be found. If not, and especially if condition is deteriorating, a vet should be called. It is helpful to the vet if careful note of all signs of illness has been taken and an account of the sufferer's recent activities made.

SKIN DISORDERS
Ringworm
Circular patches caused by fungus.
SYMPTOMS Small, round, hairless patches develop, exposing greyish, scaly skin. The horse tends to lose condition.

TREATMENT Paint iodine on to every single patch daily. It is essential that not one is missed and it is often a help to clip the horse. Ringworm is exceptionally contagious, so the victim should be isolated. Tack and grooming kit should be kept separate. Attendant should change clothes before approaching another horse. Any item that comes in contact with the victim should be disinfected. (Humans can be infected by some forms of ringworm.)

A vet should usually be consulted; he can often recommend a more effective form of treatment than the traditional iodine.
PRECAUTIONS This fungus is best prevented by thorough disinfecting of any strange tack, stable/stall or transportation, especially if there is a possibility that a horse with ringworm might have used them.

Lice
Lice-infested skin.
SYMPTOMS Itchiness; small patches, which the horse tries to rub. Careful examination reveals slate-grey lice, up to 1.5mm ($\frac{1}{16}$in) long, or nits (eggs) on the skin.
TREATMENT It is advisable to clip the horse, then apply lice-powder or -wash; repeat every few days. The horse is likely to lose condition, so he must be fed well and given mineral additives.
PREVENTION Cleanliness of horse and stable.

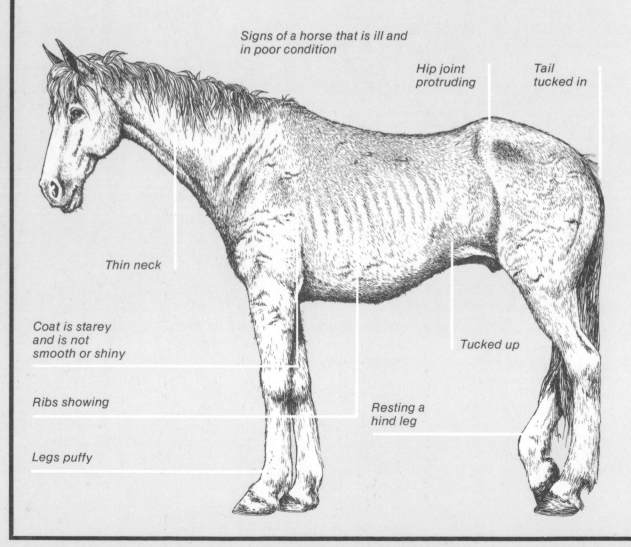

Signs of a horse that is ill and in poor condition

Hip joint protruding

Tail tucked in

Thin neck

Coat is starey and is not smooth or shiny

Ribs showing

Legs puffy

Tucked up

Resting a hind leg

Sweet itch

An irritation of the skin, usually confined to the crest, withers and croup. It tends to occur annually in the late spring and summer.

SYMPTOMS Horse rubs affected areas, eventually removing the hair and exposing a wrinkled inflamed skin.

TREATMENT Sunshine appears to agitate irritation, so keep horse stabled by day. Lotions (zinc and sulphur ointment, sulphur and tar, or calamine) applied to the area usually ease the irritation. The vet can prescribe antihistamines or cortisone.

Nettlerash

Round swellings on the skin's surface.

SYMPTOMS Round, squeezy bumps that do not cause irritation.

TREATMENT Laxative diet. Administration of antihistamine.

PREVENTION Attention to diet; avoid sudden changes in types of food. Too much high-energy food (especially accompanied by too little exercise) and lush spring grass can bring on nettlerash.

Mud fever

An inflammation of the skin occurring on the inside of limbs and/or on the belly.

SYMPTOMS Puffiness and heat in legs. Skin gets rough, scabby and sore. Occasionally horse becomes lame.

TREATMENT Essential to keep legs dry. If they get muddy, dry and brush off; or, if necessary to wash, dry thoroughly with chamois leather or warm, dry cloth.

Apply soothing lotion or cream (zinc ointment, lanolin—or other treatment, prescribed by vet).

PREVENTION Avoid riding in the muds that are known to cause it. After work, ensure legs are thoroughly dry and avoid excessive washing. Horses with white hair on legs tend to be more liable, so special care must be taken with them.

Warbles

Warble-fly maggots hatch from eggs laid on the horse. The maggots get into the horse's system and appear as small lumps under the skin.

SYMPTOMS Small lumps, usually in the saddle region.

TREATMENT Attempts to remove maggot might cause an infection. If left, the maggot bores its way out of the skin, after which iodine or antibiotic powder should be applied to the hole. A saddle should not be placed on top of a bump containing the warble maggot, as it will cause soreness.

Cracked heels

Cracks in the hollow at the back of the pastern.

SYMPTOMS Skin becomes sore, red and scabby.

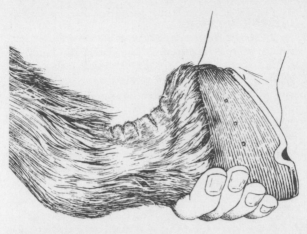

TREATMENT As for mud fever.

PREVENTION As for mud fever. Horses that tend to develop cracked heels can have their heels coated with petroleum jelly or lanolin before work.

RESPIRATORY AILMENTS

Colds

SYMPTOMS Thin nasal discharge, becoming thicker.

TREATMENT Isolate, keep warm, consult a vet who may decide to administer antibiotics if the cold is severe.

PREVENTION As for humans: avoid subjection to extremes of temperature.

Coughs

TREATMENT This varies according to cause of cough. A horse brought up from grass may develop a cough, so try to keep conditions as constant as possible (food, temperature, etc). If a sore throat or laryngitis causes cough, keep horse warm and give small doses of a good cough syrup on tongue and back of teeth, two or three times a day.

If poor condition might be cause of cough, it is wise to test for worms. In all cases, dampen food, put on laxative diet and do not over-exert. Exercise is advisable only if the cough is very mild; even then, no hard work must be undertaken.

Broken wind

Respiratory distress due to the breakdown of air vesicles or vessels (alveolar walls) of the lung.

SYMPTOMS A deep, persistent cough. Expiratory movements of chest are exaggerated and horse's flank can be seen to heave twice during exhalation.

TREATMENT Incurable unless caused by an allergy but effects can be alleviated by avoiding dust and an excess of bulk food. Linseed oil about three times a week is a help; food should be dampened and stable bedding should be of shavings or peat so that horse cannot eat straw or inhale dust.

PREVENTION Do not give dusty food, especially prior to work. Care must be taken with sufferers of a respiratory complaint; asking a horse to work with a cough can lead to broken wind.

Whistling

Caused by rupture of one of the nerves to the larynx resulting in paralysis of the vocal cord. Whistlers make a high-pitched noise when breathing in.

SYMPTOMS Whistling rarely heard until the horse is asked to work. More pronounced at the faster paces.

TREATMENT

TUBING Vet inserts into the windpipe a tube through which the horse can breathe freely.

HOBDAYING An operation to remove the membrane from the pouch behind the vocal cord. In a successful operation, the cord sticks to the wall of the larynx so that there is no obstruction to the progress of wind through the passage.

PREVENTION Can be hereditary; occurs only in larger horses.

Roaring

Due to partial paralysis of the soft palate.

SYMPTOMS Horse makes a deep, rumbling noise during exhalation at exercise.

TREATMENT Difficult to treat. Live firing of the soft palate has been recommended.

PREVENTION Avoid working too soon after an attack of strangles.

High-blowing

An abnormality of the false nostril resulting in noisy exhalation. High-blowing is not an unsoundness and does not restrict breathing.

Influenza

Contagious virus infection

SYMPTOMS These vary according to the strain of the virus; usually temperature rises, horse goes off his food, becomes lethargic and often starts to cough.

TREATMENT Isolation. Warmth, tempting food, and the attention of a vet. Rest; any exertion can lead to pneumonia and permanent damage to the respiratory passages if the cough has not gone.

PREVENTION Immunize with injections, followed by an annual booster. In the case of an outbreak, take the temperature of all horses before work (a rise in temperature is normally the first indication of influenza).

Strangles

A disease affecting the lymph glands, usually only those of horses under six years old are affected.
SYMPTOMS Lethargy, temperature rises as high as 40°C (105°F), nasal discharge, glands under jaw swell and eventually form an abscess, which usually bursts.
TREATMENT As the disease is highly contagious, isolate and disinfect all items that come in contact with the victim. Warmth, laxative diet. The attention of a vet. Convalescence must be taken slowly. The disease lasts about six weeks; this period must be followed by two to three months of very gentle work or some time out in the field.

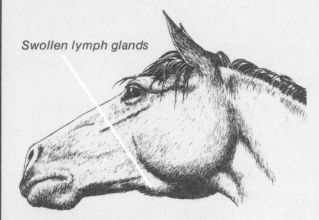

Swollen lymph glands

NON-RESPIRATORY DISEASES
Azoturia

Usually occurs after hard exercise that has been preceded by a period of rest during which the horse remained on full rations.
SYMPTOMS Stiffness of the muscles on the loins and quarters may cause staggering; eventually, horse can collapse. The horse sweats, his breathing speeds up and his temperature rises. If any urine is passed, it is brownish.
TREATMENT If azoturia starts when riding, dismount and allow horse to rest. Arrange for his transportation back to stables so he does not have to walk. Keep warm, massage tight muscles, give plenty of water and feed a laxative diet. Call a vet.
PREVENTION Always reduce diet when horse is to be rested (hence tradition of giving a mash on Saturday night, Sunday being a rest day). Azoturia is likely to recur; diet must, therefore, always be

adjusted according to work, and plenty of exercise should be given daily, by riding or turning out to grass.

Tetanus (lockjaw)

An infection caused by bacteria that live in the soil and penetrate the horse's skin through an open wound. Tetanus is fatal unless treated quickly.
SYMPTOMS Symptoms are never noticed until well after the bacteria have entered through the wound. The horse starts to move stiffly and the third eyelid flickers across the eye. Co-ordination becomes increasingly restricted. Jaws eventually lock.
TREATMENT The vet must be called, to give doses of serum. Stable must be kept darkened and absolutely quiet; diet should be laxative and plenty of water should be available.
PREVENTION Two injections followed by an annual booster, then 3- to 5-yearly boosters, provides immunity from this dreadful disease.

If any horse that has not undergone this permanent immunization is wounded (particularly a puncture wound), or if there is any doubt as to whether such a horse has been immunized, then a vet should be called to give an injection of anti-tetanus serum.

DIGESTIVE PROBLEMS
Sharp teeth

If upper jaw grows down and outward while lower jaw grows up and inward, uneven wear of teeth and formation of sharp edges that cut tongue and cheeks can result.
SYMPTOMS Chewing becomes painful so horse may not masticate food (whole oats seen in droppings) and/or not eat up and so lose condition. Sharp teeth can be felt if mouth is opened, the tongue held and finger run over teeth.
TREATMENT Floating (rasping) teeth by a vet or other specialist.
PREVENTION Regular inspection and floating (rasping) of teeth.

Colic

Abdominal pain; equine 'tummy ache'.
SYMPTOMS
SPASMODIC COLIC pain fluctuates; horse may be free from pain for up to an hour before next attack. When in spasm, horse appears unsettled, paws ground, lies down and gets up, tries to roll, may look at belly and start to sweat. Temperature may rise and breathing become hurried.
FLATULENT COLIC, or wind colic, is due to partial or temporary obstruction in the bowels, leading to a

build-up of gas. Pain tends to be continuous and not so severe. The horse rarely tries to lie down but otherwise symptoms are the same as for spasmodic colic.
TWISTED GUT occurs when the membrane suspending the bowel becomes twisted or when the bowel becomes twisted on itself, so cutting off the blood supply. The pain is much more severe and the temperature rises higher.
TREATMENT As long as the horse is not exhausted, it is best to lead him for quiet walks. He should be kept warm, the stable well bedded and he should be constantly watched to ensure no injury occurs if he should get down and roll. For wind colic, give a laxative: 0.25-0.5l (½-1pt) linseed oil depending on the size. For spasms give a colic drink, which should have been obtained from the vet and kept with the first-aid equipment. If no improvement occurs after an hour, or if pain is severe, call for professional help, and you should stay with the horse until the vet arrives.

WOUNDS AND INJURIES

TREATMENT OF WOUNDS If bleeding does not stop of its own accord, apply a pressure bandage over wound. Call the vet immediately, if stitching is required. Clean wound; clip away surrounding hair if it is in the way. Trickle cold water from a hose pipe over wound, or use salt and water. If the wound is a puncture, leave any probing to the vet. Harsh antiseptics and disinfectants are no longer recommended as they kill healing cells as well as harmful organisms. Dress the wound with antibiotic powder. Protect, if necessary and possible, by applying a bandage lightly over a layer of cotton wool, with lint next to the wound. Give anti-tetanus injection, if not already immunized. Ensure maximum cleanliness of surroundings.

If swelling is excessive, use fomentations.

Antibiotics are advisable for punctures, especially if wound is near joint, tendon sheath or foot.

Constant attention to potential signs of infection: refusing food, extension of swelling, beginning to sweat.

Mouth injuries

Use salt-and-water washes. Avoid use of bit until healed. Change bit, if injury was due to it.

Girth gall

Occurs on soft skin behind the elbow, due to the girth's rubbing. Treat injury with fomentations; when

Constipation

SYMPTOMS Droppings not passed regularly and consistency becomes hard.

TREATMENT Bran mashes, green food, 0.25-0.5l (½ to 1pt) linseed oil or 14-84g (½-3oz) Epsom salts in water or food.

Worms

Intestinal parasites found in all horses; when present in large numbers worms may cause severe problems.

The most common types are:

SMALL STRONGYLES, which rarely cause problems unless another infection impairs the horse's overall health.

LARGE STRONGYLES (red worms), reddish in colour and up to 5cm (2in) long, which spend their adult life in the bowel; earlier in their life cycle, they pass through the abdomen, where they often damage blood vessels. Because they suck blood, they can cause anaemia. These are sometimes called blood worms.

SYMPTOMS Horse loses condition, bowel movement tends to be irregular. Eggs are passed out in the droppings; a fresh dung sample can be examined under the microscope for a worm egg count.

TREATMENT The vet will recommend the most effective remedy.

LARGE ROUNDWORMS (ascarids), white or yellow and up to 7mm (¼in) in diameter and 30cm (12in) in length. They are a problem only with young horses.

TREATMENT The vet can administer dosage through a stomach tube.

WHIP WORMS, thin parasites about 25-45mm (1-1¾in) long that live in the rectum. The female lays eggs around the anal region, where they can be seen as a waxy mass. They cause irritation so horse rubs tail.

TREATMENT Vet will recommend best modern dosage.

PREVENTION Regular doses of a wormer is the best method.

Precautions must be taken against paddocks becoming 'horse sick': ie having grass on which there are many worm larvae. (Worm eggs pass out in droppings, and hatch out; hatched larvae attach themselves to grass stems; horses that eat the grass become infected.)

This state is prevented by: regular worming, which will reduce the production of worm eggs; changing the stock on particular fields on an annual basis (horse worms will not generally infect sheep and cattle, and vice versa); removing droppings from the pasture; reducing overall horse-stocking density; ploughing and re-seeding pasture.

Diarrhoea

SYMPTOMS Droppings loose.

TREATMENT Dry bran, or even kaolin, with food. Feed hay and not fresh grass.

PREVENTION Spring grass is a common cause, and hay should therefore be substituted as soon as possible.

---

healed, use salt and water or methylated spirit to harden. Avoid using saddle for a few days and after this adopt a more comfortable girth (string, or one with a sheepskin covering).

Saddle-soreness

Due to the saddle's rubbing, so do not ride in a saddle until soreness healed. Ensure cause of problem (eg badly fitting saddle) removed. Use a thick numnah with a hole cut out over the sore. Treat as for girth galls.

Broken or cut knees

Usually caused by a fall on to knees. If injury is more than skin deep, call a vet. Otherwise, treat with slow trickle of cold water from a hose pipe. Apply kaolin poultice but do not bandage.

Capped knee

A swelling resulting from a blow to the knee. Treat with rest, massage, pressure bandage and, if swelling persists, a mild blister.

Capped hock

A swelling around the point of the hock, due to a blow or kick.

TREATMENT Prevent aggravation of injury by providing thick bedding and the use of hock boots when travelling. Cold treatment followed by a poultice. If swelling persists, apply a mild blister.

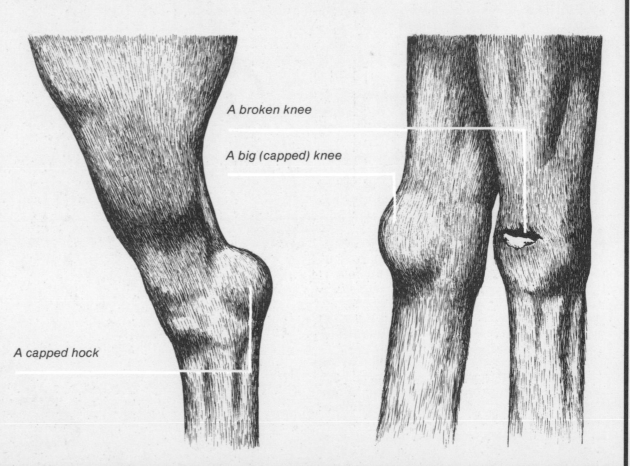

A broken knee

A big (capped) knee

A capped hock

LAMENESS

If lameness renders a horse unfit to work, he must be fed a laxative diet.

Finding the seat or place of the lameness

1. Decide which leg is causing the pain by watching horse being led at the trot (it shows best if trotted downhill).

2. Search with eyes and hands for heat, pain, and swelling. Start with the feet, as they are the most common source of lameness.

3. Call in a vet, if there is danger of infection or any doubt as to reason for lameness.

LAMENESS IN THE FOOT

Pricks and punctures

SYMPTOMS Localized tenderness, heat swelling of pastern.

TREATMENT Remove nail or other cause of puncture/prick. Scrape hole to release pus. Poultice, or submerge foot in bucket of warm salty water for 20 minutes several times a day and clean out hole. After few days, apply liquid antiseptic to a puncture. Rest patient until sound.

PREVENTION Errors when shoeing are a common cause, so care should be taken to choose a blacksmith with a good reputation.

Corns

Bruises to the sole in the heel region.

SYMPTOMS Lameness increases with work. Sensitivity to sharp blows over heels. To confirm, professional must remove shoe and pare horn away, to search for corn (red spot).

TREATMENT Remove shoe. Poultice, if severe. Re-shoe with ¾-length shoes. Rest.

PREVENTION Avoid pressure on seat of corn by: (a) careful shoeing, (b) frequent shoeing, to prevent hooves growing too long.

Founder (laminitis)

'Fever in the feet', due to inflammation of the sensitive tissue lining the inside wall of the foot.

SYMPTOMS Acute pain shown by reluctance to move; flinching observed when sole of affected foot tapped. Horse stands with weight on heels (see diagram). In chronic laminitis, ridges (due to horn being produced irregularly) form on the hoof.

TREATMENT Relieve inflammation and pain. Ask the vet to give an injection of cortisone or antihistamine. Give cold treatment (stand horse in, or hose feet with, cold water). Remove his shoes, get feet cut down and exercise him on soft going.

PREVENTION Avoid feeding too much, especially rich food (barley, wheat, etc), and take care when it is first put out on spring grass. Frequent and regular exercise. Do not go at a fast trot on hard roads. Take special care of horses with flat feet and weak horn. If disease is diagnosed, prompt treatment is essential to prevent a permanent disability due to a change in structure of the foot.

Pedal Ostitis

Bruising of the pedal bone (usually in forelegs).

SYMPTOMS 'Going short' (trotting with short strides). Heat in foot. Lameness, wearing off with exercise. X-ray to confirm.

TREATMENT Turn out to grass where land is soft, for six or more months. Introduction to work should be gradual and start with walking.

PREVENTION Avoid riding horse hard on firm or stony ground.

Bruised sole

SYMPTOMS Sole tender under pressure.

TREATMENT Rest.

PREVENTION Thin-soled horses are especially susceptible; they are less vulnerable if shod with a leather sole or pads.

Canker

A disease of the horn; tissue is secreted in and spreads from the frog.

SYMPTOMS Grey-white discharge; spongy swellings on frog. Pain is not severe.

TREATMENT As for thrush, but canker is more serious. It calls for immediate treatment and the attention of the veterinary surgeon.

PREVENTION As the cause has not been confirmed, there is no specific preventative measure, but cleanliness helps.

Thrush

A disease of the cleft of the foot, in which the glands of the region excrete excessively.

SYMPTOMS Nasty odour from discharge.

TREATMENT With brush, soap and water, clean frog and cleft. If severe, apply poultice; if mild, apply boracic powder, sulphanilamide or Stockholm tar to dried cleft. Shoe so that heels are lowered, bringing frog into contact with the ground. Keep in gentle exercise, unless lameness is severe.

PREVENTION Attention to cleanliness. Feet must be picked out regularly and bedding not allowed to

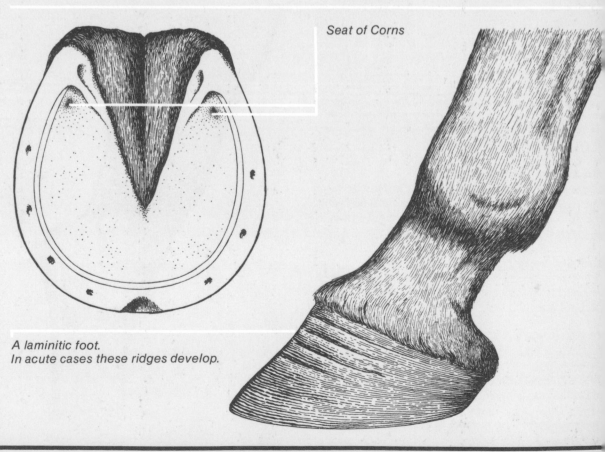

Seat of Corns

A laminitic foot.
In acute cases these ridges develop.

get dirty or damp. Care that horse is shod so that frog touches the ground and is thus able to function.

Navicular disease

The navicular bone changes in shape and texture, making it painful for the flexor tendon to run over the surface. It is suspected that the disease is hereditary and may be introduced by trotting fast on roads.

SYMPTOMS Initially intermittent lameness. Usually points the affected foot in the stable. X-ray needed to confirm diagnosis.

TREATMENT No satisfactory treatment has yet been discovered. With early diagnosis, steps can be taken to relieve the pressure of the tendon's passing over the navicular bone. Shoes with thin rolled toes and thick heels will help in this.

Neurectomy/denerving is the only means of keeping developed cases in work. In this operation, the affected sensory nerves are cut so that the horse will not feel the pain.

Sandcrack

SYMPTOMS The wall of the hoof cracks and splits.

TREATMENT Grooves can be burned into wall with a hot iron, to cross the crack at the top and the bottom. Encourage new horn to grow with applications of a mild blister to coronet band or of cornucrescine to hoof, and good food. Crack can be stopped from opening by professional insertion of a nail across the crack and clenching at both ends.

PREVENTION Weak, brittle feet especially liable. Regular applications of cornucrescine and attention to diet encourage a better growth of horn.

LAMENESS IN A LIMB

Splint

Bony enlargement of splint bones or cannon bone, or between any of these three bones. Usually found on inside of forelegs.

SYMPTOMS Pressure from fingers on area results in the horse's flinching. Splint can usually be seen.

TREATMENT It is usually only during the formation of the splint that pain occurs, unless near the knee joint or by the suspensory ligament. Normally, six weeks is enough time for recovery but if lameness persists, the splint can be blistered or pin-fired. During time of pain, cold treatment, a working

blister or an injection of cortisone can help to speed recovery. The horse should only be walked.

PREVENTION Splints can be caused by blows; brushing boots or bandages worn during work reduce this risk. Excessive work on immature legs should be avoided. NB Splints are rarely thrown by horses over six years old.

Bone spavin

Enlargement of the bone on the lower and inner side of the hock.

SYMPTOMS Lameness usually wears off with exercise. The hock moves stiffly, which usually results in the hind toe being dragged.

TREATMENT A long rest is advisable. Hot fomentations, alternated with cold-water treatment, helps to reduce the initial inflammation. Blistering or pin-firing can be of use; but surgical treatment may be necessary.

PREVENTION Bone spavin is thought to be hereditary, but excessive work or exertion, especially with young horses, may bring it on. Horses with cow, sickle or weak hocks tend to be more vulnerable to spavins because of the abnormal stress.

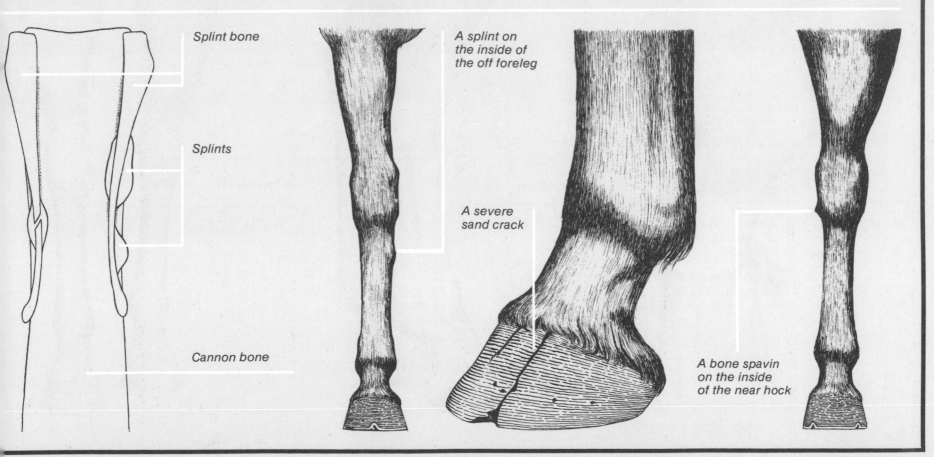

Splint bone

Splints

Cannon bone

A splint on the inside of the off foreleg

A severe sand crack

A bone spavin on the inside of the near hock

LAMENESS

Bog spavin

Fluid distension of the hock joint capsule; shows as a soft swelling on the front inner side of the hock.

SYMPTOMS Bulges can be seen. Heat is rarely present, except in acute cases. Lameness occurs only if swelling interferes with action.

TREATMENT None necessary for horse that is not lame. If needed, cold treatment, astringents and massage help. Rest and pressure bandaging may be necessary. Firing is advisable for bad cases, or injections into the area of the sprain.

PREVENTION Where there are signs of a bog spavin, shoeing with high heels and rolled toes helps to relieve the strain. As in the case of the bone spavin, horses with straight, cow or sickle hocks are more vulnerable and should not be subjected to excessive work or exertion, especially when young.

Thoroughpin

A small swelling situated above and in front of the point of the hock.

SYMPTOMS Rarely leads to lameness, except if caused by recent injury. The swelling can be seen; larger ones go through from one side of the hock to the other.

TREATMENT Thoroughpins are no problem unless very large, when the horse should be rested and blistered, or the vet can give an injection of hydrocortisone. In normal cases, massage helps to get rid of them.

PREVENTION Avoidance of exercise that might put an exceptional strain on the hocks, especially in the case of a young horse or one with weak hocks.

Curb

Enlargement, visible below the point of the hock, due to enlargement of the ligament that attaches the bones of the hock to the cannon bone.

SYMPTOMS The enlargement can be seen when looking at the hock from the side. Lameness is rare.

TREATMENT If causing lameness, inflammation should be removed with kaolin poultice or cold-water treatment, and the horse should be rested.

PREVENTION Excessive strain should not be inflicted on the hocks of young horses, especially those with weak hocks, by too much galloping and jumping. When early signs of a curb appear, the horse should be given a period of rest.

Sprained tendon

SYMPTOMS Heat and swelling always present. In bad cases, there is a bow when leg looked at from the side (in the UK referred to as 'broken down'). As foot problems often cause swelling to rise up the tendon, it is wise to remove shoe and ensure that lameness does not come from the foot, before attempting to treat the tendon.

TREATMENT Rest is most important. If swelling is slight, use cold treatment. If more severe, alternate hot poultice (animalintex, antiphlogistine or kaolin) with cold treatment. It may be advisable to follow this with blistering or firing and a long rest. The re-introduction to work should be graduated, starting

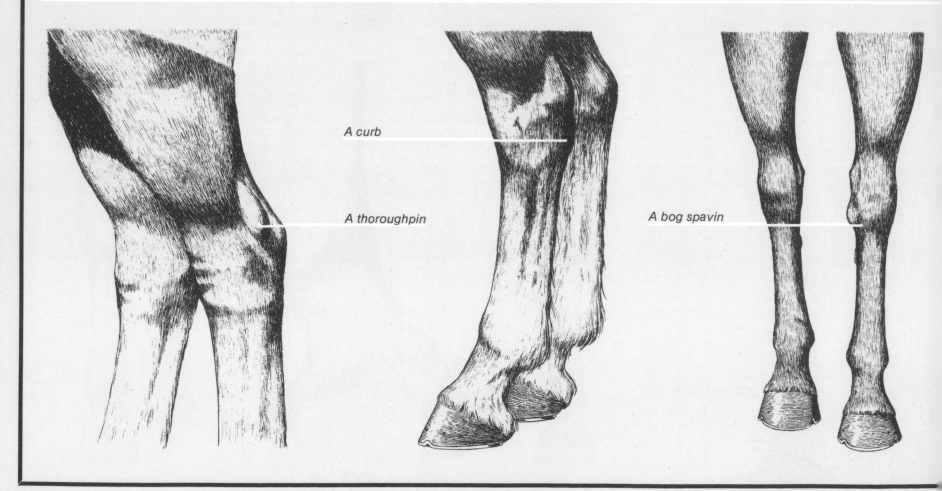

A curb

A thoroughpin

A bog spavin

with long walks on the roads to toughen up the tendons without jarring or straining.

Sprained fetlock joint
SYMPTOMS Heat and swelling around the joint.
TREATMENT Rest. Kaolin poultice, which can also be alternated with cold treatment. As for sprained tendons, the re-introduction to work must be gradual.
PREVENTION Horses with upright joints, which are not so elastic, are more liable to this injury and care must be taken to avoid jarring them on hard ground or twisting their legs in rough going.

Ring-bone
Bony enlargement of the pastern bone. A 'low' ring-bone is in the coronet region, a 'high' above the coronet.
SYMPTOMS Lameness usually occurs only if enlargement interferes with the movement of the pastern joint. Tendency for heat and pain to develop on hard ground. Eventually 'high' ring-bone can be felt but a 'low' ring-bone is more difficult and usually needs an X-ray for accurate detection.
TREATMENT Rest. Cold treatment can be used to reduce inflammation. Cortisone can be injected. If lameness persists, blistering or pin-firing may be necessary.
PREVENTION Care should be taken lest feet grow too long, which would prevent the frog from doing its work of absorbing jar. Horses with upright or very long pasterns are more susceptible; care should be taken not to work them on hard ground. Sharp blows and pulled ligaments will induce a ring-bone, so a clumsy horse should undergo corrective shoeing. It is thought to be hereditary in some cases.

Wind galls
Usually small swellings found above the fetlocks, arising from strain in the fetlock joint itself, which causes excess joint fluid to be secreted.
SYMPTOMS The swelling can be seen and felt.

TREATMENT Can be reduced with cold treatment or by using pressure bandages when at rest. Shoes with wedge heels can help; but, generally, only used if horse is lame.
PREVENTION Avoid strain and over-work, toes growing too long and heels too low.

Side-bone
Ossification of the lateral cartilages of the foot.
SYMPTOMS Can be felt. Lameness unusual, unless foot starts to contract leading to pressure on sensitive areas.
TREATMENT No need for any unless horse starts to go lame; then rest and apply cold treatment. Blacksmith can shoe so as to encourage expansion of hoof. Blistering or firing can be used.
PREVENTION Side-bone is thought to be hereditary; but concussion or a blow may bring it on.

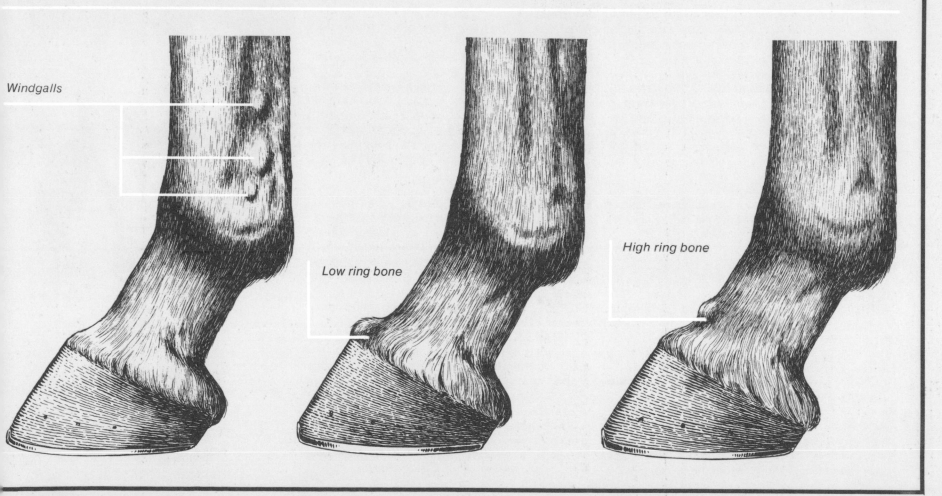

Windgalls

Low ring bone

High ring bone

VICES AND WEAKNESSES

Biting
CAUSES Ticklishness. Bad treatment. The giving of snacks. Playful nibbling not corrected.
REMEDIES **1.** Handle kindly but firmly; reprimand with voice or slap on muzzle. **2.** Take care not to irritate, especially when grooming. **3.** Incurable biters can be tied up for grooming. Muzzles can be worn.

Kicking
CAUSES Boredom as a result of too little work. A spirited nature. Fear, especially in a strange stable or when travelling. Ticklishness. Rats, mice and other animals in the stable.
REMEDIES **1.** Increase exercise to prevent boredom. **2.** Turn out to grass. **3.** Handle kindly but firmly; reprimand with voice and slap when horse raises leg. **4.** Intruding animals should be eliminated. **5.** For incurables, use a box padded with bales of straw or matting or prickly bushes (gorse). In the last resort, attach hobbles to headcollar.

Weaving
When a horse swings head, neck and sometimes forehand from side to side, usually over the stable door, it wastes energy and often loses condition. Weaving is considered an unsoundness.
CAUSES Nervousness. Imitation.
REMEDIES **1.** Exercise and turn out to grass. **2.** Attach by length of string two bricks or tyres to top of door-frame so that swaying horse hits one then the other. **3.** Various grates can be bought that prevent horse from moving when looking over top half of door.

Tearing rugs and bandages
REMEDIES**1.** Treat cause of itch. **2.** Put bad-tasting substance on clothing. **3.** Hang bib below back of headcollar or muzzle.

Eating bed and droppings
CAUSES Boredom. Lack of bulk food. Lack of mineral salts. Worms.
REMEDIES **1.** Remove cause. **2.** Bed on shavings or peat moss. **3.** Sprinkle bed with disinfectant. **4.** Use a muzzle. **5.** Tie horse up before work.

Halter-pulling
CAUSES Fear as tightening over the poll felt when pulling back. Realization that he can escape.
REMEDIES If frightened either **1.** Attach rope to ring of string that will break when he pulls back, or **2.** Stay with tied-up horse to ensure it is not frightened. If wants to get free, **3.** Use unbreakable (nylon) halter (headcollar) and rope and tie up tightly.

Brushing
When two forelegs or two hind legs brush one another, marks or damage to the fetlock joints or coronet may result.
CAUSES Conformation or action. Clenches risen on shoe. Bad shoeing.
REMEDIES **1.** Correct shoeing and/or use feather-edged shoes (inner side of shoe is built up and has no holes). **2.** Use brushing boots and/or Yorkshire boots. Bandages can also be used but they need to be put on by an expert.

Over-reaching
Hind toe/toes hit forelegs, usually on the heel.
CAUSES Horse's action results in forelegs not extending enough, or hind legs too much. Galloping and jumping.
REMEDIES **1.** Treat wound or bruise. **2.** Shoe so that hind hoof is wide, square and even concave in front. Clips must be level with hoof. **3.** Use over-reach boots.

Forging
When toe of the hind shoe strikes underneath surface of the fore shoe.
CAUSES Weak young horse. Bad conformation. Feet too long in toe.
REMEDIES **1.** None necessary for the weak or young horse who will normally just grow out of the habit. **2.** Front shoes can be made concave; hind shoes should be set well back under the wall at toe and be squared off. Hind shoe can have thin heels so that the forward action of the hind hooves is restricted.

Crib-biting and windsucking
Crib-biters or cribbers, by gripping objects with their teeth and gulping in air, can damage teeth, making it difficult to eat. Windsuckers suck in air without gripping anything; but sucking in air to stomach can cause indigestion and colic. Both habits are considered an unsoundness.
CAUSES Lack of exercise and boredom. Imitation. Irritation of stomach. Lack of bulk food.
REMEDIES **1.** Plenty of exercise. **2.** Constant supply of hay, or a salt lick to keep horse entertained in stable. **3.** Removal of projections that can be gripped with teeth. **4.** Muzzle can be worn, except when feeding. **5.** Cribbing strap (available from saddlers) can be used. **6.** Fluted bit with perforated hollow mouthpiece can be worn; prevents air from being sucked in. **7.** Paint woodwork with anti-chew mixture (available at saddlers). NB Keep horse away from others, who may quickly copy habits.

FIRST AID AND GENERAL TREATMENTS

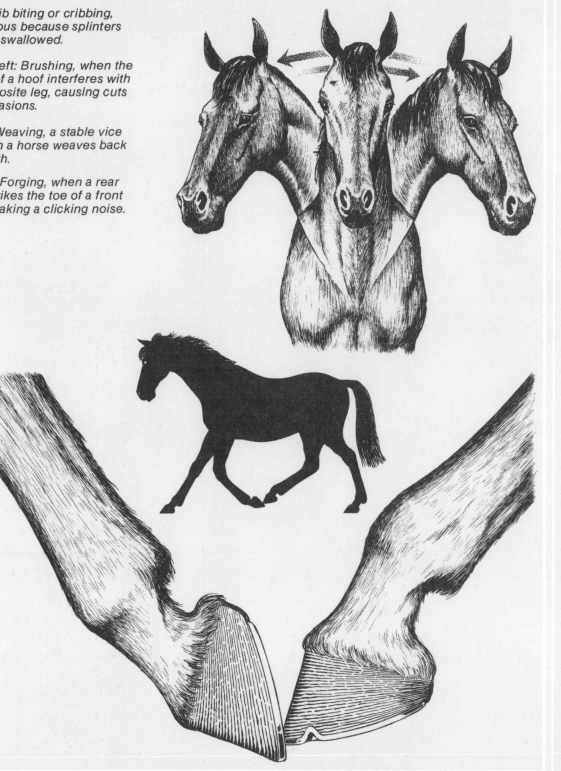

Left: Crib biting or cribbing, dangerous because splinters may be swallowed.

Below left: Brushing, when the inside of a hoof interferes with the opposite leg, causing cuts and abrasions.

Right: Weaving, a stable vice in which a horse weaves back and forth.

Below: Forging, when a rear hoof strikes the toe of a front hoof, making a clicking noise.

FIRST-AID EQUIPMENT

Items	Use
Veterinary clinical thermometer	
Pair of blunt surgical scissors	
Calico bandages five 5cm (2in) and five 7cm (3in)	
Cotton wool (in small rolls)	
25g (1oz) packets of lint	
Roll of gamgee tissue (gauze bandage)	
Cough expectorant	coughs
Colic drink (from vet)	colic
Lanolin or glycerine	sores (eg, cracked heels)
Antibiotic powder	wounds
Iodine	wounds and fungi
Boracic lotion or ointment	eyes
Animalintex or kaolin	poulticing and reducing inflammation
Lead lotion	sore back
Worming powder	worms
Epsom salts	10-60g (½-3oz) in food or water as a laxative
Methylated spirit	girth galls, etc.
Anti-parasitic dressing	ring worm
Cornucrescine	growth of hoof
Dermoline shampoo	skin disorders

Note: Store the above items in a sanitary cupboard, box, or trunk:

General treatments

POULTICING Used for bruises, abscesses, swelling and pain. Animalintex or kaolin can be applied in accordance with maker's instructions.

FOMENTATION Used for relief of pain and swellings. Cut a piece, approximately 60 × 75cm (24×30in) out of towelling or blanket. Fold into four and hold by two corners. Dip into a bucket of warm, salty water (handful of salt to half a bucket of water). Remove, wring and wrap around the injury. Repeat frequently, maintaining temperature by adding hot water to bucket. To test the temperature: before applying to injury, hold back of hand against soaked material and it should be just bearable to keep it there.

COLD TREATMENT Used for relief of pain and swelling, except in cracked heels and mud fever. Hold a hose pipe over affected area and allow a trickle of water to drop on to the injury.

Cotton wool or gamgee soaked in cold water or lead lotion can then be lightly bandaged on to the injury; renew dressing at regular intervals.

BREEDS OF THE WORLD

WESTERN EUROPE	Breed	Usual colour	Average height	Ability and purpose	Features
Austria					
Riding horses	Lipizzaner	Grey or bay	15.1hh	Intelligent and athletic used for High School work, in particular the Spanish Riding School	Originated from Spanish Breeds in seventeenth century. Compact body. Largish head
Ponies	Haflinger	Chestnut Palomino with flaxen mane and tail	13.3hh	Sure footed. Tough and hardy. General riding, transportation, agricultural work	Tyrolese breed produced for mountain work
Belgium					
Work horses	Belgian	Sorrel, dun, roan	16.2hh	Very strong and active. Heavy draught work	Feathered fetlocks, compact
	Belgium Ardennes	Any	15.3hh	Lighter type of work horse. Similar to French namesake	Early origins but recently been crossed with other breeds to increase size. Used as a cavalry horse in seventeenth century
	Brabant	Bay, dun, grey, sorrel	16.2hh	Heavy draught work	Originally known as the Flanders Horse. Thick set, stocky, heavily feathered legs. Convex head
British Isles					
Riding horses	Cleveland Bay	Bay with black points	16hh	Hardy, riding and driving	Short legs, minimum of 9in bone, relatively long back, quarters level
	Hackney	Dark brown, black, bay and chestnut	Horse 14.3hh-15.3hh Pony 14.2hh and under	Lively, harness work	Compact body, tail set high, upright feet
	Welsh Cob	Any except piebald or skewbald	14.3hh	Strong, free, forceful action, great presence and zest. Riding and driving	Strong shoulders, silky feathers on legs
	Thoroughbred	Any whole colour	15.3hh	Fast, athletic. Racing and competition riding	Developed in seventeenth and eighteenth century from imported Oriental stock. Now the most valuable breed in the world
Work horses	Clydesdale	Bay, brown, white on face and legs	16hh-17hh	Lively, active, free elastic action	Long pasterns, long arched neck, great quality, feather on legs
	Shire	Bay and brown. A few are black and grey	16.2hh-17.3hh Can be over 1 ton.	Docile, can be worked at 3 years	Wide chest, white markings, heavy feathers
	Suffolk Punch	Chestnut	16hh About 1 ton	Long life span, economical feeder, stamina	Square body, massive neck, no feathers, except tuft on fetlock
	Irish Draught	Grey, bay, brown chestnut	Mares 15.1hh Stallions 16.2hh	Good jumpers	No feathers, good shoulders
Ponies	Exmoor	Bay, brown or dun with black points, light mealy muzzle, no white	Stallion 12.3hh Mare 12.2hh	Very strong. Riding	Prominent 'toad' eyes, deep wide chest, clean legs. Winter coat thick with no bloom
	Dartmoor	Bay, black or brown	Maximum 12.2hh	Long life. Riding	Head small and fine strong shoulders, back and loins, full mane and tail. Draught work
	New Forest	Any except piebald or skewbald	13.1hh	Riding	Short coupled
	Welsh Section A	Any except piebald or skewbald	Maximum 12hh	Riding	
	Section B	Any except piebald or skewbald	Maximum 13.2hh	Excellent riding pony	Head tapering to muzzle, long neck, sloping shoulder, great quality
	Section C	Any except piebald or skewbald	Maximum 13.2hh	Sturdy, active and strong. Driving	Great substance. Silk feather on legs. Cob type
	Section D	Any except piebald or skewbald	14.2hh	Sturdy, active and strong. Driving and riding	Great substance. Silk feather on legs
	Fell	Black, brown, bay, grey	13.2hh	Strength, stamina. Riding, light draught work	Great substance, minimum of 8" of bone, fine hair on heels and long curly mane and tail
	Dale	Jet black and dark colours.	Up to 14.2hh	Strength, docility. Riding and transportation	Fine hair on heels, shoulders relatively straight, powerful hinds
	Highland a) mainland	Black, brown, varying to dun and grey	14.2hh	Riding and light draught work	Broad, short-coupled, straight, silky feather on legs, much bone
	b) islands	Has dark eel stripe along back	As small as 12.2hh		
	Shetland	Foundation colour black but now found in all colours	10.2hh	Independent and headstrong, so needs firm handling. Riding	Double coat in winter, smooth in summer, short back, deep girth, sloping shoulders
	Connemara	Usually grey, but also black, brown, bay	13hh-14hh	Riding	Compact, short-legged
Denmark					
Riding horses	Danish sports-horse	Any	16hh	General riding and competitions	New breed formed by crossing imported riding horses (Hanoverian etc) with own stock
	Fredericksborg	Chestnut	16hh	Driving	Breed nearly died out and outcrosses made with Oldenburgs and East Friesians
	Knabstrup	Spotted horse	15.3hh	Circus work and driving	Lighter but similar to Fredericksborg
Work horses	Jutland	Black, brown, chestnut	15.3hh	Agricultural work	Compact, short legs with feather

BREEDS OF THE WORLD

WESTERN EUROPE	Breed	Usual colour	Average height	Ability and purpose	Features
Finland					
Riding horses	Finnish Universal	Any	15.2hh	General purpose. Transport, military and trotting	Originally created by crossing foreign breeds and local ponies
Work horses	Finnish Draught	Any	15.2hh	Draught work, forestry	Created by crossing foreign work horses with native stock
France					
Riding horses	Anglo Arab	Any	16hh	Free paces. Racing, jumping, dressage and general riding	Based on crosses between Oriental breeds in South West France and Thoroughbred, or pure Arab and Thoroughbred
	French Trotter	Any	16hh	High action. Used for riding and competitions but main purpose is trotting races	Crosses between British Trotter and Thoroughbred, and Anglo Normans led to production of the breed in the early nineteenth century
	Selle Francais	Any	16hh	Athletic, all forms of equitation	Regional breeds (notably Anglo Norman), all of which were based on crosses between local work mares and purebreds were amalgamated under one stud book—Selle Francais in 1964
Work horses	Ardennes	Roan, iron grey, bay	16hh	Sober temperament. Draught work	Originating from the same mountains as their Belgian namesakes, they have very early origins. Flat rectangular head with short light feathered legs
	Boulonnais	Grey	16.2hh	Draught work	Arab ancestors. Elegant for their size. Clean legs
	Breton	Chestnut, grey, roan	16hh	Adaptive and energetic. Draught work	Compact bodies. Short legs, which are almost clean
	Percheron	Grey, black	16.1hh	Stamina. Active. Draught work	Bred by farmers in Le Perche last century. Now one of the most popular work horses in the world. Relatively small fine head. Well proportioned. Clean legs
Ponies	Basque	Most	13hh	Quick to mature. Used in mines and for riding	Still roams wild in Pyrenees and Atlantic cantons. Origins unknown but thought to be very ancient as it resembles primitive ponies
	Camargue	Grey	14.3hh	Most run wild. Some tamed for herding bulls	Barb origins. Large head
	Landais	Most	13.2hh	Riding and driving	Elegant strong, Arab-like head
Germany					
Riding horses	Bavarian	Any	16hh	Riding and agricultural work	Similar development to that of the Württemburg
	Hanoverian	Any	16.1hh	Very powerful with extravagant action. Riding and driving	Originally a famous carriage horse but crossed with Arab and Thoroughbred to refine. It is the most successful and numerous breed of riding horse in Germany
	Hessian Rheinlander Pfalz	Any	16hh	General riding	Similar types of horses all bred around the Rhine; but each has own stud book
	Holstein	Any	16.1hh	Strong horses. General riding and competitions	Breeding dates from 1300 when used as war horse. Oriental then Cleveland Bay and today the Thoroughbred used to upgrade
	Oldenburg	Brown, bay, black	16.2hh	Driving and riding	This is the heaviest of the German riding horses
	Trakehner	Any	16.1hh	Good action. Competition work and general riding	Refugees in West Germany as were originally bred at stud of Trakehnen in East Prussia, which was founded by Frederick William I of Prussia in 1732. Elegant horses.
	Westphalian	Any	16.1hh	General riding, competitions and driving	Developed largely from Hanoverian strains and is very similar to them
	Württemburg	Brown, bay, chestnut, black	16hh	Riding and agricultural work	The central stud is at Marbach where they have been developed by crossing many German breeds
Work horses	Noriker	Bay, brown, chestnut, spotted	16.1hh	Agricultural work. Transportation especially in mountains	Originally bred in Noricum by Romans. Heavy head on short neck
	Rhineland Heavy Draught	Sorrel, chestnut, roan	16.2hh	Powerful. Heavy draught work	Heavily crested necks. Low to ground. Feathered legs
	Schleswig	Chestnut	15.3hh	Driving and agricultural work	Similar to Jutland Cob type
Holland					
Riding horses	Gelderland	Chestnut, grey	16hh	Active types. General riding and competitions. Driving	Originated by crossing native stock in Gelderland with Trotters, Thoroughbreds and Anglo Normans
Work horses	Dutch Draught	Dun, grey, sorrel	16.1hh	Docile. One of the most massive of the draught horses.	Breed started mid-way through last century
	Friesian	Black	15hh	Very active	This breed is old and was very popular in medieval times. Particularly compact
	Groningen	Black, brown	15.3hh	Docile. Heavyweight saddle horse. Driving	Strong back and stylish action
Norway					
Work horses	Döle Horse	Black, brown	15hh	Riding and agricultural work	Short feathered legs with very thick mane and tail
Ponies	Fjord	Dun with dorsal stripe	14hh	Agricultural work and riding	Resembles horses of Ice Age. Upright mane
	Northland	Brown, bay, black	13hh	Tough and frugal. Riding and draught	After World War I in danger of extinction but now popular again
Portugal					
Riding horses	Alter-Real	Chestnut, bay, piebald	15.1hh	Extravagant action. Energetic. Famous as High School horses	Originated from Andalusians in eighteenth century. Bred in Alentejo Province

BREEDS OF THE WORLD

WESTERN EUROPE	Breed	Usual colour	Average height	Ability and purpose	Features
	Lusitano	Any	15hh	Riding and light agricultural	Fine head with full low-set tail
Ponies	Garrano	Chestnut	11hh	Hardy light build. Pack ponies, trotting races	Arab ancestry
Spain Riding horses	Andalusian	Grey, black	15.3hh	Intelligent. Attractive action made them popular High School horses in Europe	Barb origins. Still has this breed's flat, almost convex head
Sweden Riding horses	Swedish warm-blood	Any	15.3hh	Intelligent. Free paces. General riding. Good competition results	Originated from systematic crossing of native stock with Thoroughbred and German riding horses
Switzerland Riding horses	Einseidler	Any	15.3hh	Used by military, for riding and transportation.	Bred for centuries at Einseidler
	Swiss warm-blood	Any	16hh	Good action and temperament. General riding and competitions	New breed created by crossing imported French, Swedish, German and home bred riding horses, and Thoroughbreds
Work horses	Freiberger	Blue roan, grey	15.3hh	Stamina. Light agricultural work. Transportation.	Compact strong horse
EASTERN EUROPE **Czechoslovakia** Riding horses	Kladruber	Originally black or grey	17hh	Riding, driving and light agricultural work	Originated from Spanish breeds. Typically has a long straight back
Hungary Riding horses	Furioso	Black, brown	16hh	General riding and driving	Originated in nineteenth century from crosses between Thoroughbred Trotters and native mares
	Nonius	Black, brown	Large over 15.3hh. Small under 15.3hh	Reliable, active with long stride. General riding and agricultural work	The Anglo Norman was influential in development of the breed. Has an impressive head with long neck.
Work horses	Murakosi	Chestnut, bay, black	16hh	High quality draught horse	Developed this century from crossing Ardennes, Oriental and local breeds
Poland Riding horses	Malopolski	Any	15.3hh	Lighter than Wielkopolski and used mainly for riding	Originated from crosses between local mares, Arabs and Anglo Arabs
	Wielkopolsi	Any	16hh	Dual purpose horses used for general riding and driving	Breed formed by merging older breeds of Masuren and Poznan
Ponies	Konik	Yellow, grey, blue, dun	13hh	Hardy with great vitality. Valuable work ponies	Konik—meaning small horse is used to cover other types with own names ie Zmudzin, Hucul and Bilgoraj.
	Tarpan	Brown, dun with dorsal stripe	12.1hh		Primitive wild horse of northern Europe that vanished but by selective crossing of Przewalski stallions and Konik mares the breed is said to have been re-established.
USSR More than 40 recognized breeds but following most well known.					
Riding horses	Akhal-Teke	Any but with characteristic golden sheen	15.1hh	Desert horse, able to withstand great heat and lack of water. Racing, competitions and general riding	Elegant, refined horse bred in Turkemenia. Skeletons of similar fine boned horses found dating back 2,500 years
	Budjonny	Chestnut, bay	15.3hh	Good temperament with substance. Riding, competitions and racing	Created this century by crossing Thoroughbreds with Dons
	Don	Chestnut, grey	15.3hh	Great stamina. Harness work, general riding, long distance racing	Used by Don cossacks in eighteenth century
	Kabardin	Bay, black	15hh	Sure footed, good pack horse, especially able in mountains. General riding	Developed by crossing mountain breeds with southern breeds
	Karabair	Bay, grey, chestnut	15.1hh	Great stamina. Dual purpose, used for riding and driving	Bred in Uzbekistan for about 2,400 years
	Lokai	Any	14.3hh	Powerful. Used as pack horse or for general riding, especially in highlands.	Originated in seventeenth century in Tadjikistan and have Arab and Karabair ancestors
	Kirghiz	Dark colours	15hh	General riding—especially good in high altitudes and for herding stock	Improved by crossing older version of Kirghiz, which was smaller, with Don and Thoroughbred
	Orlov Trotter	Grey, black	15.3hh but up to 17hh	Harness work and Trotting races	Developed in 1770's by Count Orlov who crossed Arab, Thoroughbred, Dutch, Mecklenburg and Danish horses
	Russian Trotter (Metis)	Any	15.3hh	Trotting races	Developed by crossing American Standardbred, and Orlov when former became faster than latter. Faster but not so handsome as Orlov
	Tersk	Grey	15.1hh	Good temperament. Used for general riding, circus and dressage work	Originated from Strelets breed—Arabians that nearly died out after World War I. Outside Arabians and their cross breeds used. Larger than pure bred Arabs
Ponies	Karabakh	Chestnut, bay, dun with metallic sheen	14.1hh	Lively mountain horse used for riding and racing	Originated in Karabakh in Trans Caucasian uplands and has Arab ancestors
	Kazakh	Bay and most others	14hh	Tough, able to withstand steppe life. Herding cattle, long distance riding, especially in highlands	Originated as horses of nomads in Kazakhstan. Today are being crossed with Don to produce larger version—the Kustanair
	Yakut	Greyish, mousey	13hh	Used for riding, pack work, transportation, harness.	Long hairy coats. Survive in Yakut territory (beyond Polar circle)
Work horses	Latvian	Bay, black, chestnut	16hh	Great pulling strength—draught horses	Both horses have similar features and are bred in Baltic states by crossing local Zhmuds with larger imports—Finnish Draught and Swedish Ardennes

BREEDS OF THE WORLD

	Breed	Usual colour	Average height	Ability and purpose	Features
	Russian Heavy	Chestnut	14.3hh	Lively, fast gaits	Founded in Ukraine where local breeds were crossed with Ardennes, Percherons and Orlov Trotters
	Soviet Heavy Draught	Any	15.3hh	Active and relatively fast. The most popular heavy horse in USSR.	Developed by crossing local breeds with Belgians, Ardennes, and Percherons. Not so massive as European heavy horses
	Toric	Any	15.1hh	Agricultural work and in harness.	Originated by crossing Hackney and East Friesian with local Estonian breeds
	Vladimir Heavy Draught	Chestnut, bay, roan	15.3hh	Strong puller, energetic. Agricultural work	Created in nineteenth century by crossing local horses with Clydesdale and Shire
Turkey Riding horses	Karacabey	Solid colours	15.3hh	Riding and harness work.	Developed from native horses crossed with Nonius from Hungary
Iran Riding horses	Turkoman	Any	15.2hh	Floating action. Long-distance racing, endurance rides, and general riding	Originated, like the Akhal Teké, from the Turkmene horse
Yemen Riding horses	Arab	Originally bay and chestnut, grey is now common	15hh	Light, graceful action; fast, with great stamina. General riding and racing	Origins vague but thought to have roamed wild in Yemen until tamed c. 3000BC. Oldest pure breed and has had great influence on all other breeds. Typically has a concave head; croup level with the back
Morocco and Algeria Riding horses	Barb	Bay, brown chestnut, grey	14.3hh	Fast. Used for general riding	An old breed with Arab blood. Typically has the tail set lower than Arab. Convex ram-shaped head
South Africa Ponies	Basuto	Chestnut, bay	14.2hh	Riding and general transportation	Thick set and long in the back. Originated from Arab and Barb stock
Australia Riding horses	Australian Stock Horse	Any	16hh	Riding, herding and campdrafting	Originated by crossing Arab, Anglo-Arab and Thoroughbreds with local stock in last century. Became known as the Waler.
Ponies	Australian pony	Any	13hh	General riding	Foundation stock was Welsh
SOUTH AMERICA **Argentina** Riding horses	Criollo	Dun, sorrel, palomino	14.3hh	Great stamina. Used for endurance work and for general riding	Short head, stocky. Originated from Andalusians, imported in sixteenth century, which ran wild on the pampas
Brazil Riding horses	Crioulo	Dun, sorrel, palomino	14.2hh	General riding and herding	Similar background to Criollo but original stock mainly Alters from Portugal
	Mangalarga	Grey, sorrel, roan	15.3hh	General and long-distance riding and harness work.	Originated from Crioulo crossed with imports from Spain and Portugal. Also selective breeding of Mangalarga has produced a heavier breed—the Campolino
Peru Riding horses	Peruvian Stepping Horse	Dun, sorrel, palomino	14hh	Especially smooth gaits; the amble (a pace) enables the rider to cover great distances at speed and in comfort	Developed, like Criollos, from Spanish and Portuguese horses that ran wild
Venezuela Riding horses	Llanero	Light colours, pinto, with dark mane and tail	14hh	Great stamina; used for endurance riding	Smaller and finer than other Criollos but from similar origins
NORTH AMERICA Riding horses	Appaloosa	White coat with black or brown spots	15.1hh	Used by Indians who took advantage of camouflage colouring. Now popular for Western riding.	Developed by Nez Percé Indians in Palouse, Idaho
	Morgan	Any	15hh	Short active stride; great stamina. Very versatile, used for riding and harness work	Originated in New England from the Justin Morgan Horse (1789). Particularly short in the back and legs
	Quarter-horse	Any	15hh	Sure footed with great acceleration; excellent ranch horses. Racing, rodeo work, polo and general riding	Developed as quarter-mile sprinters. Foundation sire was the Thoroughbred 'Janus'. Largest stud book in the world. Stocky with powerful hindquarters
	Palomino	Golden with light mane and tail	Any	All types of use	Not yet an established breed as not yet breeding true to type but stud book now exists for which horses qualify through colour
	Pinto	White splashes on black (piebald) or on other colours (skewbald)	Various	Tough. Used by Indians. General riding horse	Not a true breed. Defined by colour like palominos
	Saddle-bred	Any	15.2hh	High action; either 3-gaited, when mane is roached, or 5-gaited. Riding and driving	Short back, long tapering neck. Foundation stock was Thoroughbred and Arab
	Standard-bred	Any	15.3hh	Tough. Can trot nearly as fast as Thoroughbred can gallop. Some pace rather than trot when they move lateral rather than diagonal pairs	Foundation sire was the Thoroughbred 'Messenger' imported from UK in 1795. Strong hindquarters and long back
	Tennessee Walking Horse	Any	15.2hh	Comfortable paces. High-stepping gaits with fast running walk. General riding and driving	Developed as hacks for plantation owners in nineteenth century from a mixture of US breeds
Ponies	Pony of Americas	Any	13hh	Riding	New breed developed by crossing Quarter-horse, Arab and Appaloosa

RIDING FOR THE DISABLED

The value of riding for the handicapped was realized long ago. At the healing festivals of Ancient Greece, incurables were given exercises on horseback and rides in the country to help raise their spirits; and the Romans, French and Germans later practised such treatment. In recent times, however, little was done until Liz Hartel, a Danish woman stricken by polio, got out of her wheelchair to ride her horse at the 1952 Helsinki Olympics. Despite her physical handicap, she won the silver medal, repeating her success in the 1956 Olympics in Stockholm, and so gave inspiration to all those interested in riding as a therapy.

A Norwegian hospital was the first to start handicapped children riding, but groups were soon organized in the UK. In 1966, these groups formed an advisory council, and in 1969, the Riding for the Disabled association was established. A registered charity, the association has its headquarters at the National Agricultural Centre. Other countries followed suit; in Scandinavia, Australia, Bermuda, Lesotho, Malta, New Zealand, Canada, Rhodesia and the USA, ponies are now giving a new dimension and inspiration to the lives of handicapped people.

Benefits

The continuous motion of riding is the therapeutic equivalent of frequent and often tedious exercises in hospital or school. Also the mental and emotional effects are thought to be of greatest benefit. Riding gives the disabled great pleasure: any control he can exercise over the pony gives an inordinate sense of achievement to the handicapped who may have little control over his own body. Riding has an added psychological value, in that it brings the handicapped into contact with the normal world. The riders must have their doctor's permission to take part, and are often referred to the riding centres from hospitals and special schools.

Equipment

An enclosed space (preferably an indoor arena, as children in particular cannot ride in the rain) must be found. The horses and ponies need to be very quiet and their saddlery simple. Occasionally, adaptations are advisable, such as long looped reins for armless children and a basket saddle for the legless. The children should have a belt that can be held and a hard hat. A qualified riding instructor must be present; the presence of a physiotherapist or a member of the medical profession is desirable. Up to three helpers per pony are needed when the child is just starting, or is severely handicapped. One leads the pony; and the others steady the rider. These helpers, who need not be 'horsey', come from all walks of life, and there is always an urgent need for volunteers prepared to give up a few hours a week.

The work

The ride usually starts with progressive exercises and ends with mounted games. Many groups, however, like to take their children for rides in the countryside; an increasingly popular idea is to take them for holidays, on which they can ride every day of the week instead of the mere hour. Groups of volunteers may get together and offer to have a party of children for a working holiday. They provide the ponies and arrange accommodation, and the children are encouraged to learn how to care for their mounts.

THE UK

The Riding for the Disabled association had 80 groups to organize when it started; now, there are close to 400. The groups help about 9,500 riders, all of whom can be awarded competency certificates as an incentive to improve their riding. There are seven grades of certificate. Although some of the groups have very little money and few facilities, large centres are now springing up. One hundred thousand pounds ($200,000) was raised to start the Diamond Riding Centre for the Handicapped in Surrey.

THE USA

The North American Riding for the Handicapped Association (NARHA), formed in 1969, has the following aims: the establishment of standards and techniques for teaching the handicapped; the provision of appropriate manuals for those interested in starting programmes; approval of training programmes and provision of certification of instructors planning to work with the handicapped; the maintenance of co-operation with members of the medical profession, to ensure the safety and well being of handicapped riders and to gain approval and recognition of riding as a valuable therapeutic activity; the provision of experienced consultants for lectures and discussions; and the promotion and publication of responsible research.

BIBLIOGRAPHY

BREEDS:
Mellin, J. The Morgan Horse Handbook (Stephen Greene Press)
Summerhays, R. S. Observer's Book of Horses and Ponies, Observer's Pckt S. (Warne) (1957)
Silver, S. Guide to Horses of the World (Elsevier/Phaidon)
Glyn, Sir R. (Ed.) World's Finest Horses and Ponies (Harrap)
MacGregor Morris, P. and **Lugli, N.** (Eds) Horses of the World (Orbis)
Summerhays, R. S. The Arabian Horse (Wilshire Bk Co. L.A.)
Clabby, J. The Natural History of the Horse (Weidenfeld & Nicolson)

BREEDING AND MANAGEMENT:
Leighton Hardman, A. C. Stallion Management (Pelham)
Finney, H. A Stud Farm Diary (J. A. Allen)
Wynmalen, H. Horse Breeding and Stud Management (J. A. Allen)
Dougal, N. Stallions: Their Management and Handling (J. A. Allen)
Andrist, F. Mares, Foals and Foaling, Tr. fr. German by Dent, A. (J. A. Allen)
Dougall, N. Stallions Their Management and Handling (British Book Centre)

VETERINARY
Straighton, E. TV Vet Horse Book (Farming Press)

Codrington, W. S. Know Your Horse (J. A. Allen)
Rossdale, The Horse From Conception to Maturity (J. A. Allen)
Lyon, W. E. First Aid Hints for the Horse Owner (Collins)
Miller, W. C. and **West, G. P.** (Eds) Black's Veterinary Dictionary (A. C. Black)

HORSE MANAGEMENT
Hayes, M. H. Stable Management and Exercise (S. Paul)
Manual of Horsemanship (British Horse Society)
Tuke, D. R. Bit by Bit: Guide to Equine Bits (J. A. Allen)
Rose, M. Horsemaster's Notebook, and **Smith, R. N.** Anatomy of the Horse (P. Barker)
Hartley Edwards, E. Saddlery (J.A. Allen)
Wiseman, R. F. Complete Horse Shoeing Guide (Univ. Oklahoma P.)
Sophian, T. J. Horses and the Law (J. A. Allen)
Wheatley, G. Stable Management for the Owner-Groom (A. S. Barnes)
Leighton Hardman, A. C. Young Horse Management (Pelham)

HORSE BUYING:
Posey, J. K. Horse Buyer's Guide (Yoseloff)

TRAINING:
Handler, H. The Spanish Riding School (Thames & Hudson)
Museler, W. Riding Logic (Eyre Methuen)

Podhajsky, A. W. S. Complete Training of Horse and Rider, Tr. fr. German (Harrap)
Littauer, V. S. Development of Modern Riding (J. A. Allen)
Wynmalen, H. Equitation (J. A. Allen)
Froissard, J. Equitation, Tr. fr. French Froissard, L. P.
Froissard, J. Equitation: Learning and Teaching, Tr. fr. French Froissard, L. P. (Wilshire Bk Co. L.A.)
Wright, G. Learn to Ride, Hunt, and Show (Doubleday)
Seunig, W. Horsemanship (Doubleday)
Jacobson, P. and **Hayes, M.** A Horse Around the House (Crown)
Dickerson, J. Make the Most of Your Horse (Doubleday)
Dent, A. The Horse Through Fifty Years of Civilization (Holt, Rinehart & Winston)
Stanier, S. The Art of Lungeing (J. A. Allen)
Podhajsky, A. The Art of Dressage (Doubleday)

EQUESTRIAN SPORTS:
Ansell, Sir M. Riding High (P. Davies)
Steinkraus, W. Riding and Jumping (Pelham Bks)
Wilcox, S. Event Horse (Pelham Bks)
Hope, C. E. G. Horse Trials Story (Pelham Bks)
Walrond, S. Guide to Driving Horses, Horsemaster S. (Warne)
Vickers, W. G. Practical Polo (J. A. Allen)
'Marco' Introduction to Polo (J. A. Allen)

(continued on page 208)

COLOURS AND MARKINGS

Star

Stripe

Blaze

White face

Snip

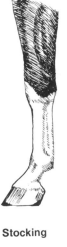

Stocking

MARKINGS

Sock

Markings are areas of white on the head, body and limbs. The different markings on the legs and head are illustrated above.

Head
Star is a white mark on the forehead.
Stripe is a narow white mark down the face.
Blaze is a broad white mark down the face, usually extending from eyes to muzzle.
White face is white forehead, eyes, nose and parts of muzzle.
Snip is a small area of white in the region of the nostrils.

Wall eye is white or blue-white colouring in the eye, due to lack of pigment in the iris.

Legs
Stocking is white on the leg, from coronet to knee or hock.
Sock is white covering the fetlock and part of the cannon region.

Body
Zebra marks are stripes on the limbs, neck, withers or quarters.
Whorls are patterns formed by hairs around a small central spot.

If there is any doubt as to the colour of the coat, then the colour of the points (muzzle, tips of ears, mane and tail and extremities of the four legs) is the deciding factor.

Bay
Brownish colour (shades very from reddish and yellowish to approaching brown). The points are black.

Black
Coat, limbs, mane and tail are black. Any markings are white.

Brown
Dark brown or nearly black, with brown to black points.

Sorrel (Chestnut)
Ginger, yellow or reddish colour, with similarly coloured mane and tail. The three shades of chestnut are dark, liver and light chestnut.

Dun
Blue dun is a diluted black, with black points, and may or may not have a dorsal band and a withers stripe.
Yellow dun is a yellowish on a black skin. Points are normally black and there is often a dorsal band and stripes on withers and limbs.

Cream
Cream-coloured on an unpigmented skin. The eye often has a pinkish appearance.

Grey
Hairs are white and black, on a black skin. There are many shades, including flea-bitten grey (dark hairs occurring in tufts) and iron grey (black hairs more numerous).

Roan
A blue roan has a basic colour of black or brown and a sprinkling of white.
A strawberry or chestnut roan has a basic colour of chestnut with sprinkling of white.

Palomino
Golden colour with flaxen mane and tail.

Pinto or calico
A piebald has large, irregular patches of black and white.
A skewbald's coat has large patches of white and any colour but black.
Odd-coloured, with patches of more than two colours.

COLOURS

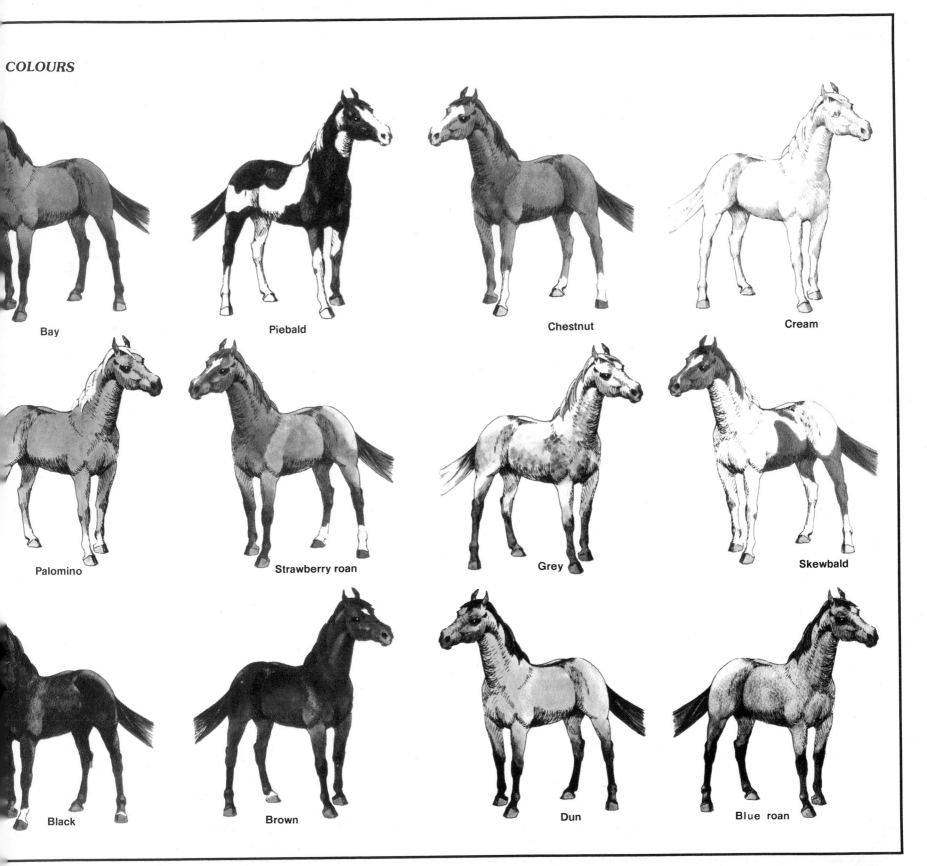

Bay

Piebald

Chestnut

Cream

Palomino

Strawberry roan

Grey

Skewbald

Black

Brown

Dun

Blue roan

(continued from page 205)

Bent, N. American Polo
Blake, R. L. V. F.-Dressage for Beginners (Seeley Service)
Dwyer, Ted, Show Jumping Down Under (R. Hale)
Friedlaender, E. Vaulting (S. Green)
Saare, S. Endurance Riding and Management (Appaloosa Horse Club, US)
Morris, H. Hunt Seat Equitation (Doubleday)
Crabtree, K. Saddle Seat Equitation (Doubleday)
Spector, D. A. Grand Prix Jumping (Abingdon Press)
Batchelor, V. The Observor's Book of Show Jumping & Eventing (F. Warne)
Clayton, M. and **Steinkraus, W.** The Complete Book of Show Jumping (Crown)

WESTERN HORSEMANSHIP:
Nye, N. C. Your Western Horse: His Ways and His Rider (Wilshire Bk Co., L.A.)
Price, E. F. and **Collier, G. M.** Basic Horsemanship: Western and English (Doubleday, NY)
Taylor, L. Ride Western: A Complete Guide to Western Horsemanship (Harper & Row)
Weikel, Bill (Ed.) How to Break and Train the Western Horse (Farnham)
McGann, T. How to Train a Reining Horse (Farnham)
Smith, B. The Horse in the West (World)
Brander, M. The Complete Guide to Horsemanship (A & C Black)

HUNTING:
Hayes, M. H. Riding and Hunting (S. Paul)
Clayton, M. A-Hunting We Will Go (J. A. Allen)
Williams, J. Introduction to Hunting (J. A. Allen)
Baily's Hunting Directory (J. A. Allen)
Moore, D. Book of the Foxhound (J. A. Allen)
Carr, R. English Fox Hunting: A History (Weidenfeld & Nicolson)

PONY TREKKING
Spooner, G. Pony Trekking (J. A. Allen)·
Saare, S. Know All About Trail Riding (Farnham)
Price, S. D. Horseback Vacation Guide (Stephen Greene Press)
Hart, E. Pony Trekking (David & Charles)

EQUESTRIAN ORGANIZATIONS

THE UNITED KINGDOM
Arab Horse Society, The, c/o Lt Col. J. Denney, Sackville Lodge, Lye Green, Crowborough, Sussex
Association of British Riding Schools, The, Chesham House, Green End Road, Sawtry, Huntingdon, Cambridgeshire PE17 5UY
British Driving Society, The, 10 Marley Avenue, New Milton, Hampshire
British Veterinary Association, The, 7 Mansfield Street, Portland Place, London W1
Combined Driving Committee, The The National Equestrian Centre, Kenilworth, Worcestershire CU8 2LR
Combined Training Committee, The, The National Equestrian Centre, Kenilworth, Worcestershire CU8 2LR
Dressage Committee, The, The National Equestrian Centre, Kenilworth, Worcestershire CU8 2LR
Horse and Hound, King's Reach Tower, Stamford Street, London SE1 9L5
Horse and Pony Breeds Committee, The National Equestrian Centre, Kenilworth, Worcestershire CU8 2LR
Horsemanship and Examinations Committee, The, The National Equestrian Centre, Kenilworth, Worcestershire CU8 2LR
Hunter Improvement Society, The, National Westminster Bank Chambers, 8 Market Square, Westerham, Kent
Hurlingham Polo Association, The, 60 Mark Lane, London EC3R 7TJ
Master of Foxhounds Association, The, c/o Col. Chamberlayne, The Elm, Chipping Norton, Oxfordshire OX7 5NS
Ponies of Britain, c/o Miss G. Spooner, Brookside Farm, Ascot, Berkshire
Pony Club, The, The National Equestrian Centre, Kenilworth, Worcestershire CU8 2LR
Riding Clubs Committee, The, The National Equestrian Centre, Kenilworth, Worcestershire CU8 2LR
Riding for the Disabled Association, The, The National Agricultural Centre, Kenilworth, Worcestershire CV8 2LY
World Arabian Horse Organisation, c/o R. M. Kydd, Esq., Thujas, Bisley, Surrey

THE UNITED STATES OF AMERICA
American Association of Equine Practitioners, The, Route 5, 14 Hillcrest Circle, Golden, Colorado 80401
American Dressage Institute, The, 249 Round Hill Road, Greenwich, Connecticut 06830
American Driving Society, The, c/o Robert Heath, 339 Warburton Avenue, Hastings-on-Hudson, New York 10706

American Horse Council, Inc., The, 1700 K Street, Washington DC 20006
American Horse Shows Association, The, 527 Madison Avenue, New York 10022
American Morgan Horse Association, The, PO Box 265, Hamilton, New York 13346
American Quarter Horse Association, The, PO Box 200, Amarillo, Texas 79168
American Standardbred Breeders' Association, The, PO Box 667, Pine Bush, New York 12566
American Vaulting Association, The, PO Box 1307, San Juan Batista, California 95045
American Veterinary Medical Association, The, 600 South Michigan Avenue, Chicago, Illinois 60605
Appaloosa Horse Club, Inc., PO Box 8403, Moscow, Idaho 83843
Arabian Horse Registry of America, The, 1 Executive Park, 7801 East Belleview Ace, Englewood, Colorado 80110
National Cutting Horse Association, The, PO Box 13486, Fort Worth, Texas 76118
National Cowboy Hall of Fame, 1700 NE 63 Street, Oklahoma City, Oklahoma 73111
National 4-H Service Committee, The, 150 North Wacker Drive, Chicago, Illinois 60606
National Steeplechase and Hunt Association, The, PO Box 308, Elmont, New York 11003
North American Riding for the Handicapped Association, The, Cheff Foundation, RR1, PO Box 171, Augusta, Michigan 49023
Palomino Horse Association, The, PO Box 324, Jefferson City, Missouri 65101
Professional Rodeo Cowboys' Association, The, 2929 West 19 Avenue, Denver, Colorado 80204
Rodeo Information Commission, The, 2929 West 19th Avenue, Denver, Colorado 80204
Tennessee Walking Horse Breeders' Association, The, PO Box 286, Lewisburg, Tennessee 37091
Thoroughbred Owners' and Breeders' Association, The, PO Box 4038, Lexington, Kentucky 40504
United States Combined Training Association, The, 1 Winthrope Square, Boston, Massachusetts 02110
United States Dressage Federation, The, c/o Lowell Boomer, Box 80668, Lincoln, New Brunswick 68501
United States Equestrian Team, Inc., The, 292 Bridge Street, South Hamilton, Massachusetts 01982
United States Polo Association, The, 1301 West 22nd Street. Suite 706, Oak Brook, Illinois 60521

United States Pony Clubs, 303 South Street, West Chester Pennsylvania 19380

AUSTRALIA
Adelaide Hunt Club, The, Main Road, Cherry Gardens, South Australia 5157
Adelaide Polo Club Inc., The, 34 Pirie Street, Adelaide, South Australia 5000
Australian Horse and Rider (NSW), PO Box 360, Avalon, NSW 2107
Australian Stock Horse Society, The, PO Box 288, Scone, NSW 2337
Dressage Club of South Australia, The, c/o K. Guster, Esq., 9 East Terrace, Henley Beach, South Australia 5022
Equestrian Federation of Australia, The, Royal Show Grounds, Epsom Road, Ascot Vale 2, Victoria 3032
Hoofs and Horns, 194 Prospect Road, Prospect, South Australia 5082
Horse Riding Clubs' Association, The, c/o Miss D. Mansom, 5 Rose Terrace, Wayville, South Australia 5034
Light Horse Breeders' Association of South Australia, The, c/o Mrs M. Potts, Revlis Park, Gawler Ricer, South Australia 5118
MacTaggarts, 12 Creek Street, Brisbane 4000, Queensland
Riding for the Disabled Association of Western Australia, The, 140 Forrest Street, Peppermint Grove, Western Australia
South Australian Bloodhorse Breeders' Association, The, Morphettville, South Australia 5043
South Australian Horse Driving Society, The, c/o P. Fincher, Esq., 1090 South Road, Edwardstown, South Australia 5039
Trail Riding Club, The, c/o B. Virgo, Esq., Headquarters, South Australian Police Force
Victoria Harness Society, The, c/o Mrs B. Byron, PO Box 220, Berwick Victoria

SOUTH AFRICA
Horse and Hound, PO Box 78317, Sandton 2146
Jockey Club of South Africa, The, PO Box 3409, Johannesburg 2000
South African National Equestrian Federation, 17 Tulip Avenue, Sunridge Park, Port Elizabeth
South African Veterinary Association, The, PO Box 2460, Pretoria 0001
Thoroughbred Breeders' Association (South Africa), The, PO Box 7679, Johannesburg 2000

proost Turnhout (Belgium)

INDEX

PICTURE CREDITS

The publishers would like to thank Gidden's of London for supplying tack and a grooming kit for photography, and Ackerman's for supplying a sporting print. We should also like to thank Bruce Scott for the commissioned photography, and the following photographers and organizations who supplied photographs for this book.

Photographs have been credited by page number. Where more than one photograph appears on the page, references are made in the order of the columns across the page and then from top to bottom. Where all the photographs on a page or spread are the work of one photographer, the pictures are not credited individually.

Front cover: E. D. Lacey
1: Robert Estall. 3: Picturepoint. 4/5: J. Kidd. 6: National Army Museum. 7: Popperphoto/Popperphoto/Wallace Collection. 8: Mansell Picture Library. 9: Arthur Ackerman & Son Ltd.. 10-15: Bruce Scott. 16: E. D. Lacey. 17: E. D. Lacey. 18: W. Rentsch. 19: W. Rentsch. 20-33: Bruce Scott. 34: E. D. Lacey. 35: E. D. Lacey. 36: ZEFA. 37: L. Lane. 38: J. Kidd. 39: J. Kidd. 40-45: Bruce Scott. 46: Mike Roberts/E. D. Lacey. 47: E. D. Lacey. 50-61: Bruce Scott. 63: J. Kidd. 64: John Barrow. 65: Tony Stone. 66: Animal Photography. 67: John Barrow. 68: Animal Photography. 69: Tony Stone. 70: E. D. Lacey. 71: E. D. Lacey. 73: Tony Stone. 74: E. D. Lacey/W. Rentsch/W. Rentsch. 75: W. Rentsch. 76: Bruce Scott/E. D. Lacey. 77: ZEFA. 78: W. Rentsch. 79: Tony Stone. 80: Mike Roberts/E. D. Lacey. 81: E. D. Lacey. 82-87: Bruce Scott. 88: J. Kidd. 89-91: E. D. Lacey. 92: J. Kidd. 93: Bruce Scott. 94: J. Kidd. 95: J. Kidd. 96: E. D. Lacey/E. D. Lacey/Freudy Photos. 98: L. Lane. 99: Picturepoint. 100: Mike Roberts. 101: J. Kidd. 102: Mike Roberts. 103: Freudy Photos/Freudy Photos/Mike Roberts. 104: Animal Photography. 105: E. D. Lacey/Mike Roberts. 106: J. Kidd. 107: E. D. Lacey/Jim Meads. 108: Bruce Scott/J. Kidd. 109: Bruce Scott. 110: Freudy Photos. 111: Freudy Photos/Freudy Photos. 112: Freudy Photos. 113: Freudy Photos. 114: Dave Jones. 115: Spectrum. 116: Picturepoint/Picturepoint/Colour Library International. 117: Colour Library International. 118: ZEFA. 119: Spectrum. 127: E. D. Lacey. 128: Bruce Scott. 129: 132-133: J. Kidd. 136: J. Kidd. 139: E. D. Lacey. 140: J. Kidd. 143: Mike Roberts. 146: E. D. Lacey. 149: E. D. Lacey. 150-151: Bruce Scott. 153: E. D. Lacey. 154: J. Kidd. 160-161: Bruce Scott. 164-166: Bruce Scott. 168-169: E. D. Lacey. 177-178: Bruce Scott. 180: Bruce Scott. 184: Bruce Scott. 187: J. Kidd. 200: L. Lane. 208-209: E. D. Lacey. 211: Keystone.